Asylum Seekers

Asylum Seekers:
International Perspectives on Interdiction and Deterrence

Edited by

Alperhan Babacan and Linda Briskman

Cambridge Scholars Publishing

Asylum Seekers: International Perspectives on Interdiction and Deterrence,
Edited by Alperhan Babacan and Linda Briskman

This book first published 2008 by

Cambridge Scholars Publishing

15 Angerton Gardens, Newcastle, NE5 2JA, UK

British Library Cataloguing in Publication Data
A catalogue record for this book is available from the British Library

Copyright © 2008 by Alperhan Babacan and Linda Briskman and contributors

All rights for this book reserved. No part of this book may be reproduced, stored in a retrieval system, or transmitted, in any form or by any means, electronic, mechanical, photocopying, recording or otherwise, without the prior permission of the copyright owner.

ISBN (10): 1-84718-491-X, ISBN (13): 9781847184917

TABLE OF CONTENTS

Acknowledgments vii

Chapter One... 1
Turning Away Thy Neighbour
Linda Briskman and Alperhan Babacan

Chapter Two 10
A World Turned Down: Risk, Refugees and Global Security
in the 21st Century
Paul Battersby

Chapter Three 28
Securing Borders: Interdiction and Deterrence in Australia and Canada
Alperhan Babacan

Chapter Four.. 45
Exporting the Border: Immigration Detention and "Juxtaposed Controls"
Madeleine Byrne

Chapter Five 63
Australia's Border Control and Refugee Protection Capacity-Building
Activities in the Asia–Pacific Region
Savitri Taylor

Chapter Six 82
Out of Sight, Out of Right? Who Can Be Held Accountable
for Detainees Harmed on Nauru?
Azadeh Dastyari

Chapter Seven.. 97
Beyond the Clinical Contract: Restoring Asylum Seeker Health
through Advocacy and Care
Deborah Zion and Bebe Loff

Chapter Eight 112
Enemies Everywhere: (In)security Politics, Asylum Seekers
and Other Enemies Within
Jude McCulloch

Chapter Nine 128
Detention As Deterrence
Linda Briskman

Chapter Ten 143
New Racisms and Asylum Seekers in Australia
Hurriyet Babacan and Narayan Gopalkrishnan

Chapter Eleven 158
The Future for Asylum Seekers in a Changing World
Alperhan Babacan and Linda Briskman

Bibliography 166

Editor and Contributor Biographies 194

Acknowledgments

We wish to thank our universities for their financial support in making this publication possible. The Centre for Applied Social Research at RMIT University provided a grant for a conference from which the vision for the book emerged. The Division of Humanities at Curtin University gave a publication grant and the Curtin Centre for Advanced Studies in Australia, Asia and the Pacific supported attendance at an international refugee conference in the United Kingdom. Thank you to Mar Bucknell for his fine editing. We wish to also acknowledge the role of the many academics and advocates who are working tirelessly to expose unjust policies and who are involved in global and national dialogue in order to create a just system for asylum seekers.

Alperhan Babacan and Linda Briskman

CHAPTER ONE

TURNING AWAY THY NEIGHBOUR

LINDA BRISKMAN AND ALPERHAN BABACAN

Introduction

Enshrined in the 1951 United Nations convention on refugees is the right of people with a well-founded fear of persecution to seek asylum. Despite this imperative, many countries are increasingly finding means to push away asylum seekers from their national borders. A fear engendered of invasion by strangers permeates countries that have signed up to the refugee convention under a range of guises including the sacrosanct nature of the nation state, fear of disruption of monocultural interests, the so-called war on terror and a socially engineered immigration regime based on the myth of consummate order and control. Presented is a visual display that each state retains control of the "illegal" movement of people and people smuggling (Babacan 2007, 179). The various attempts at deterrence by western countries in particular reveal capricious and cruel policies that not only flout international conventions, but defy commonly accepted standards of tolerance, humanity and decency. The national measures that are now enshrined in laws, policies and practices obfuscate the quest by many for a common humanity (Briskman 2007a, 164).

Refugees are manifestly a product of our world, "of the modern system of states and its technologies of government, geopolitics, citizenship, border control and exclusion" (Burke 2002, 22). Regrettably, the general public in refugee-deterring countries has been duped by a range of unifying forces that border on what McGhee (2005) refers to as asylum hysteria. These include governments and their propaganda-generating machinery, with which refugee scholars and advocates cannot compete due to the massive resources needed to counter the dominant discourse. Sections of the media collude with governments to paint a fear-producing depiction of asylum seekers. This results in the community at large readily adopting the terminology of "illegals", "queue jumpers", "economic migrants" and "bogus claimants", language that reconstructs social reality.

In the current world order, the fear of Islam combines with the fear of asylum seekers. As Kundnani (2007, 2) explains, we are confronted by a dichotomy of Islamic extremism and its supposed envy and hatred of the West on one side and, on the other, the "liberating" forces of the United States, Britain and their allies. Underpinning this discourse is a belief in the incapacity of "the other" to be absorbed into Western societies as their value base is seen to be at odds with Western value systems. These factors deny the reality that many refugees have no choice but to put their lives, and often entire family savings, into the hands of people smugglers in order to escape from persecution and serious human rights violations (UNHCR 2007).

The politics of governments and community

With nationalism becoming a major world force, Delanty (2000, 96–7), argues that this is a product of the internal crisis of the state in the age of globalisation, with the "new nationalism" directed at immigrants rather than towards competing nation states. With the decline in the multicultural project in Australia and elsewhere, the competing discourses of assimilation and exclusion, thought to be shed in the annals of history, are now thematically unified by restriction of refugee rights. This is further shrouded in what McGhee (2005, 1) sees as the common place in the world of "hatred, prejudice, intolerance and antagonism", positing that hatred embodies a set of fears about difference forming around the "unknown". This is underpinned by fears about loss of identity and security, which are at the root of conflict within and between societies, and are manifest at a micro level by taunts at people with dark skin, non-Anglo names and "strange" food in their lunchboxes (Lawrence 2006, 28; 30). Translating this into broader political behaviour, Alan Touraine (2000), in his aptly named book, *Can We Live Together?*, speaks of how the ideal of the nation state has degenerated into an aggressive nationalism. The unfinished project for the west is to critically interrogate the pervading nationalism in order to move policy and political consciousness into an ethical realm.

A content analysis of tabloid newspapers illuminates the extent of the ignorance, fear and support for policies underpinned by both xenophobia and a racism or its extension into the blurred boundaries of culture and religion. Race thinking still dominates the way contemporary society views human difference (Ratcliffe 2004, 16) and such thinking is readily transferable to refugees as a site of exclusion, dehumanisation and denigration. The views expressed contrast starkly with post-colonial propositions that transnational communities have multiple loyalties that are likely to be more negotiable than those of the majority culture (Delanty 2000, 64). According to McGhee (2005, 90), there are a number of threats, risks and sources of anxiety that are associated with fear that a country will be engulfed by strangers who will bring their crime, their neediness and their sinister anti-western malcontent. The following examples documented by Iain Lygo (2004, 1–3) in the Australian context are transferable to populist views that are increasingly expressed in other parts of the world.

So how do we educate Islamic asylum seekers who are clearly opposed to all things Western? How do we educate a group of people who uphold the beliefs of barbaric human rights abuses?

It would be better for all concerned, if asylum seekers were refused entry ...as the mix will never work as long as Middle Eastern boat people refuse to assimilate...

Boat people are illegal refugees, a majority are fraudulent rabble who come here illegally on illegal boats.

Most of us don't want liars, cheats, frauds, criminals, terrorists and all-round losers coming here in rusty boats.

Islam is a religion still rooted in the Dark Ages and has no place in a modern, democratic society like ours.

Ethics, the strangers and the other

Stratton and McCann (2002) ask what kind of ethics are being deployed to legitimise existing policies and how might an alternative ethical lens refocus the policies. They suggest that the current guiding ethic is utilitarian and majoritarian, steered by a principle of the greatest good for the greatest number and in line with public opinion. How might things look if we were to adopt an ethics of responsibility proposed by Levinas, which is a way of locating ourselves in relation to other people, including strangers; what he calls an ethics of alterity (Stratton and McCann 2002).

A song titled *Anytime the Wind Can Change*[1] depicts the story of the kind deeds of the townsfolk of Zakynthos, a neighbouring island of Ithaca in the Ionian Sea. In November 2001, the townsfolk extended helping hands to more than 700 refugees who were rescued offshore by the Greek coastguard. "Seven hundred rolls did the baker bake today/Seven hundred guests did the town receive today" are among the inspiring words written by Kavisha Mazella and Arnold Zable (Boite 2003).

Why is it that such welcoming of stranger is not the norm? What is it that makes nations repel strangers and summons a politics of fear to support inhumane policies? As UK Prison Ombudsman Stephen Shaw says "the strength of a liberal democracy is measured not by how it treats the majority but how it cares for minorities and those at the margins of society" (Medical Justice Network 2007).

The landmark work of Palestinian writer, Edward Said (1995), offers leads on how society misrepresents non-Western cultures. The notion of postcolonial societies is far from realised and empire, history and current politics all converge in Said's construction of those represented and pathologised in their "otherness" from accepted norms. Barthes uses the term inoculation to emphasise a desire to immunise society against difference (cited in Sandoval 1997, 88), something that is clearly evident in the way many societies and political structures reinforce the power hierarchy that characterises relationships with those "othered" in the discourse of the desired citizen (Briskman 2007b), including refugees. The values, beliefs, meanings and practices from the dominant culture become the benchmarks against which other values and meanings are measured and those outside the mainstream are deemed inferior (Quinn 2003). For Burke (2002, 25), what is required is a new kind of encounter with "otherness", which seeks neither to fix "others" onto a plane of sameness nor prevents them from entering a nation's physical, economic and existential space.

The book

Our treatise examines the themes and trends apparent in refugee treatment today. It is problematic to dismiss the trends as mere cause and effect rather than recognising that how we have reached this exclusionary state of existence is in fact multi-faceted with both over-arching themes and contextual layers. Within the unifying theme of deterrence and

---

[1] This song was first performed in the play Kan Yama Kan, in which refugees from Iran, Iraq and Afghanistan told their stories to Australian audiences.

interdiction, each author contributes to providing understandings of the underpinnings of the policies using specific and timely examples. These cohere with what Peter Ratcliffe (2004, ix) sees as societal divisions rooted in forms of difference that are conceptualised in terms of race, ethnicity, culture, religion and nation and which are mediated by issues of class, status, power and gender. His conjecture is that none of these factors have a reality independent of history and an appreciation is needed of the impact of colonialism, imperialism and slavery. Although it is beyond the scope of the book to examine all these elements in detail, they need to be kept in mind as we ponder how we came to be politically entrapped in this parlous state of exclusion, globally and nationally.

The book begins by delving into the heart of the global issues that represent the push factors that are refugee creating in a "world turned upside down" as Paul Battersby proclaims. Here we are exposed to the reality of the mass movement of people as migrants, guest workers and refugees, which is a globalising phenomenon to which governments in the developed world have reacted with tightened border controls, a fortress mentality and selective immigration. Rights of passage are today determined substantially by wealth and educational attainment. Reactions against a parallel trend towards greater global openness reflect "national security" concerns framed negatively as the protection of domestic living standards or the defence of the majority against subterranean challenges to national identity and "social cohesion". Millions of people in developing and less developed countries cope daily with major economic, political and environmental stresses without any hope of immediate relief. A fraction of these arrive as asylum seekers or illegal migrants in Western countries and present at worst a negligible security burden to recipient countries. A much greater security challenge arises from the failure of the international community and the developed world in particular to alleviate the social, economic and political conditions that provoke social dislocation in many parts of the world. This chapter sets the scene for those that follow.

From Battersby's chapter, Alperhan Babacan moves on to some specifics of tightened border controls. Through an analysis of interdiction and deterrence in Australia and Canada, Babacan explicates how in recent decades Western industrial states have increasingly resorted to the use of interdiction and deterrence to "combat" the arrival of asylum seekers. It argues that the harsh measures adopted by Australia and Canada are contrary to the fundamental principles of justice and the spirit of the refugee convention and are bound to fail as they reinforce the political and economic divide across the world.

Moving to Europe, Madeleine Byrne examines the harshness of immigration detention and "juxtaposed controls". Despite a dramatic fall in asylum applications across Europe, immigration detention is on the increase. Tens of thousands of asylum seekers are detained in airport holding centres, detention facilities and prisons while their claims are processed, or before deportation. The chapter investigates the diverse range of immigration detention facilities in European nations and analyses why detention is seen as an effective way of controlling the "disorderly" movement of people across borders. It also explores recent controversies about immigration detention in Europe, including concerns about substandard conditions and inhumane treatment.

Savitri Taylor's chapter discusses how Australia and other developed countries regard irregular immigration as a threat to national security against which defence is required. One defensive strategy which Australia has in common with other developed countries is that of attempting to create an "offshore" border for itself in the countries of origin and the transit of potential irregular entrants including asylum seekers. This chapter presents the findings of a preliminary investigation into Australia's border control and refugee protection capacity building cooperation with countries such as Papua New Guinea and Indonesia, and considers the implications of those activities for asylum seekers. Concern is expressed that Australia puts more effort into border control rather than taking responsibility for those affected by its actions.

Shifting focus to the country of Nauru, Azadeh Dastyari contemplates the question of accountability. Immigration detainees held in the offshore processing centre in Nauru are caught within a complex arrangement between the Australian government, the International Organization for Migration, private contractors and the government of Nauru. Recent compensation cases in Australia suggest that the Australian government must accept ultimate responsibility for detainees who are physically or psychologically harmed in immigration detention centres run by private contractors in Australia. However, the complicated arrangement for the detention facility in Nauru makes it more difficult for detainees to seek compensation for physical or psychological damage caused by their incarceration in Nauru. This chapter explores the question of who can be held accountable for detainees who are harmed in Nauru and how detainees may achieve redress for their suffering.

The use and abuse of health care as a deterrent tool, and the associated ethics of the practices, are critically examined by Deborah Zion and Bebe Loff. Both medical ethics and human rights literature stress the importance of the primary duty of healthcare workers to their patients, rather than to the states in which they reside or the employers who provide remuneration for them. Inadequate healthcare provision for asylum seekers has been used as a form of deterrence in Australia and elsewhere. This chapter examines the ethical issues that this raises for healthcare professionals, and some solutions based upon a human rights approach to health.

The manner in which refugees have been constructed is subject to analysis by Jude McCulloch. In her chapter "Enemies Everywhere" that focuses on Australia but has broad application elsewhere, she looks at the politics of fear and the way that fear of asylum seekers is manufactured and manipulated to further a range of vested interests. The chapter seeks to describe the dynamics of (in)security politics in Australia and places the manufacture of the threat of asylum seekers in a broader context of fear and moral panic attending to "dangerous others", in the "war on crime" and the "war on terror". The chapter argues that the politics of fear, while extracting a high cost in terms of human security, yields benefits in terms of neo-liberal political agendas and the expansion of state's coercive capacities.

Also on Australia, Linda Briskman expands on how the type of politics outlined by McCulloch. are played out in the flawed policy of using immigration detention for the purposes of deterrence. The employment of immigration detention to deter other asylum seekers from arriving by boat is lauded by the Australian government and critiqued by academics, advocates, lawyers and human rights bodies. The policy is flawed because evidence suggests that it does not work as intended and, more importantly, because of the manner in which this policy breaches international human rights obligations.

The role of the new racisms permeates asylum seeker policy, with Hurriyet Babacan and Narayan Gopalkrishnan exploring how these are played out in policy and practice. After outlining the characteristics of the new racisms in Australia, the authors argue that the negative portrayal of asylum seekers to justify the Australian government's policies relating to the war on terror and border control has resulted in the racialisation of the asylum seeker issue in Australia and the criminalisation and marginalisation of asylum seekers .

The chapters should be read against an ever-changing global order where the refugee "crisis" and the responses of governments are continually re-worked according to perceived opportunities and threats. The book is a contribution to academic, political and community debates through its exposure and analysis of the illegality and immorality of deterrence and interdiction that permeates industrialised countries.

References

Babacan, A. 2007. Regulating asylum in the aftermath of September 11: The case of Australia, Canada and New Zealand. In *Racisms in the New World Order: Realities of cultures, colours and identity*, ed. N. Gopalkrishnan and H. Babacan, Newcastle: Cambridge Scholars Publishing.
Boite, The. 2003. *The Fig Tree*, CD recording, Collingwood: The Boite.
Briskman, L. 2007a. A tale of two racisms. In *Racisms in the New World Order: Realities of cultures, colours and identity*, ed. N. Gopalkrishnan and H. Babacan, Newcastle: Cambridge Scholars Publishing.
—. 2007b. *Social work with indigenous communities*. Sydney: The Federation Press.
Burke, A. 2002. Prisoners of paradox: thinking for the refugee. *Social Alternatives*, vol. 21, no. 4, 21–7.
Delanty, G. 2000. *Citizenship in a global age: Society, culture, politics*. Buckingham: Open University Press.
Fanon, F. 2006. *The Fanon reader*. London: Pluto Press.
Kundnani, A. 2007. *The end of tolerance: racism in 21st century Britain*. London: Pluto Press.
Lawrence, C. 2006. *Fear and politics*. Melbourne: Scribe Short Books.
Lygo, I. 2004. *News overboard: The tabloid media, race politics and Islam*. Sydney: Southerly Change Media.
McGhee, D. 2005. *Intolerant Britain: Hate, citizenship and difference*. Maidenhead: Open University Press.
Medical Justice Network. 2007. *Beyond comprehension and decency: An introduction to the work of Medical Justice*. MJN, London, July.
Quinn, M. 2003. Immigrants and refugees: Towards anti-racist and culturally affirming practices, in *Critical social work: An introduction to theories and practices*, ed. J. Allan, B. Pease and L. Briskman. Sydney: Allen and Unwin.
Ratcliffe, P. 2004. *'Race', ethnicity and difference: Imagining the inclusive society*, New York: Open University Press.
Said, E. 1995. *Orientalism*. London: Penguin.
Sandoval, C. 1997. Theorising white consciousness for a post-empire world: Barthes, Fanon and the rhetoric of love. In *Displacing whiteness: Essays in social and cultural criticism*, ed. R. Frankenburg, London: Duke University Press.
Stratton, J. and S. McCann. 2002. Staring into the abyss: Confronting the absence of decency in Australian refugee law and policy development. *Mots Pluriels*,

http://www.arts.uwa.edu.au/MotsPluriels/MP2102jssmc.html (accessed 1 October 2007).

Touraine, A. 2000. *Can we live together?: Equality and difference*, Cambridge: Polity Press.

United Nations High Commission for Refugees. 2007. *Refugee Newsletter*, UNHCR Regional Office for Australia, New Zealand, Papua New Guinea and the South Pacific.

CHAPTER TWO

A WORLD TURNED UPSIDE DOWN: RISK, REFUGEES AND GLOBAL SECURITY IN THE 21ST CENTURY

PAUL BATTERSBY

Introduction

At the beginning of the twenty-first century military affairs returned to the top of the international agenda. This triumphal resurgence is buttressed by the enduring assumption that "hard security," relating to power balances, military strategy and the like, outweighs the supposed "soft security" concerns of poverty, environmental degradation and human rights in the calculation of national interests. Yet, if security in its broadest sense means the maintenance or restoration of social, economic and cultural conditions that restrain resort to political violence, then there is an urgent need for governments to adequately address the human dimension to "global security". Not least, the plight of the world's refugees should be recognised as a major global security concern rather than an irksome immigration burden for recipient countries in the developed world.

As the world becomes increasingly complex and interconnected, so people choose in ever-increasing numbers to relocate to new countries. Right of movement around a rapidly shrinking globe is, however, constrained by the capacity and willingness of receiving countries to absorb new arrivals. While tourists, business travellers, highly qualified professionals, even guest workers, are welcomed by countries eager to attract foreign exchange, capital and expertise, refugees are greeted with at best suspicion and at worst resentment. For the millions that travel as voluntary migrants there are millions more who move not by choice but at best out of necessity; to escape war, famine, or fear of persecution or at worst tricked or sold into varying forms of slavery, or forcibly removed from their homes and villages by agents of the state or their opponents.

A World Turned Upside Down: Risk, Refugees and Global Security   11
in the 21st Century

Endemic instability in the Middle East, East Africa and Central and South Asia,[1] exacerbated by external military interventions, is largely responsible for the current flows of persons seeking asylum. While responsibility for such human suffering is popularly sheeted home to military dictators and their corrupt regimes, modern mass refugee movements highlight significant structural weaknesses in the evolving global system which governments in the developed world and global institutions are best placed but reluctant to tackle.

The global wrap

Human mobility is synonymous with contemporary globalisation. Industrialisation brought rapid demographic change to Western Europe with far reaching consequences for the rest of humankind. In 1750 at the dawn of the Industrial Revolution estimated world population was 700 million rising to 900 million by 1800. Over the next 200 years, world population rose by more than five times to 6 billion people, with the most rapid increase occurring after 1950 and mainly outside the industrialised or developed world. This global population explosion coincided with increased population transfers from Europe to the Americas, and from China to European colonies in Southeast Asia. From 1840 to 1940 some 56 million Europeans migrated with more than two-thirds bound for North America aided by relaxation of emigration restrictions by Western European governments to ease their domestic population pressures (Held, McGrew, Goldblatt and Perraton 2000, 292–3). Over that hundred-year period more than 140 million people moved around the world as migrants travelling in the wake of European and American expansion (Manning 2005, 146). By comparison, in 2005 alone, some 191 million people were classed as international migrants by the International Organization for Migration (IOM) (UNPD 2005). Contemporary migration patterns, however, display a South–North bias, mirroring a major shift in global economic prosperity.

Global travel pre-dates the dawn of the industrial era but the laying down of a new global communications infrastructure in the nineteenth century gave fresh impetus to the human propensity to move and greater opportunity to cross entire continents and oceans in rapid time. The

---

[1] Afghanistan sits astride the boundaries of the Middle East and South Asia. In this paper it is treated as a part of the modern Middle East but with due weight and attention given to the humanitarian and military implications of the country's ongoing civil war for neighbouring Pakistan.

"speed," "intensity," "rapidity" and "range of repercussion" of nineteenth-century international economic exchange, writes historian Eric Hobsbawm, brought about a world "transformed from a geographical expression into a constant operational reality" (Hobsbawm 1985, 63, 78). Advances in transport technologies and electronic communication contributed to world economic expansion but also hastened the catastrophic displacement of indigenous peoples in the Americas and Australasia.

The spread of this European-centred world system across the Americas, Africa and Asia disrupted long-established political traditions and economic patterns. Historical wealth distribution data from Maddison (2003) for the period 1500–2001 highlights the shuddering impact of globalisation upon Asian productivity relative to Western Europe and North America (261). Accounting for nearly two-thirds of global GDP at the beginning of the eighteenth century, Asia's share fell below one-quarter by 1913. Productivity climbed back above one-third in the late twentieth century led by Japan, but in Africa, however, the share of global GDP remained virtually stagnant throughout with, as of 2001, a paltry 3.3 per cent for a continent of 1.2 billion people and rising (259).

Two world wars caused the fatal haemorrhaging of the European imperial order. In its place the United States and the former Soviet Union engaged in "hegemonic competition" across the globe. For the next four decades a tense nuclear balance of terror maintained relative peace and stability in the geographical heartlands of the West and the former Soviet Bloc. But while prosperity rose and wars declined in frequency in the West and East Asia, violent conflict became endemic elsewhere. European colonialism facilitated economic and cultural globalisation but also introduced new social stresses into colonised worlds, between coloniser and colonised, immigrant and "indigenous" and between ethno-linguistic communities thrown together by unwelcome colonial state formations.

Since 1945 an estimated 41 million people, civilians and combatants, have died as a result of interstate conflict and bitter civil wars fought across the Middle East, Asia, Latin America and Africa, in the name of nationalism and anti-colonialism, socialism or purely for private gain (Leitenberg 2006). Superpower rivalry turned civil wars into proxy wars prolonging armed conflicts to the greater emiseration of those caught in the crossfire. It is no coincidence that, acknowledging the violent disintegration of the former Yugoslavia, the frequency of intra-state conflicts declined appreciably over the 1990s as the Soviet system crumbled. But, at the start of the twenty-first century, conflicts in

Afghanistan, Iraq, Sudan and state repression such as is occurring in Zimbabwe, create new global security challenges and new refugee crises.

Suffering by numbers

Refugee flows can be read as indices of the intensity of conflict or political oppression. The United Nations High Commissioner for Refugees documented 8.5 million refugees and asylum seekers at the end of 2005; 2.5 million in Africa, and a further 2.45 million in Central Asia, North Africa and Middle East (UNHCR 2006, 2). UNHCR refugee statistics recognise both internationally and internally displaced persons (IDPs) including stateless peoples and returned refugees. The UNHCR recorded 19.2 million such "persons of concern" in 2005 of which only 5.6 million IDPs were under UNHCR protection out of an estimated global total of 25 million. By the beginning of 2006 there were fewer still refugees but the total number of persons under UNHCR protection reached 20.8 million; a rise of 1.2 million almost entirely attributable to the escalating counter-insurgency in Iraq (UNHCR 2006). More alarming are estimates that undocumented and unregulated population movements could range from 45 to 65 million persons globally (UNFPA 2006; CHS 2003, 41). These statistics represent an unacceptable social, and for the most part hidden, cost of power politics at the local and global level.

Unregulated population movements constitute the underside side of globalisation. The promise of better living standards draws thousands of illegal migrants from North Africa into Spain from where they disperse throughout Europe. This clandestine migration creates friction at the interstate level between Spain and Morocco, especially given the latter's proximity to the Iberian Peninsula (Driessen 1998, 100–2). More subtle forms of displacement render people vulnerable to kidnapping and trafficking. Searching for higher wages to supplement meagre agricultural earnings or compensate for the lack of economic opportunity at home, seasonal urban workers are vulnerable to exploitation. In Indonesia, the Philippines and Thailand, the capital cities have attracted masses of rural people who congregate around the city centres and on the city outskirts in slum areas—living in appalling squalor. Young village girls sold by their parents or kidnapped into the commercial sex industry swell the ranks of the estimated 700,000 persons trafficked internationally each year (Shifman 2003, 126–7). Because they are not in imminent danger of being killed, people trapped in these patterns of displacement lie outside the scope of the present global refugee regime.

Created to protect people displaced by war, the 1951 Refugee Convention and the UNHCR confront escalating responsibilities in an increasingly volatile global system. According the Michael Barnett and Martha Finnemore (2004) the global policy balance has, over the course of the last sixty years, tilted against resettlement towards "voluntary" repatriation of refugees (93). This shift in emphasis, they argue, is due to increased reluctance of developed countries to accommodate refugees following the mass exodus from Indochina after 1975 (94–103). Indeed repatriation is celebrated by the UNHCR as a "durable solution" to refugee crises and the measure most responsible for a decline in refugee numbers in recent years (UNHCR 2005; 2006)

Globally, as many as 6 million refugees returned home during 2002– 05, of which 4.6 million Afghans now confront a resurgence of violence and renewed persecution, as the Taliban intensifies its campaign against Kabul and international forces stationed in Afghanistan (UNHCR 2006). The plight of refugees is not helped by the narrow framing of national political debates around immigration and humanitarian assistance.

Globalisation and identity

Globalisation is miscast by its critics as a challenge to the security of national communities and by liberal advocates who portray it as a linear process leading to the creation of a "global village" where cultural differences are diluted by a common propensity to consume. Instead, globalisation displays both centrifugal and centripetal tendencies. Many people in Western societies affected by the rapid internationalisation of national economies, opened to the vicissitudes of unpredictable and volatile global markets, sense globalisation as an assault on their national identity (Ruggie 2003, 102–3). Technological innovations and deepening economic interconnectedness bring people into closer proximity but few are prepared intellectually for the cultural challenges posed by these globalising trends. The reassertion of religious identity across the Middle East, South and Southeast Asia is a reaction to the pervasiveness of Western culture and the implications of this "cultural imperialism" for traditional values and beliefs (Giddens 2000; Gray 2002).

In the West, public perceptions of risk associated with refugee and minority migrant groups are easily manipulated by extremists in receiving states who imply that each new arrival poses a threat to "national cohesion". Anti-cosmopolitans, from white supremacists to Al-Qaeda, welcome any hardening of identities wrought by fear and revulsion of cultural or religious difference in a world of seeming chaos and deepening insecurity.

Immigration is bound tightly to concerns about national identity. All states bear the imprint of human migrations, forced and free, making cultural diversity the international norm rather than the exception. And yet, today, the prevailing cultural reflex is to assert singular and exclusive identities. A fraction of the world's vulnerable or "at risk" persons arrive as asylum seekers or illegal migrants in Western countries, four per cent in 2005, and present at worst a negligible economic burden to the receiver (Costello 2002, 197; UNHCR 2005). Australia's record on asylum seekers is poor by world and regional standards, both in terms of absolute numbers accepted, as well as per capita refugee resettlement overall (Singer and Gregg 2004, 72–5). In Australia at the end of 2005 there were 1,822 asylum seekers awaiting the outcome of applications for refugee status compared to 40,710 in Austria, 71,624 in Germany and 20,552 in Canada (UNHCR 2006).

Stigmatised as "queue jumpers" by a bellicose Australian government, "boatpeople" from the Middle East passing through the Indonesian archipelago were intercepted and either sent to remote detention centres in Australia or shipped off to neighbouring Pacific island states where hundreds languished, in some case for several years, before their refugee status was confirmed. Denying displaced peoples from the Middle East any shred of legitimacy the Howard government chose instead to heighten public anxiety with allegations that those cast adrift along Australia's extensive northern maritime border might harbour terrorists in their midst; an argument that struck deep into the Australian psyche following the events of September 11, 2001.

Both the policies and the rhetoric deployed by Western governments against asylum seekers are designed to dampen public sympathy for genuine and extreme human suffering. The chaotic nature of refugee dispersal and the geographical location of refugee camps mean that the resettlement process does not function according to developed country notions of efficient social service, thus rendering as absurd the notion of an orderly "queue" of refugees waiting patiently to be called forward. "Frontline" camps in countries bordering on to "hot" combat zones countries can be extremely unsanitary and dangerous; doubly so if the receiving country adopts a hostile attitude and uses force to expel or deter refugees, as often happens in the early stages of a refugee crisis.

More than half of all refugees are women who, along with children, bear the greatest burden of forced migration. Violence against women, including rape, is commonplace in central African camps and those in

Central and West Asia, meaning that women are exposed to severe risks ranging from physical harm to contracting sexually transmitted diseases (UNFPA 2006). Unsurprisingly, people with sufficient economic means will take extraordinary steps to ensure that they and their families find safe haven. Were governments to focus on the reasons why people risk all to escape war and its consequences, they might create broader public support for more effective and more expensive forms of intervention.

Displacement effects

Cambodia

Refugee emergencies capture public attention for barely a moment and yet the conditions that generate each new displacement can endure for decades. There is no single explanation for Cambodia's descent into darkness in the 1970s. Politically and culturally the country made sense as a nation state. A Cambodian state preceded the imposition of French colonial rule. A common language, Khmer, and a common historical tradition dating back to the time of Angkor, complemented the relative prosperity which the country enjoyed following independence in 1953. Yet Asian Cold War politics played out in the domestic sphere with tragic consequences. A coup by General Lon Nol in 1970 transformed the government into a US-subsidised military dictatorship allowing a small group of insurgents, the Khmer Rouge, to gather revolutionary momentum (Evans and Rowley 1990). An urban–rural divide caused resentment but of insufficient intensity to ignite a general insurgency. Rather, as David Chandler writes, the central government collapsed under the weight of its own incompetence (Chandler 1991).

Cambodia was caught in the updraught of war in Vietnam and the strategic rivalry between China, the former Soviet Union and the United States. Out of a population of roughly 7 million when Phnom Penh fell to the Khmer Rouge in April 1975, it is conservatively estimated that at least 1.7 million perished during three and a half years of Communist rule. Under the direction of the notorious Pol Pot, the Party announced a new beginning for the Khmer nation, Year Zero. Their aim: to turn Cambodia into a modern agrarian society by first purging the country of all corrupting outside influences. Cities were depopulated as millions were forced to endure, on pain of death, the purifying experience of hard physical work in the countryside. As many as one million Cambodians failed to meet the exacting demands of Party overseers and were murdered in the Killing Fields or tortured to death. As many as half a million died from starvation or disease.

The end to the holocaust came with the Vietnamese invasion in December 1978 which ended the Pol Pot era but led to a humanitarian crisis in neighbouring Thailand, to which the international community was slow to respond. In response to the influx of Cambodian refugees, Thailand temporarily closed its border with Cambodia. An experience repeated in many refugee emergencies across the Third World, Cambodian asylum seekers were met at gunpoint by Thai border guards and forced to return across open minefields or face being shot (Seng 2005, 162–6).

Civil war between the Vietnamese-backed Cambodian government and nationalist groups aligned with remnants of the Khmer Rouge forced hundreds of thousands more to flee to Thailand where camps were reluctantly established. The Thai government baulked at the costs of assistance, which included damage to agricultural and forest resources near to the refugee camps and the inflationary effect on local village economies caused by the increased demand for supplies (Monhathai 1999). Further, government obstruction of international agencies, which included denial of access to some camps, occasioned major logistical breakdowns in the provision of relief (Nattinee 1999). Over 200,000 Cambodian refugees were resettled in third countries from camps in Thailand which remained active well into the 1990s despite the 1992 Paris peace accords which opened the way for Cambodia's rehabilitation.

The ironies of the Cambodian refugee crisis are manifold. Cambodia's civil war was prolonged by Beijing's support for the Khmer Rouge and Washington's hostility towards the Vietnamese-backed government of Heng Samrin. It took more than thirty years to bring internal conflict to an end and to re-establish a working political equilibrium in Cambodia. The deeper the fault lines within a state, however, the more protracted and brutal civil or secessionist wars become thus prolonging the displacement effect of armed conflict. This is evident in protracted intra-state conflicts in Myanmar, Indonesia, and Afghanistan while in Iraq, the country's descent into internal chaos highlights the limits of intervention, humanitarian or otherwise.

Myanmar

European colonialism left behind multiethnic states saddled with deep ethnic rivalries across Asia and the Middle East. The presence of ethnically diverse populations is not in itself a weakness of these states; rather, former colonial authorities and independence governments failed to adequately address the demands of those opposed to new state formations.

Claiming a right to self-determination, the Christian Karen have fought against central authority since the formation of the Federation of Burma in 1948. The Karen National Union (KNU) continues its armed resistance, but the fall of the Karen National Union's stronghold of Mannerplaw in 1995 allowed the Burmese army to penetrate deeply into the Karen homeland pinning down KNU forces along the Thai–Burma border. Repeated Burmese dry-season offensives drove Karen refugees into Thailand where they comprise the vast majority of Thailand's 149,351 refugee population (UNHCR 2006).

The presence in Thailand of Karen and other refugee groups from Myanmar exposed the Thai government to allegations from Burma's military junta that it is harbouring KNU insurgents at a time when Thai business interests are pursuing legal access to Burmese timber and energy resources. Denied even basic services by the Thai state and subject to periodic shelling and guerrilla incursions from across the border, the Karen, like Cambodians before them, are regarded as an unwelcome security burden.

West Papua

Even minuscule numbers of refugees can generate political friction between neighbouring countries. In 2006, 42 asylum seekers from the Indonesian province of Irian Jaya, also known as West Papua, made landfall on Australian territory sparking a diplomatic dispute between Canberra and Jakarta, which withdrew its ambassador in protest at the Howard government's swift decision to accord the new arrivals refugee status amid claims of Indonesian human rights abuses. The Australian government's decision fuelled Indonesian suspicions that some influential sections of Australian society favour the break-up of Indonesia. At the end of 2005 there were 9,991 "Indonesian" refugees in Papua New Guinea, the majority of which undoubtedly originated from West Papua where a low-level secessionist insurgency has simmered for the last forty years (UNHCR 2006).

The Free Papua Movement, *Organisasi Papua Merdeka* (OPM) grew out of the popular movement for West Papuan independence that emerged under Dutch rule but which was ignored by the international community and Indonesia after the former colony was incorporated into the Indonesian state in 1962 (King 2004, 20–25, 27–51). Australia's tightening of immigration laws to deflect future West Papuan asylum seekers was widely interpreted as a capitulation to Indonesian diplomatic pressure and reaffirmed the salience of geo-strategic priorities relative to humanitarian values in Australian foreign policy.

Afghanistan

In the Middle East, from Iraq to Afghanistan, ethnic and sectarian violence appears intractable. A Pashtun-dominated Afghanistan emerged towards the end of the eighteenth century and survived as a buffer state between British India and the Russian Empire becoming a British protectorate in 1907. From gaining its political independence little over a decade later until the Soviet invasion of 1979, the country's ethnic divisions and tribal loyalties were subordinated to the idea of a modernising Afghan state. Afghanistan was all but a Soviet satellite state in 1979 when Soviet troops moved in to prop up the country's increasingly unpopular communist government.

Muslim resistance to secular socialism escalated into all-out civil war driving millions to seek refuge in neighbouring Pakistan where Islamabad nurtured the Taliban and then turned it against Soviet troops (Schmeidl 2002, 25–6). Covert United States assistance for the Muslim *mujaheddin* fighting the Soviet invasion was predicated on the notion that Islam could be mobilised to counter the appeal of Marxist ideology and arrest communist expansion. Washington determined to turn Afghanistan into a quagmire; a Soviet Vietnam that would further degrade Moscow's capability to challenge US interests elsewhere (Coll 2005).

Anarchy ensued after the Soviet withdrawal in 1989. Diminishing and selective US assistance to the *mujaheddin* factions encouraged those out of favour in Washington to turn to the illegal opium trade to fund their struggle for control of the state, feeding a cycle of violence and corruption that engulfed neighbouring Pakistan (Rasanayagam 2005, 138–41, 184–8). American and Pakistani strategic interventions simply exacerbated the political crisis in Afghanistan and the Afghan refugee crisis along Pakistan's Northwest Frontier which remains a seedbed for Islamic radicalism. Focused upon ejecting the Soviets, US strategists misread the dynamics of instability in South Asia and the catastrophic consequences this would have for US and global security. Backed by Pakistan's intelligence agency, the Taliban gained the ascendancy and imposed a harsh Islamic regime over much of the country, including the capital, Kabul, which fell in 1996. Genocidal acts against minorities like the Hazara and continued fighting between the Taliban and the Northern Alliance sustained a cycle of population displacement that only ended when the Taliban capitulated to the Alliance and a US-led international coalition in late 2001 (157).

The risk of fragmentation in Afghanistan remains high as an elected government has so far failed to earn political legitimacy or create a sense of national unity. Persisting ideological, factional and economic divisions and a resurgent Taliban suggest the reconstruction of Afghanistan is a substantial and long-term challenge (Maley 2006).

Iraq

Armed interventions, humanitarian or strategic, do not in themselves end conflicts or resolve conflict dynamics. The US invasion and occupation of Iraq in 2003 has so far displaced at least 1.2 million Iraqis into neighbouring countries with a further 700,000 displaced internally by rising sectarian violence (Pollack and Byman 2006; UNHCR 2007). Iraq, formerly Mesopotamia, is one of Britain's more enduring colonial legacies. Split into three distinct regions, dominated by Kurds to the north, Sunni Muslims in the centre around Baghdad and Shi'ite Muslims to the south, the former British protectorate was predominantly tribal. The rationale for the creation of an Iraqi state was undoubtedly influenced by the presence of substantial oil reserves which Britain hoped to secure for British oil interests.

The country was born out of and into violence. Britain used military force to compel warring factions to accept their incorporation into the Iraqi state in 1920 (Fromkin 449–54). Aided by the former Soviet Union, the Baath Party regime of Saddam Hussein proved to be particularly brutal. Iraq made extensive use of chemical weapons against Iranian forces during Iran–Iraq war (1980–88) with full knowledge of Moscow, London and Washington. Both the US and Britain subscribed financially and politically to the Iraqi war effort in a vain attempt to bring down the Islamic theocracy of the Ayatollah Khomeini (Hiro 2003).

This First Gulf War writes Dilip Hiro, turned Iraq into a heavily militarised country which both enabled and emboldened Hussein to invade neighbouring Kuwait in 1990 to expropriate additional oil revenues with which to settle war debts and maintain a large standing army. Defeated by a US-led international coalition in the 43-day Second Gulf War (1991), Iraq's independence was preserved because neighbouring Arab states feared a popular backlash were the US to occupy the country. The Bush administration failed to support popular uprisings in the north and south of Iraq that might have eliminated Saddam Hussein (Galbraith 2007, 56–60). Instead the US, acting through the UN, sought to bring Saddam down with the imposition of sanctions and through clandestine moves to foment first rebellion and then a coup; measures which failed utterly (Hiro 2003, 71–94).

Responding to public outcry over the plight of ordinary Iraqis dying for lack of medical treatment, medicines and food, the UN allowed limited sales of Iraqi oil, the proceeds of which could be used to purchase food and essential medical supplies. The Oil for Food Scheme was, however, widely abused. For geo-strategic reasons, the US tolerated sanction-busting by Iraq's neighbours and much illegally purchased Iraqi oil found its way to the West. Sanctions were designed to bring down Hussein without recourse to armed intervention, which, when it eventuated in 2003, precipitated a major humanitarian and geo-political crisis (Meyer and Califano 2006, 74–5; 120–34).

Realising global security

The application of force to fashion a solution to endemic instability in the Middle East and South Asia did not yield anticipated results. Insurgent groups in Iraq and Afghanistan proved adept at using violence to block essential political reconciliations. As the international community struggles to come to terms with the sharp transition to a volatile post–Cold War world, questions must be asked about the serviceability of *Realpolitik*. By seeking to understand how and why countries lapse into chaos forcing people to relocate, we can gain insights into the dynamics of refugee crises. Two-thirds of the world's population live outside the industrialised world in countries where political, social, economic and environmental stresses are becoming more acute (Maddison 2003, 259). As this proportion rises over the next half century the displacement effects of new and unresolved intra-societal conflicts are likely to be greater in scope and impact.

In the logic of traditional security studies, peace is interpreted as the absence of armed conflict or war, which can only be sustained if states maintain sufficient armed force to deter or repulse an attack by one or more hostile powers. The international environment is therefore cast negatively as a source of potential harm against which states must frame their security policies and act individually or through strategic alliances to reduce the risk of attack through diplomacy or, paradoxically, the use of force. According to this crude logic, security is gained through strength measured in tangible military assets and the less tangible national unity of purpose, with varying degrees of importance attached a nation's economic base. Perversely, as discussed above, balance of power principles promote tolerance for civilian casualties and the traumatisation of whole populations as unavoidable "collateral damage" in the great game of power politics.

By categorising security crises as either "hard" or "soft", policy makers, researchers and development practitioners alike ensure that war and human development remain conceptually detached. From different starting points, security analysts and economists identify a series of conditions or "risk factors" that lead, in combination, to a breakdown in government and of law and order, ranging from extreme disparities in wealth, the economic and political marginalisation of ethnic or religious minorities, to low levels of educational attainment, poor nutrition and high maternal and infant mortality rates (Goldstone et al. 2000, 17; Sachs 2005). Feminist writers foreground a gender dimension of security and emphasise the greater exposure of women to security risks ranging from systematic political violence, systemic oppression and sexual exploitation (McKay 2004, 155–7). There is an urgent need to reconceptualise security and to re-tool or re-calibrate the apparatus of national and global security to accommodate the proliferation of global security risks.

Human security is a concept framed as much in opposition to traditionalist or Realist ideas as it is defined to establish a new cognitive map for security analysts to follow. Human security risks are "polymorphous" in that they are many-sided and can quickly change in shape, scope and trajectory. The United Nations Commission on Human Security, handing down its report, *Human Security Now* (2003), detailed the interrelated global challenges of endemic poverty, disease, illiteracy, degraded natural environments and poor nutrition and their correlations with the incidence of armed conflict and societal collapse (CHS 2003, 6). Rejecting the UN's holistic approach to global problem solving, critics argue the sheer breadth of issues encompassed by the UN's broad conception of human security carries the risk of being too cumbersome to serve as an operational definition (Paris 2004, 254–5). Researchers at the Canadian Human Security Centre at the University of British Columbia in their *Human Security Report 2006* limit the scope of human security to the study of the "incidence, severity, causes and consequences of global violence" (HSC 2006, 18–20). Placing human security squarely within the orbit of conflict studies, their approach attaches greatest importance to humanitarian assistance for victims of war and to the conditions that promote peace within and between states. But narrowing our focus to the immediate causes and consequences of conflict we lose sight of the long-term trajectories of risk that can culminate in societal breakdown and humanitarian crises.

The limits of liberalism

Gaping wealth disparities between urban and rural populations mirror wealth disparities between developed and developing countries but are masked by aggregate per-capita purchasing power parity or productivity ratios. A global poverty line of US$1.07 per day is cold comfort for those on or just above this level whose economic prospects and those of their family are limited. If we accept that pressure to migrate mounts in those parts of the global system where economic, political and environmental stressors are not addressed at the national, regional or global levels, the present low rate of international development assistance paid by developed countries like Australia is both short-sighted and self-defeating. The UN recommends that donor countries allocate 0.7 per cent of their annual Gross National Income (GNI) to overseas development assistance (ODA). Globally, however, ODA has fallen in percentage terms with OECD countries averaging 0.25 per cent of GNI in 2003 down from 0.33 per cent in 1990 (World Bank, 2005). Economic transfers from developed to developing countries through foreign direct investment, tourism and the consumption of low-cost manufactures, in part counteracts in aggregate terms this decline. Guest-worker remittances too, rising from a little over US$100 billion in 2001 to US$233 billion in 2005, of which 71 per cent was transferred to developing countries, highlight further compensatory income flows (IOM cited in CHS 2003, 51). The reality is however that market returns are unevenly distributed across the developing world creating pockets of prosperity while leaving vast areas in absolute or near-absolute poverty.

Even in middle-income countries, large sections of society can be marginalised or deprived of opportunity because their country's natural capital is degraded by population pressures or poor management, or there are insufficient funds to invest in education and industry, because these funds are siphoned off by vested interests. In underdeveloped and heavily indebted countries there is little or no manufacturing, little or no foreign investment to generate wealth because foreign corporations, unless they happen to be resource companies, prefer to invest in economies with more tolerable levels of political risk, better health standards and higher literacy rates for working age people. In combination these disadvantages contribute to patterns of aid dependency, paradoxically high population growth amidst galloping disease infection rates in Africa, Asia and the Pacific, material and psychological deprivation, and severe trauma from political instability and in many instances protracted social conflict (Harrison 1993; Diamond 2005; Sachs 2005).

The success of East Asian economies in the late twentieth century demonstrates the benefits but also the risks of dependence upon foreign direct investment. In addition to its severe social impacts, the 1997 Asian financial crisis threatened to politically destabilise an entire region and strengthened anti-Western sentiment, some of which surely translated into support for terrorist elements in Indonesia and the Philippines. Economic issues loom large in any security equation. Those countries most severely affected by endemic conflict bear a heavy burden of foreign debt, disease, severe environmental stress and extreme poverty and are in no position to lift themselves up the development ladder without substantial external assistance (Sachs 2005). But the extent that liberal economic prescriptions can alleviate pressures leading to societal breakdown is limited.

We are witnessing a resurgence of power politics, writes John Gray (2002). After a brief summer of international cooperation in the 1990s, the "Washington consensus" on market liberalisation is in danger of unravelling (88). In a world where international prestige and influence derive from military capability, any hope for a humanitarian consensus around refugee protection, in all its dimensions, is tragically slipping from view.

Conclusion

We have never been so well equipped to study the causes and consequences of refugee movements and to identify those most at risk and those most in need. Yet governments in the developed world are unprepared to deal humanely with the human debris of globalisation. This blinkered self-interest leaves refugees "buried" in countries ill-equipped or ill-governed to deal with such crises. Security policies articulated at the national level factor-in human suffering, but in an unpredictable world it is unlikely that humanitarian crises can be kept within a "tolerable" bandwidth of risk. Even if conflicts decline in frequency, the potential for environmental or major health emergencies to displace entire populations should not be underestimated. The risk to global security lies in the subordination of long-term practical and sustainable development goals to ideology-driven economics and to *Realpolitik*. Globalisation has many paradoxes but one of the most glaring is the inability of governments in the developed world to recognise and respond to a new global security landscape where people matter, not for moral, but for the most pragmatic of reasons.

References

Barnett, M. and M. Finnemore. 2004. *Rules for the world: International organizations and world politics.* Ithaca: Cornell University Press.

Chandler, David P. 1991. *The tragedy of Cambodian history: Politics, war and revolution since 1945.* New Haven: Yale University Press.

Coll, Steve. 2005. *Ghost wars: The secret history of the CIA, Afghanistan and Bin Laden, from the Soviet invasion to September 10, 2001.* London: Penguin.

Commission on Human Security. 2003. *Human security now.* New York: United Nations.

Costello, T. 2002. Seeing the whole: Population policy in a global context. In *Australia's population challenge: The 2002 Australian Population Summit*, ed. S. Vizard, H. J. Martin and T. Watts. Melbourne: Penguin.

Diamond, J. 2005. *Collapse: How societies choose to fail or survive.* London: Allen Lane.

Driessen, H. 1998. The "New Immigration" and the Transformation of the European–African frontier. In *Border identities: Nation and state at international frontiers*, ed. T. M. Wilson, H. Donnan. Cambridge: Cambridge University Press.

Evans, G. and K. Rowley. 1990. *Red brotherhood at war: Vietnam, Cambodia and Laos since 1975.* London: Verso.

Fromkin, D. 1989. *A peace to end all peace: Creating the modern Middle East, 1914–1922.* London: Penguin.

Galbraith, P. W. 2007. *The end of Iraq: How American incompetence created a war without end.* London: Pocket Books.

Giddens, A. 2000. *Runaway world: How globalisation is reshaping our lives.* Cambridge: Polity.

Goldstone, J. A. et al. 2000. *State Failure Taskforce report: Phase Three Findings.* College Park, MD: Centre for International Development and Conflict Management, University of Maryland.

Gray, J. 2002. *False dawn: The delusion of global capitalism.* London: Granta.

Harrison, Paul. 1993. *Inside the Third World.* London: Penguin.

Held, D., A. McGrew, D. Goldblatt and J. Perraton. 2000. *Global transformations: Politics, economics and culture.* Cambridge: Polity.

Hiro, D. 2003. *Iraq: The report from the inside.* London: Granta.

Hobsbawm, E. 1985. *The age of capital.* London: Abacus.

Human Security Centre. 2006. *Human Security Report, 2005.* Vancouver: University of British Colombia.

King, P. 2004. *West Papua & Indonesia since Suharto: Independence, autonomy or chaos?*. Sydney: UNSW Press.
Klaits, Alex and Gulchin Gulmamdova-Klaits. 2005. *Love and war in Afghanistan*. New York: Seven Stories Press.
Legrain, P. 2006. *Immigrants: Your country needs them*. London: Little, Brown.
Leitenberg, Milton. 2006. *Deaths in wars and conflicts in the 20th century*, Occasional Paper no. 29, Peace Studies Program, Cornell University.
McKay, S. 2004. Women, human security and peace-building: A feminist analysis. In *Conflict and human security: A search for new approaches to peace-building*, ed. H. Shinoda and H. Jeong. Hiroshima: Institute for Peace Science, Hiroshima University.
Maddison, A. 2003. *The world economy: Volume 2, historical statistics*. Paris: OECD.
Maley, William. 2006. *Rescuing Afghanistan*. Sydney: UNSW Press.
Manning, Patrick. 2005. *Migration in world history*. London: Routledge.
Meyer, J. A. and M. G. Califano. 2006. *Good intentions corrupted: The oil-for-food scandal and the threat to the UN*. New York: Public Affairs Reports.
Monhathai Pundrikabha. 1999. The Royal Thai Government's policy towards Cambodian refugees, 1978–98. *Asia Pacific School of Economics and Management Working Papers*, Canberra: Asia Pacific Press.
Nattinee Marakanond. 1999. Coordination of humanitarian aid for Cambodian refugees in Thailand: Reasons for ineffectiveness. *Asia Pacific School of Economics and Management Working Papers*, Canberra, Asia Pacific Press.
Paris, R. 2004. Human Security: Paradigm shift or hot air? In *New global dangers: Changing dimensions of international security*, ed. M. E. Brown, O. R. Cote jr, S. M. Lynn-Jones and S. E. Miller. Massachusetts: MIT Press.
Pollack, K. M. and D. L. Byman. 2006. Iraqi refugees: Carriers of conflict, *The Atlantic Monthly*, November. http://www.brookings.edu/views/articles/byman/2061101.htm (Accessed 7 February 2007).
Rasanayagam, A. 2005. *Afghanistan: A modern history*. London: I. B. Taurus.
Ruggie, J. G. 2003. Taking embedded liberalism global: The corporate connection. In *Taming globalization: Frontiers of governance*. ed. D. Held and Mathias Koenig-Archibugi, 93–129. Cambridge: Polity.
Sachs, J. 2005. *The end of poverty: How we can make it happen in our lifetime*. London: Penguin.

Schmeidl, S. 2002. (Human) security dilemmas: Long-term implications of the Afghan refugee crisis, *Third World Quarterly*, vol. 23, no. 1, February, 7–29.

Seng, Theary, C. 2005. *Daughter of the killing fields: Asreai's story.* London: Fusion.

Shifman, P. 2003. Trafficking and women's human rights in a globalised world, *Gender and Development*, vol. 11, no. 1, May, 125–32.

Singer, P. and T. Gregg. 2004. *How ethical is Australia? An examination of Australia's record as a global citizen.* Melbourne: The Australia Collaboration and Black Inc.

UNHCR. 2005. *Refugees by numbers.* Geneva: Media Relations and Public Information Service.

—. 2006. *2005 global refugee trends.* Geneva: UNHCR

—. 2007. *The Iraq situation.*
http://unhcr.org/cgi-bin/texis//vtx/iraq?page=intro (Accessed 10 July 2007).

United Nations Population Division. 2005. *World migrant stock: 2005 revision database.* http://esa.un.org/migration/p2k0data.asp (accessed 12 September 2006).

UNFPA. 2006. *State of the world population 2006: A passage to hope: Women and international migration.*
http://www.unfpa.org/swp/2006/english (accessed 12 September 2006).

World Bank. *World Development Indicators, 2005.*
http://www.devdata.worldbank.org/wdi2005/section6_1.htm (accessed 10 December 2007).

Chapter Three

Securing Borders: Interdiction and Deterrence in Australia and Canada

Alperhan Babacan

Introduction

Australia and Canada are comparable countries as they have similar legal and political traditions and rights discourses. They are both relatively young nations, were former British colonies and share a British heritage, legal and political system. Each country is also party to all major United Nations (UN) human rights treaties and share a history of mass migrations. Both countries now promote skilled migration and have explicit policies concerning the inflow of immigrants and refugees.

Until the 1970s and early 1980s, Australia and Canada had reasonably generous refugee and asylum policies. From the 1980s, each country began to tighten its asylum policies. By the 1990s and into the post-2000 period, the once generous and accommodating asylum policies in each country were transformed through legislative enactments, into policies of containment directed at interdicting and deterring asylum seekers from arriving on each country's shores. Two macro factors which led to the tightening of asylum in each country were economic globalisation and geo-political changes. This is further complicated by the fact that the Refugee Convention lacks appropriate safeguards to prevent states from implementing many harsh measures. After providing a broad overview of the profound impact of these factors on asylum policies, an overview of the interdiction and deterrence policies in each country is provided.

Economic globalisation

The refugee and asylum policies of each country were built on healthy economies of the postwar period and the ability to interview and select refugees from abroad, with very few asylum claims being made until the latter part of the twentieth century. These countries accordingly developed generous refugee policies when their economies were healthy during the postwar boom period. Refugees and asylum seekers could be absorbed into the unskilled sectors of industry. Historically these were the manufacturing and construction sectors.

The latter part of the twentieth century saw entire nations and continents being economically locked out of the new global world order through the process of economic globalisation. Accompanying the process of economic globalisation was that the first world replaced Keynesian and social democratic policies with severe budgetary cutbacks and placed emphasis on economic rationalism (Whitaker 1998). Structural shifts in the economies of first world countries (including Australia and Canada) resulted in an intense competition for investment capital and skilled labour. High unemployment and inflationary pressures, a growing emphasis on economic rationalist policies and "market forces" resulted in the tightening of immigration and refugee policies (Richmond 1995). Immigration control mechanisms to secure borders were instituted to regulate and manipulate the movement of people from Third World countries, to restrict the migration of unskilled people and to select from the pool of highly skilled or wealthy immigrants who were suitable for resettlement (Cheran 2001). The closing of borders by the more advanced industrial countries of the world has been described as a "new serfdom" (Dowty 1987) or as "global apartheid" (Richmond 1994).

Cold War

Economic developments cannot be treated independently of major political changes that have occurred internationally. The global political order for most of the twentieth century was structured around the Cold War. Most contemporary asylum policies were formulated following the Second World War with the Cold War in mind. To a significant extent, refugee policy and the admission of refugees from the communist bloc countries was an instrument of foreign policy because it was seen as part of the fight against communism (Shukre 1995).

Ideological considerations during the Cold War were so powerful that the discriminatory immigration policies of first world governments were occasionally overshadowed. An example is provided by Indo-Chinese boat people in the 1970s and 1980s, who were accepted in large numbers in Canada and Australia, not only on humanitarian grounds, but because they were fleeing "communist oppression" (Whitaker 1998). Other examples of this ideological influence include the state response to refugees from Eastern Europe between the 1940s and 1960s and acceptance of Afghan refugees after the Soviet invasion of Afghanistan.

The collapse of communism after the end of the Cold War (1989–92) brought a new political world order and, as a result, new economic relationships. The ensuing emergence of new states, coupled with civil wars and conflicts around the globe on the one hand (Inglis 1994), and economic restructuring in the former eastern bloc countries, on the other, resulted in considerable population displacement and the emergence of new patterns of immigration (Gould 1994; Held et al. 1999).

The Refugee Convention and interdiction

Although the two broad macro developments have contributed to regressive policies in each country, part of the problem also lies in the inadequacies in the Refugee Convention. Notwithstanding the Convention's definition of "who is a refugee" and the standards for treatment that must be accorded to refugees, both the Convention and Protocol remain silent on the procedures that are to be adopted in the determination of refugee status (Goodwin-Gill 1996). The international instruments leave the means of implementation to each state (Watson 1998). International refugee law differs from the UN human rights regime in that international refugee law does not provide a mechanism for individuals and states to make complaints. Further, very few safeguards are built into international refugee law to prevent state abuse or non-compliance (Loescher 1999).

The Refugee Convention is silent or not totally clear on some of the measures adopted by states to prevent asylum seekers from arriving on their shores or having the right to seek asylum. Such measures include visa requirements, carrier sanctions, and other interdiction measures such as turning around people at ports and airports (Cronin 1994). The Convention's silence on these matters and the absence of an enforcement mechanism has allowed each state to enact and implement harsh measures.

The combined result of these factors, coupled with a sharp increase in asylum claims from the mid-1980s in Canada and the 1990s in Australia, resulted in each state blocking the asylum route through the enactment of obstacles known as interdiction. This led to further asylum claims.

Immigration controls, border controls, bureaucratic procedures, incarceration, punitive treatment and quasi-military measures began to be used by each country to deter repatriate "illegal" or unwanted boat people (Richmond 1995). Each country portrayed the increased numbers of unauthorised arrivals as a threat to their sovereign right to decide who can enter and remain in their respective territories. Along with the legislative hurdles began a process of deterring unwanted immigrants and refugees through negative discourses: the "other", the "illegal", "queue jumpers" (Simmons 1997; McMaster 2001) and the "potential terrorist" since 2001.

There is a vast range of interdiction measures which aim to directly prevent (through physical and legal obstacles) or indirectly prevent (for example, by deterring through discursive labelling) asylum seekers from arriving on each state's borders. The Canadian Council for Refugees divides interdiction into pre and post-arrival measures. Some of the measures fall into both categories whilst some also act as a deterrent (Canadian Council for Refugees 2007a). Pre-arrival interdiction measures include the imposition of visas, carrier sanctions and fines for people smuggling, the placement of immigration officials at international ports and airports, entering into border cooperation agreements, intervention on the high seas, sharing of immigration intelligence, imposition of detention, the safe first or third country rules and excising migration zones. Some post-arrival interdiction measures include removing or reducing welfare and/or settlement services available to asylum seekers, speeding up the refugee determination process, barring rights to appeal decisions or accessing the court and resort to detention and discursive labelling.

Interdiction and deterrence in Canada

As a result of its geographical location, Canada had very few asylum claims until the 1980s. However, commencing in 1980, the number of asylum claims began to increase, reaching several thousands of claims by the late 1980s. In the changed economic and political climate of the 1980s and 1990s, and in an era of increased numbers of asylum claims, Canada's humanitarian response to asylum seekers began to be questioned (Lippert 1998). Rather than being able to select refugees from abroad, Canada, like Australia, found itself having to cope with a large number of asylum seekers arriving spontaneously. Lippert partly attributes this increase to the reduction in the cost of air travel and increased dissemination of information about Canada as a safe haven for refugees (Lippert 1998). As a result of the increased number of asylum claims, the refugee system that was designed primarily to handle small numbers of individual asylum claims developed a huge backlog (UNHCR 2000). In an attempt to curb the rising numbers of asylum claims in the 1980s, Canada imposed transit visa requirements on 17 countries in 1985 (Lippert 1998).

On 21 July 1988, Bill C55 and Bill C84 were enacted in a further attempt to reduce the increased number of asylum applications (Richmond 2001). The Canadian government justified the new legislation on the basis that it had to combat the increased numbers of illegal entrants (Elliott and Fleras 1992) and that the increased numbers of asylum seekers undermined Canada's sovereignty to decide who entered and who became a member of Canadian society. Bill C55 and Bill C84 were aimed at deterring unauthorised arrivals and the restoration of "control" over Canada's borders (Hanks 1989; Richmond 1991).

Bill C55 (*An Act to Amend the Immigration Act 1976*) was passed following the extensive media coverage of the arrival of the Sikh boat people in Nova Scotia in 1987 (Dirks 1995). It overhauled and streamlined the refugee determination procedures (Richmond 2001). It created the Immigration Review Board (IRB) and a two-stage determination process with a "credible basis" screening process being resorted to in the first instance (Dirks 1987). Within 72 hours after entry, each asylum seeker's "credibility" had to be assessed by an adjudicator. Only claims assessed as being genuine were to appear at a more detailed hearing held by the IRB. This process was said to be aimed at reducing the backlog of cases before the IRB (Knight 1993). Bill C55 also elaborately defined circumstances where a person would cease to be a Convention refugee (such as when the reasons for the person's fear or persecution no longer existed in the home country). In addition, the Act empowered immigration officers to refuse entry to asylum seekers who arrived in Canada from a safe third country (Hounslow 1988).

Bill C84 (*The Refugee Deterrents and Detention Act*) focused on security concerns, border protection and organised people smuggling (Hanks 1989). Although the *Immigration Act 1976* did contain provisions for carrier sanctions, Bill C84 significantly increased the penalties for the transportation of refugees lacking "proper" documentation (Lippert 1998). It also imposed penalties for organised people smuggling (Elliott and Fleras 1992). Immigration officers were given increased powers to board and turn ships around (Lippert 1998).

Virtually all travellers from the Third World countries that had generated refugee flows were required to obtain visitors' or transit visas (Richmond 2001). Media coverage depicted asylum seekers as illegal migrants and queue jumpers (Gorman 1993). Several polls and surveys revealed that Canadians were concerned with the rise in immigration numbers during periods of economic recession and with refugee admission (Jakubowski 1997).

The increased number of asylum claims in the 1990s resulted in the introduction of two further pieces of legislation that curtailed the rights of asylum seekers. Bill C86 (*An Act to Amend the Immigration Act and Other Acts in Consequence Thereof*, 1976 (Bill C86), 1992) came into force in early 1993 and was dictated by changing world conditions (Dirks 1995). The world in which Canada delivered its immigration and refugee program was very different from that which existed at the time when the *Immigration Act* of 1976 came into force. There were more people on the move, especially after the collapse of the Soviet Union (Knowles 1997). In an attempt to deter and prevent uncontrolled and/or unwanted immigration, other developed countries had imposed strict entry and visa requirements (Dirks 1995). The Charter of Rights and Freedoms was not in force in the 1970s and its enactment meant that refugee claimants could challenge the rules governing immigration and refugee policies, resulting in refugee and asylum claims being dealt with in a more litigious manner. Furthermore, the years between 1978 and 1993 witnessed the globalisation of finance and crime, increased terrorism and a decline in the manufacturing sectors as a result of economic restructuring. All of these factors "necessitated" Canada to manage its refugee and asylum policies in a different manner (Dirks 1995).

Bill C86 extended criminality-based grounds for exclusion from the refugee system (ss. 19 and 27). It also introduced a new discursive era in immigration and refugee law. It focused on criminality and abuse and increased the powers of immigration officers to enforce the Act. Bill C86 inserted a "terrorism" clause into the *Immigration Act* rendering refugees (and immigrants) as inadmissible if there were reasonable grounds to believe that they would engage in terrorism or were members of a terrorist organisation. The Act did not, however, specify or define what constituted terrorism or a terrorist group and what role a person had to play or undertake to be classed as "inadmissible" under this provision (Aiken 2001).

Bill C86 allowed for the increased use of visa requirements for nationals of countries that were prone to the use of 'fraudulent' documents, as well as the fingerprinting and photographing of asylum seekers whose cases were pending. The credibility hearing was abolished in order to expedite cases before the IRB (Dirks 1995). The Bill further tightened the safe third country provisions whereby asylum seekers who entered Canada through a safe third country could be returned after an administrative decision (Young 2001). The government justified Bill C86 on the grounds that it would lead to the improved efficiency and effectiveness of the refugee status determination system without compromising the protection obligations (Lippert 1998).

The bombing of the Twin Towers in 2001, coupled with an increased number of asylum claims during the 1990s, allowed the government to easily pass the *Immigration and Refugee Protection Act 2001* (IRPA) through parliament. Overall, the Act focused heavily on criminality, security and border control at the expense of protecting refugees and asylum seekers (Macklin 2001). Several key provisions of the IRPA were directed at tightening access to the refugee determination system including a more extensive initial screening of claimants and limitations on the appeal processes (Reitz 2002). Interdiction methods were strengthened by way of increased penalties for offences related to illegal entry and trafficking and the retainment of the safe third country provisions (Dench 2001).

Powers of detention were strengthened including detention for administrative convenience. The Act also expanded the provisions for detention without a warrant and for detention on the grounds of identity. The legislation did not impose time limits on detention. The principle of *non-refoulement* has also been eroded through section 115(2) which makes an explicit exception to the principle of non-refoulement, allowing the government of Canada to refoule a person on the basis of allegations of criminality or security. This was affirmed in *Suresh v. Minister of Citizenship and Immigration* [2002] 1SCR 3, where the Supreme Court of Canada held that in exceptional circumstances, the Canadian government can send an asylum seeker back to their country origin, notwithstanding that the person sent back faced the risk of being subjected to torture.

Coupled with the physical policies of exclusion and deflection of asylum seekers came the discursive portrayal of asylum seekers as "illegals", "criminals" or people who "abused" the system. The IRPA was portrayed by the Minister for Citizenship and Immigration as a new Act directed at preventing criminal abuse of the immigration and refugee system, while simultaneously being directed at attracting the world's most highly skilled and qualified people to Canada (Macklin 2001, 2). The human rights and humanitarian discourse normally associated with refugees and refugee movements was replaced by the discourse of security, criminality and abuse. (Whitaker 2002; Harvey 2002; Dench 2001).

Apart from the above measures, Canada has a large global network of Migration Integrity Officers who work under the Intelligence Branch of Citizenship and Immigration Canada (Brouwer 2002). Between 1996 and

2002, some 40,000 "improperly documented" travellers were interdicted and denied the right to board on flights bound for Canada. In 2004 the figure was 5,644. The Canadian government has failed to provide information regarding nationality, the exact grounds of interdiction, which countries they were sent to or what happened to them (Canadian Council for Refugees 2007b).

After September 11, Canada took a number of steps to tighten security measures directed at the unauthorised movement of people to its borders. These include the implementation of the IRPA; introduction of a new fraud-resistant Permanent Resident Card; the creation of an intelligence branch within the CIC; an increase in the number of overseas screening officers; the establishment of the Advanced Passenger Information (API) and Canadian Passenger List and the initiation of early security checks on refugee claimants. Part 9 of the *Public Safety Act*, which was passed after September 11, included amendments to the former *Immigration Act* whereby refugee proceedings could be stopped and terminated if the refugee claimant was discovered to be a member of an inadmissible class or there were reasonable grounds to believe that the claimant was a terrorist. In addition to the enactment of the above legislation, Canada added a further list of countries to its list of countries whose citizens had to obtain a visa to travel to Canada (the countries being the Dominican Republic, Grenada, Kiribati, Nauru, Tuvalu, Vanuatu, Zimbabwe and Hungary) (Adelman 2002). The US–Canada Safe Third Country Agreement was entered into on 29 December 2004. Under this agreement, each country treats the other as a country of first asylum so that each country is able to summarily return to the other refugees who had travelled from the other country. While the Canadian government justified the agreement on the basis that it would reduce abuse of Canada's refugee determination system, the US was in favour of the agreement as it formed a further plank of its anti-terror strategy (Canadian Council for Refugees 2007c).

Interdiction and deterrence in Australia

Similar developments occurred in Australia. From the late 1980s onwards, the Australian government signalled its firm stance against asylum seekers by the introduction of the *Migration Legislation Amendment Act 1989*, which strengthened border controls and introduced mandatory detention (Parliament of the Commonwealth of Australia 2003). Further reforms to curb the increased number of asylum claims occurred in 1994 after the passage of the *Migration Legislation*

Amendment Act 1992, which included a bar on the review of mandatory detention. The *Migration Amendment Act (No. 4) 1994* introduced the safe third country provisions (Poynder 1995) which were applied to people covered under the Comprehensive Plan of Action (CPA) and all non-citizens for whom there was a safe country. The introduction of this provision was a direct response to the arrival of a boat on 7 July 1994, which carried a small number of Vietnamese asylum seekers from Indonesia (Poynder 1995). The Act provided that a person who had access to protection in a safe third country would be denied entry to Australia's onshore refugee process.

Discontent at people arriving in Australia with a valid visa (e.g. a student or tourist visa) and subsequently claiming asylum, led to the government making important changes to the Asylum Seeker Assistance Scheme (ASAS) in 1996 and 1997. Prior to 1997, people who arrived in Australia with a valid visa and who subsequently applied for asylum were granted a Bridging Visa and were authorised to work and were eligible for Medicare (being medical treatment paid for by the Australian government) and a fortnightly payment (Australian Catholic Migrant and Refugee Office 2002). In 1996, the ASAS was changed so that community-based asylum seekers whose cases had been rejected by the Department of Immigration and were awaiting a review by the Refugee Review Tribunal (RRT) were no longer entitled to such payment or employment authorisation (Amnesty International Australia 2003). In a further attempt to deter so called "non-genuine" refugee applicants, the regulations regarding work rights were changed. As from 1 July 1997, people who arrived in Australia with a valid visa and who failed to apply for asylum within 45 days of arrival were denied work authorisation and access to Medicare (Australian Catholic Migrant and Refugee Office 2003).

Despite the Australian government displaying a firm stance against asylum seekers during the 1980s and 1990s, the increased number of asylum claims in 1999 resulted in additional tightening of Australia's asylum laws that further curtailed the legal and social citizenship rights afforded to asylum seekers. In 1999, Australia witnessed the highest number of unauthorised boat arrivals. The Australian government responded with even tougher measures. The *Migration Legislation Amendment Act (No. 1) 1999* created new offences for migrant trafficking and repealed the Government's obligations to provide unlawful non-citizens with visa and refugee status information unless explicitly requested (Schloenhardt 2000; Parliament of the Commonwealth of Australia 2003).

In October 1999, the Migration Amendment Regulations (No. 12) created a new Temporary Protection Visa (TPV) for successful onshore asylum seekers (Subclass 785). Most of the people who were granted a TPV were onshore asylum seekers who had been kept in immigration detention and subsequently deemed to be "genuine" refugees. The TPV was the centrepiece of the government's deterrence strategy (Esmaeli and Wells 2000). The government justified the introduction of the TPV on the grounds that it would curb the "increasing misuse of Australia's onshore protection arrangements by organised people smuggling rackets" (Catholic Commission for Justice, Development and Peace 2003). The TPV restricted welfare benefits and family reunification and excluded asylum seekers' rights to citizenship through the limitation of the protection period offered to a maximum of three years (Wong 2003; DIMA 2002). This effectively created two classes of refugees in Australia (that is onshore and offshore refugees) as the visas provided different access to benefits.

The government also entered into a regional cooperation agreement with Indonesia which allowed for the interception, detention and screening of all asylum seekers who travelled through Indonesia en route to Australia (UNHCR 2000). The *Border Protection Legislation Amendment Act 1999* (Cth) empowered Australian authorities to intercept boats suspected of people-smuggling and strengthened the safe third country provisions (Kneebone 2004).

In public discourse initiated by the Australian government, asylum seekers were depicted as people who abused Australia's refugee determination process and threatened the Australian community. The government manipulated the increased arrivals of boat people to move its policy agenda forward. Through their association with people-smugglers, asylum seekers and refugees were depicted as criminals (Pickering 2001; Van Acker and Hollander 2003).

For many years, Australia was in search of a system of deterrence that successfully prevented asylum seekers from arriving in Australia. It was clear in mid-2001 that mandatory detention and the TPV had not acted as a successful deterrent as asylum seekers continued to arrive on Australia's northern shores in the period 1999–2001 (Brennan 2003). Triggered by the *Tampa* incident, more reforms designed to interdict and deter asylum seekers were enacted.

Australia's post 2001 deterrence policy consists of four main components:

(1) authorities were granted with extended powers of interception at sea;

(2) "excising" certain Australian islands from its national immigration law and processing asylum seekers there;
(3) subcontracting the detention to poorer neighbouring states (the Pacific Solution); and
(4) rules denying permanent protection in Australia to virtually all refugees who were in third countries prior to arrival (Human Rights Watch 2002).

Frank Brennan refers to these policies as the "closing of Australia's national borders" (Brennan 2003).

The legislative changes followed closely after the Tampa incident of August 2001 and several weeks prior to the November 2001 federal election. The government's decision to include asylum seekers at the centre of its election campaign (justified in terms of "defending Australia's borders") marked a shift in the practices of past Australian governments (Philpott 2002). The Pacific Solution developed in the immediate aftermath of September 11 resulted in a shift in the way asylum seekers were represented from a cultural threat to that of a potential terrorist threat. The then Defence Minister Peter Reith warned that refugees arriving by boat could "be a pipeline for terrorists to come in and use your country as a staging point for terrorist activities" (Kyriacou 2002, 9).

During the election campaign of 2001, the government manipulated the terrorist attacks of September 11 and "successfully" linked the asylum seeker issues to the terrorist threat and matters of national security. The government resorted to a language of fear and set the public debate on asylum seekers (Wong 2003). Playing on people's feelings of insecurity (Hugo 2002) allowed the government to win the election with the asylum seeker/security issue, border protection and Australia's sovereignty being crucial to its victory (Taylor 2002; Gibney 2004).

Several measures were passed in direct response to the September 11 terrorist attacks. These included the establishment of a Movement Alert List (DIMIA *Factsheet 77*) and the entering into of cooperation agreements with source countries such as Indonesia, Pakistan, Iran, China, (Mason 2002; Kyriacou 2002) Under the *Migration Act*, mandatory minimum sentences were prescribed for people-smuggling (s. 232A of the *Migration Act* (Cth)).

These measures and the raft of legislation passed in 2001 were presented by the Government as "homeland defence"—defence against unauthorised and uncontrolled movement of people into Australia and a defence of Australia's right to existence (Taylor 2002). Through the introduction of a comprehensive border protection regime, interdiction and mandatory detention, Australia has managed to insulate itself from unauthorised boat arrivals of asylum seekers and has unfortunately proved to be a unique world model.

While the 2001 legislative amendments required that only people who arrived on islands which had been excised from Australia's migration zone were subjected to offshore processing, in April 2006, the government proposed legislation which would extend the offshore processing to all "unauthorised" boat arrivals who reached Australia's mainland. The Migration Amendment (Designated Unauthorised Arrivals) Bill 2006 was withdrawn by the government after dissent from some government MPs and opposition from human rights groups.

Some of the common approaches to interdicting or deterring asylum seekers in each country include entering into agreements with neighbouring countries, resort to detention, transit visas, border controls, anti-smuggling laws, the placement of migration officers at international ports and airports, a negative portrayal of asylum seekers as criminals or queue jumpers and the conjoining of asylum to security issues in the post–September 11 climate. Australia, however, is a unique model in terms of its mandatory detention policy, temporary protection, excision of its migration zones and its Pacific solution. While the Australian state has expanded in terms of extra-territorial immigration control operations, it has shrunk in terms of the territory for which it is responsible (Morris 2000). The manner in which Australia negatively portrays asylum seekers is also excessively harsh when compared with Canada, which arguably stems from Australia's isolation as a nation with a European culture situated in the Asian region.

Conclusion

As is clear from the legislative enactments in each country, interdiction (and deterrence) measures are a unilateral implementation of measures which fail to incorporate any safeguards for refugees and asylum seekers. Such measures work against the spirit of the Refugee Convention and ultimately erode the institution of asylum. The engagement in heavy handed legislation and adoption of harsh measures against asylum seekers has, however, jeopardised Canada's and Australia's human rights standing in the international community. There is an urgent need for states to adopt a two-pronged approach if they are serious about addressing the worldwide refugee problem: meaningful national policies which recognise human dignity and the plight of the persecuted need to be adopted on the one hand and policies which address the factors that cause refugee movements in source countries on the other.

References

Adelman, H. 2002. *The new immigration regulations*. 1–20, www.yorku.ca/crs/publications/articles.htm (accessed 2 August 2004).

Aiken, S. J. 2001. *Comments on Bill C11 related to national security and terrorism*. Submission to the House of Commons Standing Committee on Citizenship and Immigration, 26 March 2001, Ontario: Centre for Refugee Studies.

Amnesty International Australia: Fact sheet 14: *Community based asylum seekers*. 1–4. www.amnesty.org.au/refugees/ref-fact14.html (retrieved 13 March 2003).

Australian Catholic Migrant and Refugee Office. 2002. *Background paper on asylum seekers in Australia*. Australian Catholic Migrant and Refugee Office, 25 August 2002, www.acmro.catholic.org.au/index.htm, (accessed 24 February 2003).

—. 2003. *Welfare issues and immigration outcomes for asylum seekers on Bridging E Visas*. Asylum Seeker Project, April 2003 www.acmro.catholic.org.au/index.htm, (accessed on 24 February 2003).

Brennan, F. 2003. *Tampering with asylum. A universal humanitarian problem*. St Lucia: University of Queensland Press.

Brouwer, A. 2002. *The new Immigration Act. More questions than answers*, 1–8, The Maytree Foundation, www.maytree.com/HTMLFiles/publications_immigration_Act.html, (retrieved 13 November 2002).

Canadian Council for Refugees. 2007a. *Interdiction and refugee protection: Bridging the gap*, www.ccr.web.ca/interdiction.proceedings.PDF, (accessed 2 February 2007).

—. 2007b. *Submission of the Canadian Council for Refugees on the occasion of the visit to Canada of the UN Working Group on Arbitrary Detention*, 8 June 2005, www.ccr.web.ca/WGAD. HTM, (accessed 2 February 2007).

—. 2007c. *Safe third country*, www.ccr.web.ca/S3C.HTM, (accessed 2 February 2007).

Catholic Commission for Justice, Development and Peace. 2003. *Hordes or human beings? A discussion of some of the problems surrounding Australia's response to asylum seekers and possible solutions to those problems.* 1–20, Occasional Paper no. 8, Melbourne: Catholic Commission for Justice, Development and Peace. www.melb.catholic.aust.com/ccjdp/op08-200003.htm, (accessed 11 October 2003).

Cheran, R. 2001. Xeno racism and international migration. *Refuge*, vol. 19 (6) August, 1–3.

Cronin, K. 1994. Links between human rights instruments and the Refugee Convention, 116–24. Paper presented at Old Problems, New Directions, Conference on Refugee Protection, University of Sydney, 18 February 1994, convened by the Australian Council of Churches and the Refugee and Migrant Services.

Dench, J. 2001. Controlling borders: C31 and interdiction, *Refuge*, vol. 19 (4), February, 34–40.

Department of Immigration and Multicultural Affairs. 2002. *Consultations on the 2001–2002 migration and humanitarian programs.* Discussion Paper. Canberra: Australian Government Publishing Service.

Department of Immigration, Multicultural and Indigenous Affairs. 2002. *Fact sheet 77: The movement alert list.* 21 August 2002. Canberra: Australian Government Publishing Service.

Dirks, G. E. 1995. *Controversy and complexity. Canadian immigration policy during the 1980s.* Montreal: McGill Queens University Press.

Dowty, A. 1987. *Closed borders: The contemporary assault on freedom of movement.* New Haven: Yale University Press.

Elliott, J. L. and A. Fleras. 1992. *Unequal relations. An introduction to race and ethnic dynamics in Canada.* Ontario: Prentice Hall Canada Inc.

Esmaeli, H. and B. Wells. 2000. The 'temporary' refugees: Australia's legal response to the arrival of Iraqi and Afghan boat people. *University of NSW Law Journal*, vol. 23 (3), 224–5.

Gibney, M. J. 2004. *The ethics and politics of asylum. Liberal democracy and the response to refugees.* Melbourne: Cambridge University Press.

Goodwin-Gill, G. S. 1996. *The refugee in international law.* second edition, Oxford: Clarendon Press.

Gorman, R. F. 1993. Introduction: Refugee aid and development in a global context. In *Refugee aid and development: Theory and practice.* ed. R. F. Gorman. Westport Connecticut: Greenwood Press.

Gould, W .T. S. 1994. Population movements and the changing world order: An introduction, 3–14. In *Population migration and the changing world order.* ed. W. T. S. Gould and A. M. Findlay. Chichester: John Wiley & Sons.

Hanks, P. 1989. Immigration history and policy: Australia and Canada. Paper from the conference held on 2 August 1989, Working papers on migrant and inter-cultural studies, Centre for Migrant and Inter-cultural Studies, Monash University, Melbourne.

Harvey, C. 2002. Securing refugee protection in a cold climate, *Refuge*, vol. 20 (4), August, 2–4.

Held, D., A. McGrew, D. Goldblatt and J. Perraton. 1999 *Global transformations: Politics, economics and culture.* Cambridge: Polity Press.

Hounslow, B. 1988. *Immigration law and policy—learning from the experience of Canada, the United States and Britain.* Public Interest Advocacy Centre, A Report to the Law Foundation of New South Wales, Sydney, March 1988.

Hugo, G. 2002. Australian immigration policy: The significance of the events of September 11. *International Migration Review*, vol. 36, no. 1, Spring, 37–40.

Human Rights Watch. 2002. *Not for export. Why the international community should reject Australia's refugee policies.* Human Rights Briefing Paper, 1–21, www.hrw.org/press/2002/09/ausbrf0926.htm, (retrieved 14 October 2002).

Inglis, C. 1994. Australia's refugee policy in an international context. *Australian Quarterly*, Summer, 15–25.

Jakubowski, L. M. 1997. *Immigration and the legalisation of racism.* Halifax: Fernwood Publishing.

Kneebone, S. 2004. The rights of strangers: Refugees, citizenship and nationality. *Australian Journal of Human Rights*, vol. 10 (1), 33–61.

Knight, S. B. 1993. The international refugee crisis: The Canadian response, 17–25. In *The international refugee crisis. British and Canadian responses*, ed. V. Robinson. London: Macmillan.

Knowles, V. 1997. *Strangers at our gates. Canadian immigration and immigration policy 1540–1997.* Toronto: Dundurn Press.

Kyriacou, L. 2002. *The human face of Australia's refugee policy.* Executive Committee of the UNHCR Programme Annual Meeting. Background papers, www.unhcr.org/publ.html (accessed 10 December 2002).

Lippert, R. 1998. Canadian refugee determination and advanced liberal government. *Canadian Journal of Law and Society*, vol. 13 (2), 177–207.

Loescher, G. 1999. Protection and humanitarian action in the post cold war era. In *Global migrants, global refugees. Problems and solutions*, ed. A. Zolberg and P. M. Benda, 171–205, London: Berghabn Books.

Macklin, A. 2001. New directions for refugee policy: Of curtains, doors and locks. *Refuge*, vol. 19 (4), February 2001, 1–4.

Mason, J. 2002. Sea change: Australia's new approach to asylum seekers, US Committee for Refugees, www.safecom.org.au/Australia.pdf (accessed 18 November 2002).

McMaster, D. 2001. *Asylum seekers: Australia's response to refugees*. Melbourne: Melbourne University Press.

Morris, T. 2000. Australia and asylum: No longer land of the fair go?, *Forced Migration Review*, no. 8, August, 31.

Parliament of the Commonwealth of Australia. 2003. *Australia and refugees: 1901–2002: An annotated chronology based on official sources*. Canberra: Department of Parliamentary Library, AGPS.

Philpott, S. 2002. Protecting the borderline and minding the bottom line: Asylum seekers and politics in contemporary Australia, *Refuge*, vol. 20 (4), August, 63–75.

Pickering, S. 2001. Common sense and original deviancy: News discourses and asylum seekers in Australia, *Journal of Refugee Studies*, vol. 14 (2), 2001, 167–85.

Poynder, N. 1995. Recent implementation of the Refugee Convention in Australia and the law of accommodations to international human rights treaties. Have we gone too far? *Australian Journal of Human Rights*, vol. 2 (1), 1–16.

Reitz, J. G. Immigration and Canadian nation building in the transition to a knowledge economy. Paper prepared as a contribution to *Controlling immigration: A global perspective*, second edn, ed. W. A. Cornelius, P. L. Matin and J. F. Hollifield, Stanford University Press, 1–46, www.utoronto.ca/ethnicstudies/research.htm, (retrieved 13 November 2002).

Richmond, A. H. 1991. Immigration and multiculturalism in Canada and Australia: The contradictions and crises of the 1980s. *International Journal of Canadian Studies*, no. 3, Spring, 87–110.

—. 1994. *Global apartheid: Refugees, racism and the New World Order*, Oxford: Oxford University Press.

—. 1995. International migration and global change. In *Crossing borders: Transmigration in Asia Pacific*, ed. O. J. Hui, C. K. Bun and C. S. Beng, 33–48, Sydney: Prentice Hall.

—. 2001. Refugees and racism in Canada. *Refuge*, vol. 19 (6), August, 12–20.

—. 2002. Globalisation: Implications for immigrants and refugees, *Ethnic and Racial Studies* vol. 25 (5), September, 707–27.

Schloenhardt, A. 2000. Australia and the boat people: 25 years of unauthorised arrivals. *University of NSW Law Journal*, vol. 23 (3), 33–55.

Shukre, A. 1995. Who is a refugee? The definition of beneficiaries revisited. In *Crossing borders: Transmigration in Asia Pacific*, ed. O. J. Hui, C. K. Bun and C. S. Beng, 125–39, Sydney: Prentice Hall.

Simmons, A. B. 1997. Globalisation and backlash racism in the 1990s: The case of Asian immigration to Canada. In *The silent debate: Asian immigration and racism in Canada*, ed. E. Laquian, A. Laquian and T. McGee, 29–50. Vancouver BC: Institute of Asian Research.

Taylor, S. 2002. Reconciling Australia's international protection obligations with the war on terrorism, *Pacifica Review*, vol. 14 (2), June, 121–40.

UNHCR. 2000. *The state of the world's refugees 2000. Fifty years of humanitarian action.* Oxford: Oxford University Press, UNHCR.

Van Acker, E. and R. Hollander. 2003. Protecting our borders: Ministerial rhetoric and asylum seekers. *Australian Journalism Review*, vol. 25, no. 2, 103–19.

Watson, V. 1998. Interpreting asylum, reinterpreting refugees: An Australian case study, *Australian Journal of Social Issues*, vol. 33 (2), May, 133–54.

Whitaker, R. 1998. Refugees: The security dimension. *Citizenship Studies*, vol. 2 (3), 413–34.

—. 2002. Refugee policy after September 11: Not much new. *Refuge*, vol. 20 (4) August, 29–33.

Wong, L. 2003. Immigrants, the contract state and rights, *Just Policy*, no. 29, April, 47–56.

Young, M. 2001. *Canada's immigration program*, 1–29, Parliamentary Research Branch, Law and Government Division, Parliament of Canada, www.parl.gc.ca/information/library/PRBpubs/bp190-e.htm, (retrieved 10 December 2002).

CHAPTER FOUR

EXPORTING THE BORDER: IMMIGRATION DETENTION AND "JUXTAPOSED CONTROLS"

MADELEINE BYRNE

Introduction

Following the closure of the reception centre at Sangatte, administered by the International Committee of the Red Cross, the governments of Britain and France announced the establishment of a policy called "juxtaposed controls", which would allow British immigration officers to work in the ports of northern France (and the French officers to conduct inspections at Dover). This chapter will consider the ambiguous legal protections afforded immigration detainees at Coquelles Freight terminal and the other offshore detention facilities. It will argue that the impetus behind the policy—to stop "clandestine entrants" who might also be asylum applicants appearing on the British mainland—is inherently punitive and jeopardises core human rights, such as the right to asylum.

> Britain is now laying the foundation stone for offshore borders all over the world.
> —Liam Byrne, British Minister for Immigration, Citizenship and Nationality (Home Office, 2007c)

Coquelles Freight Terminal, France 2005

In the European summer of 2005, a team of British inspectors visited three non-residential holding centres at Coquelles and Calais in northern France. The centres, established under international treaty, allow Britain's Immigration and Nationality Directorate (IND) to detain "clandestine entrants" en route to the United Kingdom. No distinction is made between categories of entrant; yet it is likely that asylum applicants are among those detained.

Under the Le Touquet treaty, which came into effect in March 2004, detention is allowed for a period of up to 24 hours and can be extended to 48 hours in exceptional circumstances (HM Chief Inspector of Prisons 2006b, appendix). These detention centres, according to the report by Britain's Chief Inspector of Prisons, Anne Owers, are largely "out of the public gaze" (HM Chief Inspector of Prisons 2006b, 5). Immigration detainees are picked up from trucks, or caught while trying to cross the Channel without valid documents.

To reach the accommodation block at Coquelles Freight terminal, the inspectors entered an external pathway between the building and perimeter that was covered by insubstantial roofing sheets, with wire fencing on the open side. Opaque gauze covered the fencing, to provide some protection from the elements. At the end of the path, the team found a block of six almost identical rooms—measuring four metres by three. These were the rooms that the staff called "dog kennels". During the inspection the rooms were empty—though wet after being hosed down that day. In the corner of each was a hole-in-the-ground toilet, with three-quarter length screening, and a small stainless steel sink with a single tap (HM Chief Inspector of Prisons 2006b, 23).

Solid block benches, covered by thin plastic-covered pads, ran along three walls. Apart from a tiny heater, there was no furniture "offering any comfort in the room".

Staff told us that people emerging from under lorries, or after long periods of living rough, were often unclean and sometimes infected. As a consequence, rooms were routinely hosed down. No spare clothing was on offer to replace dirty or infested clothing. We saw some paper suits but no staff member asked could recall one being handed out. No blankets were available (in winter) despite the cold weather. (HM Chief Inspector of Prisons 2006b, 24)

The staff confirmed that when they were occupied the rooms became extremely smelly. With the door closed, the only ventilation was a vent above the toilet and a mesh-covered hole (17 cm by 12 cm) at the bottom of the door. Air-conditioning was due to be installed (HM Chief Inspector of Prisons 2006b, 24). On a busy day, six people could occupy the room, and yet there was no room-sharing risk assessment. Rooms had no alarms, but staff checked them every 20 minutes. No light filled the rooms, other than that which entered through the small hole in the door and the one external wall. "The strip light outside threw some light into the room, if custody officers turned it on. With the door closed it was extremely gloomy even in day time" (HM Chief Inspector of Prisons 2006b, 24).

Immigration detainees with children could stay together in one of the holding rooms, but there were no toys, reading material or games. Children could not go outside for fresh air. From May to July 2005, the facility had been occupied on 43 days, with a total of 202 people. Nine were women; 33 were minors or possible minors with given ages ranging from 10 to 17. The largest number held on any one day was 24. In June, a family with a ten-year-old child was detained for eight hours (HM Chief Inspector of Prisons 2006b, 27). Limited documentation was available on-site regarding detention, but incomplete records provided by the private contractor, Securicor (G4S) indicated an average duration of seven and a half hours; the longest detention period was 11 hours 45 minutes (HM Chief Inspector of Prisons 2006b, 27). None of the detainees, in the three months' records provided, entered Britain.

Exporting the border, or undermining international law?

The Coquelles Freight Terminal detention centre is one of the detention facilities operating under the system of "juxtaposed controls" which allows for British immigration officers to conduct their duties on French soil. The British Home Office has called this policy a success, while critics argue that it has engendered a situation where international law is routinely undermined. In the following section I will consider how the uncertain protections afforded those held in the detention centres in northern France reflect a broader emphasis upon interdiction and deterrence.

The Home Office, in its response to the HM Chief Inspector of Prisons report, noted that the detention was for "inadequately documented passengers and illegal entrants attempting to enter the UK, prior to their being handed over to French authorities" (Home Office Speeches and Statements 2006). The government stated that the facilities were intended to hold people "very briefly", while acknowledging that with arrivals at ports operating 24 hours a day people could be held overnight. The government acknowledged that it needed to clarify the "primacy" of UK law in the centre's operation. It also recognised that there might be a need for a system of independent monitoring of the short-term facilities, comparable to that on the British mainland, and signalled that the use of Coquelles Freight—the site of the so-called "dog kennels"—might be reviewed.

Within these two recommendations—the need to assert the primacy of UK law and for enhanced scrutiny—we find the basis of criticism levelled at the arrangement between Britain and France called juxtaposed controls. The 2003 *Treaty between the Government of the United Kingdom and Northern Ireland and the Government of the French Republic Concerning the Implementation of Frontier Controls at the Sea Ports of Both Countries on the Channel and North Sea* was negotiated after the closure of the controversial Red Cross Sangatte centre near Calais.

The Treaty, signed at Le Touquet, France on 4 February 2003, allows British immigration officers to exercise full immigration control procedures at the ports of northern France: at Calais, Coquelles, Dunkirk, Boulogne and other sites as necessary. French immigration officers can do the same at Dover. The legislation builds on that relating to the Channel Tunnel, which similarly established a process where British officers could check departing passengers and freight before arrival in the United Kingdom. More recently, the Home Office has called for this power to be expanded so that private contractors, employed by the British Border and Immigration Agency, can fingerprint, escort and detain suspected "clandestine entrants" until a UK immigration officer arrives.

The significance of this legislation is twofold. First, it epitomises the growing trend of "internationalisation" in immigration control (Oxfam 2005), what the British Immigration Minister, Liam Byrne, has called "exporting the border". Inherent in this arrangement are legal ambiguities that affect due process and threaten international human rights protections. Yet, it also represents one of the more surprising aspects of globalisation; that is, despite repeated calls to uphold national sovereignty and "maintain the security of borders", states are increasingly looking towards others to do this work for them in the area of immigration. Arguably, this weakens the very principle of national sovereignty that such legislation purports to uphold.

According to the *Nationality, Immigration and Asylum Act 2002* (Juxtaposed Controls) Order 2003, within the "Control Zone" in the "State of Departure" (France) officers of the "State of Arrival" (Britain) can carry out their immigration responsibilities. However, it also states that French officers have the power to arrest and detain a person for a period of 24 hours for the "purposes of immigration," which can be extended (Home Office 2003, 1). The fact that a person can be detained for the purposes of investigation, rather than a suspected offence, is significant. Moreover, French officers, according to the law, are immune from prosecution for any offence committed in the UK control zone.

British law relating to detention and terrorism, broadly applies in the offshore detention centres at Calais and Coquelles. However, it is not clear whether the safeguards stipulated within section 38 of the *Operation Enforcement Manual*—information used by British immigration officers when deciding to detain—informs such parallel operations in the French control zone. In Britain, considerations that might lead to a decision not to detain include whether the person is under 18, has a history of torture or shows signs of physical or ill-health. The manual includes other statements relating to the treatment of vulnerable groups, such as pregnant women, children or people suffering from chronic mental illness. Arguments can be made about whether or not these directives are followed (HM Chief Inspector of Prisons 2006a, 64). But on the question of grounds for detention, and possible exemptions, the juxtaposed controls legislation is strikingly non-specific in comparison to that which applies in Britain.

Following the refusal to enter the United Kingdom, British officers inform French border police who organise removal. If the person is of no interest to French police and legally in France, they are released. From this description it appears that British officers, not French police, are responsible for the decision to detain. Most importantly, the HM Chief Inspector of Prisons report states that British immigration officers do not accept applications for asylum on the basis that the claimant is on French territory. No exception is made for asylum applicants seeking to be reunited with close family in Britain (HM Chief Inspector of Prisons 2006b, appendix).

The question of who detains—a French or British contractor, French police officer or British immigration officer is important as each operates under different legal codes and cultural practices. Relevant parts of British immigration law—including those relating to detention powers and the prevention of terrorism are applied by British immigration officers, supported by police officers from Kent and the Special Branch (HM Chief Inspector of Prisons 2006b, appendix). But it is not clear how this affects French contractors or police.

The lack of clarity as to which country's law is responsible has two primary outcomes. First, it affects the operation of the centres—a situation that is further complicated by the involvement of a private corrections company, Securicor (G4S). Second, it creates a situation where the people held in the centres have little understanding of how to enforce their legal or human rights.

Among the Securicor (G4S) staff working at Coquelles Freight terminal, there was also confusion as to *which* law applied—French or British—in terms of their daily duties and responsibilities. Many did not know what their powers were in terms of the use of force, or what they should do in response to suspected acts of self-harm or suicide. They also largely worked in isolation from local authorities and emergency services that could have indicated how to meet French health and safety, healthcare, child protection or disability obligations (HM Chief Inspector of Prisons 2006b, 5).

Securicor (G4S) information refers to the company's involvement in the "operation of holding facilities and holding rooms at ports, which provide temporary, secure accommodation for immigration detainees awaiting decisions or action on their right to enter and remain in the country" (Securicor G4S, accessed 25 May 2007). This description makes their role seem rather passive, but this could soon change following the introduction of mooted legislation that would give them the same responsibilities as UK immigration staff.

The proposed order would allow the UK immigration service to employ "suitably qualified and trained personnel through a private contractor" to complete the "important but straightforward" function of apprehending, escorting and detaining someone suspected of committing an immigration offence. Under this legislation, contractors would be able to search vehicles at Calais, Dunkirk and Boulogne, physically search "clandestine entrants", then detain and escort them to an immigration officer. Detention should not exceed three hours, or be "as speedily as is reasonably practicable, pending the arrival of the immigration officer" (Home Office 2006d, 2).

The London-based Immigration Law Practitioners' Association (ILPA) has issued a statement expressing its concern about this proposals to authorise private contractors to act independently in circumstances defined (that is, in the searching vehicles, the detention and escort of individuals to the nearest facility where they can be held for three hours and fingerprinting of individuals) without British or French officials being present (ILPA 2006, 1). Dominating the Association's July 2006 statement is concern about what it calls an uncertain legal framework.

Laws and controls relating to "Frontier Controls" of the "state of arrival" (in Calais, those of the UK) apply for breaches of applicable laws relating to related immigration matters. However, in the instance of any other suspected offence, the laws and regulations of France apply. Of central concern to the Association is the uncertain status of the private contractors. Under which system of laws and regulations, it asks, would they be acting? Added to this is the fact that some of the private contractors will be French nationals. Who would then be responsible for any breach: the contractor or the British immigration officer purportedly directing and supervising them? (ILPA 2006, 5).

The Association acknowledges that, according to the Council of Europe, detention is considered to be the "most severe penalty" European member states are permitted to exercise against individuals. As a result of this the ability to detain an individual is "jealously guarded" by member states and seen to be a key element of its functioning as a sovereign state (ILPA 2006, 5). Yet, what dominates in the documentation relating to this arrangement of "juxtaposed controls" between Britain and France is not so much a highly codified process preceding detention, but rather vague statements, which assume that detention has become a predictable first rather than last resort.

Another outcome of the uncertain legal framework governing the centres is that it was unlikely that immigration detainees at Coquelles Freight received any documents about their status until after they had left, according to the report on the 2005 inspection, aside from some verbal explanation (HM Chief Inspector of Prisons 2006b, 26). On occasion, immigration detainees were given a form which explained that they were illegal entrants into Britain, with limited right of appeal, liable to detention and return by French authorities. They were not necessarily given documentation, as would be the case in Britain, providing information on how to challenge their detention, or complain about conditions (HM Chief Inspector of Prisons 2006b, 26). No free telephone call was offered to contact a lawyer or embassy official, and there was no public pay phone.

Immigration detainees, moreover, lacked adequate information about reasons for their detention and access to qualified advisers on British immigration law (HM Chief Inspector of Prisons 2006b, 5). Yet, potential asylum applicants would be barred from making a protection claim in Britain because of their location on French territory. This is in keeping with the Dublin Convention, signed in 1990, that requires asylum seekers to lodge their applications in their "first country of entry" in the European Union. This principle remains highly contested as a reason for a state not assessing asylum applications (Thompson 2003, 15). Not only does it deny the possibility of valid reasons for an asylum seeker to lodge an application in one country, rather than another—close family ties; historical and linguistic links; a lack of adequate protection and assessment capability in the second state; or other risks that may endanger the applicant's human rights or safety—but it also "shifts" the responsibility without taking into account individual circumstances.

More subtly, the transfer of immigration controls to a third state has the potential to undermine local examples of good practice. France has traditionally had one of the most codified systems within the European Union in terms of detention. France does not allow the indefinite detention of asylum applicants at the start of their claim, or prior to deportation. In France there are two kinds of detention centres where asylum seekers, and other irregular immigrants, can be held: *zones d'attentes* (short-term holding centres) located at airports and ports and detention centres that hold people prior to deportation. In the short-term holding centres asylum seekers can be held for four days before judicial intervention is required. The maximum duration for detention is twenty days (République française, Art. L.222-1 and L.222-2 *Code de l'entrée et du séjour des étrangers et du droit d'asile*) In detention centres, immigration detainees can be held for a maximum of 32 days before deportation or they are released into the community. Any further detention requires approval from a tribunal judge (République française, Art. L.552-1 and L.552-7 *Code de l'entrée et du séjour des étrangers et du droit d'asile*).

In contrast, Britain does not have any statutory limit on the length of detention and asylum applicants, particularly under its accelerated or "fast-track" processing, are routinely held. Seventy per cent of the 1,435 immigration detainees in Britain in the first quarter of 2007 had claimed asylum at one stage (Home Office 2007a, 10). It is important to note that Britain does not maintain annual detention statistics. This figure was accurate as of 31 March 2007 and does not include those being held in police cells and prisons, which the Chief Inspector of Prisons has estimated understates the actual figure by 60 per cent (HM Chief Inspector of Prisons 2006a, 65).

It is difficult to assess the direct impact of the juxtaposed controls legislation on French asylum and immigration policy. However, there is evidence to show that in other contexts—most notably when similar arrangements were developed on the German–Polish border and in central and eastern European states prior to their accession to the European Union—the outsourcing of immigration control has led to a toughening of immigration measures, designed at stopping arrivals in the receiving state (Rigo 2005, 10; Byrne 2007 passim).

French asylum statistics do not specify whether applicants passed through the Coquelles Freight terminal as a result of juxtaposed controls; nor does the information available indicate how many people detained at Coquelles terminal later applied for asylum in France. However, approximately the same time as the Le Touquet Treaty was negotiated, a detention centre was opened in the town of Coquelles. Designed to hold 75 people, it is often overcrowded with people sleeping on folding beds in the television room and, on occasion, the isolation cell. Instances of verbal and physical abuse are not uncommon, although the conditions are generally considered to be better than other centres in France, which have been called among the worst in Europe (Les Invisibles website, accessed 1 June 2007). Twenty-seven children with their families were held there in 2005, as well as a number of heavily pregnant women with young children. None of the information available notes the percentage of asylum applicants.

Of the 2,322 people held in the Coquelles detention centre in 2005 more than half were sent there from other European countries; of these 523 were returned to their country of origin and another 758 sent to another European state (Cimade 2005, 106). The first country of return for the immigration detainees was neighbouring Belgium, then Germany and Italy, with Britain low on the list (11 people were returned there in 2005). The largest group of those held at Coquelles were Indians trying to get to Britain (509 people, or 21.95 per cent). Most were stopped on trucks coming from Belgium, returned, only to try again (Cimade 2005, 106). The centre at Coquelles has become controversial in France because of its on-site court, located near a police shooting range and bus station, which opened in June 2005. The court does not decide asylum applications, but rules on detention matters. Judges and lawyers have boycotted a similar plan to locate a court within the detention centre at Roissy airport, which has delayed its opening (Gil-Robles 2005, 49). One man detained at Coquelles described the experience of appearing before the court:

> I was in the tribunal; it's completely closed with police spread out all around the room. I thought I was back at the police station. It's not a court; there are police everywhere (Cimade 2005, 106).

In one newspaper report, the court is described as a room without windows. Sitting in the court one day in June 2005 was a badly shaved Turk called Ali Youskaia, who nervously pinched his cheek as he listened to the judge and lawyers. Youskaia had spent seventeen days in detention and was waiting on a reply to his asylum claim (Saberan 2005). The local government had asked to extend his detention so that it could organise his deportation. "I want to be freed"—this was the only phrase the man kept repeating, before he was eventually released.

In 2006, 2,556 people asked for asylum at the French border, a 12.2 per cent increase on 2005, but lower than the figure of 6,000 in 2003 and 10,000 in 2001 (Ofpra 2006). The bulk of the applications were made at Roissy airport in Paris (96 per cent), with a tiny fraction being made at regional airports and ports, which possibly include those of northern France (0.5 per cent). This small number of border applications corresponds with the report of a visit to France by the European Union's Commissioner for Human Rights, Alvaro Gil-Robles, in September 2005 where he expressed surprise at the "very low" number of applications at French ports:

> When I visited Arenc (Marseilles), I learnt that there were only some twenty applications a year. Only seven had been made from January to September 2005. On examining the register of entries and exits, I realised that illegal immigrants spent very little time in the waiting zone before being expelled. The average length of time they are kept at Arenc is between two and three days. As the senior officer who showed me around explained to me, illegal immigrants arriving by boat are often sent back the same day on the same boat they arrived on (Gil-Robles 2006, 52).

"This makes me wonder whether foreigners are really given the opportunity to apply for asylum," he continued. "It would seem that some stowaways are not even allowed to disembark from the ship on which they are discovered and are detained on board until the ship sets sail again." Gil-Robles noted the case of two Congolese citizens, without documents, who were expelled before they could lodge a claim. In protest against their treatment they leapt out the portholes of the ship and were seriously injured.

Success

Britain has heralded its juxtaposed controls with France as an unquestionable "success" (Home Office 2007d). "Tougher checks abroad" before people can arrive in Britain, as under the juxtaposed controls arrangement in France and Belgium have led to a reported 70 per cent "reduction in unfounded asylum applications for the whole of the UK" (Home Office 2007d). The British government also states in a press release that the system has led to an 88 per cent fall in the number of clandestine entrants in Kent in 2006 compared with the same period in 2002 (Home Office 2007c). However, it is possible that the 2002 figure is not representative of typical trends as that year had a "high" of 50,360 people refused entry and removed, as compared with 31,930 refusals in 2004 and 17,220 at port in 1994 (United Kingdom Parliament, Select Committee on Home Affairs, Fifth Report 2006).

The catchphrase for restrictive pre-entry measures, which include 34 British Airline Liaison Officers (ALOs) in 32 international airports (The United Kingdom Parliament 2006); the juxtaposed controls in France and Belgium; ID cards for foreign nationals living in Britain and the introduction by April 2008 of biometric visas for nationals of 135 countries is "exporting the border" (BBC 2007). By the end of 2008 citizens of half of the countries in the world—that is, three-quarters of the world's population—will be issued with biometric visas before they enter the UK (Home Office 2007d). These visas will consist of digital finger scans and a full-face digital photograph, which will be sent to London to be checked against a central government database. Such information will become useful for immigration officers during operations seeking out "illegal workers", a Home Office spokeswoman explained. "Staff can take readers with them—they look a bit like games consoles. Then when they get to say a factory or a restaurant, they can check people's fingerprints there and then," the spokeswoman said. "Someone might say, 'I've got a work visa,' but in five minutes the officer will know if they've actually got a tourist visa. Then we can detain them there and then." (BBC 2007).

However, it is difficult to assess the "success" of the juxtaposed controls in northern France because of the absence of official statistics from these locations. The British Home Office does not maintain data on asylum-seeking immigration detainees held at Coquelles or Calais. The *Asylum Statistics* for the first quarter of 2007 (January–March) show a fall in asylum applications, which are 1 per cent lower than the previous quarter and 12 per cent lower than the first quarter of 2006 (Home Office 2007a, 2). In terms of asylum seekers in detention, the data only refer to those in mainland centres and "short-term holding facilities" on the mainland at Colnbrook, Manchester Airport, Dover Harbour and Harwich (Home Office 2007a, 10). Statistics from France are similarly general, but do provide information about applicants at the border requesting admission on protection grounds.

The British Immigration Minister, Liam Byrne, has stated that international alliances, such as the juxtaposed controls between Britain and France close routes to those attempting to abuse the system, while enabling legitimate travellers to pass freely. Tackling "illegal immigration" is also cited as an important way of maintaining public confidence in the country's system. "It is essential that we have a fair and effective system, trusted by the public as a whole and those who rely on it," he said (Home Office 2007d). "The days when border control started at the white cliffs of Dover are over," he added. "Our immigration control needs to start well before people come anywhere near British shores" (Home Office 2007d).

Much criticism has been made of this policy of "exporting the borders" with opponents describing the initiatives as "blunt instruments" that risk barring genuine refugees and undermining Britain's international obligations. Even though a report by the British House of Commons Home Affairs Committee on Immigration Control praised the series of checks at Calais by French and British authorities it noted that equipment in use was not entirely reliable or effective and that "no efforts" had been made by the government to determine how many people stopped from travelling to the United Kingdom might have a legitimate claim to protection (House of Commons 2006, 53).

A 2004 Select Committee on Home Affairs from the British House of Commons found that it has become "increasingly difficult" for asylum applicants to enter the UK (United Kingdom Parliament, Select Committee on Home Affairs Fifth Report 2006). Moreover, as a result of such restrictive measures those who manage to make an asylum claim in the UK tend to be "young, male, healthy, educated and with access to significant financial support and less likely to be old, female, ill, uneducated and poor" (United Kingdom Parliament, Select Committee on Home Affairs Fifth Report 2006)—and therefore not representative of the world's refugee population. Because of this, the Committee argued that the British government had a "moral responsibility" to provide alternative and legitimate means for asylum seekers to enter its territory, while also assisting refugees closer to their country of origin and tackling the roots of enforced migration.

A 2005 Oxfam/Refugee Council report has argued that there are a number of serious problems with the juxtaposed controls in France and Belgium. First, it leads to a displacement of people to countries on the edges of the European Union, and also shifts the responsibility to poor countries closer to the refugees' regions of origin. It also encourages asylum seekers to take more dangerous risks; UNITED for International Action, a European anti-racism network, has documented more than 6,300 deaths of non-European citizens trying to get to the EU since 1993 that it attributes to the toughening of asylum laws (Oxfam/Refugee Council 2005, 8). Such measures have also, the organisations argue, led to an increased reliance on smugglers and traffickers, while undermining shared notions of refugee protection and international law.

And as the 2005–06 inquiry by the House of Commons Committee found, people are still trying to cross the Channel. At Calais there were 9,652 detections of "clandestine entrants" in 2005 (which might include multiple attempts by the same person) a trend that continued into the first three months of 2006, with almost a third of that number again trying to cross the border (House of Commons 2006, 54).

"Burden-sharing" between Britain and France post-Sangatte

The logic behind the move towards juxtaposed controls is not new. A 2004 explanatory memorandum relating to the extension of the administrative arrangement between Belgium and the United Kingdom—at Brussels' Gare du Midi and London's Waterloo expresses the idea of "burden sharing" succinctly:

> Anyone trying to claim asylum at United Kingdom juxtaposed controls abroad will be directed to the authorities of that member state country. This encourages asylum applicants to claim international protection at the earliest opportunity (Home Office 2004, 7.1).

Elsewhere, the Home Office referred to "clandestine entrants" at the ports in northern France being handed over to the French authorities for "processing" (Home Office Border and Immigration Agency 2007). This idea of obstructing the onward movement of asylum applicants was made explicit during parliamentary debate in 2002 when the former Home Secretary, David Blunkett, stated that the "shifting of border controls" to France has "shifted the immigration and security check and ensured that people will not get here; stopping people entering clandestinely has to make more sense than trying to process them and send them back whence they came" (Refugee Council 2002, 3).

This logic that asylum applicants en route to Britain are the responsibility of France betrays the legacy of Sangatte, the Red Cross-administered centre that became a source of tension between Paris and London. Located half a mile from the Channel Tunnel and thirty miles from Britain, the centre also came to represent the worst fears of an anxious British electorate. Designed to house 600 people, the centre provided basic conditions—no heating, only a few showers—for a population of approximately 1,500 mostly Afghans and Iraqis at any one time. Over the life of the camp's existence an estimated 50,000 people were housed there (Fassin 2005, 363). Figures relating to the number of people caught trying to enter Britain are equally striking; in the first half of 2002, Eurotunnel management claimed that it had stopped 18,500 people trying to smuggle themselves into Britain, which equated to 200 people a night (Guardian 2002).

Only 350 of the asylum applicants at Sangatte sought protection from France (Fassin 2005, 363). Whether this was because of ignorance—only 11 per cent of residents surveyed in 2002 knew of their rights to apply for asylum in France—or other factors, such as family and community ties in

Britain, is difficult to assess. However, the impact of this fact on British public opinion, media coverage and political discourse continues to inform contemporary policy decisions, such as juxtaposed controls. Thompson found that the concept of "choice and asylum seeking" dominated in public discourse between March 2001 and April 2002, with the result that the entire asylum seeker population at Sangatte was tarred as undeserving and their claims deemed "bogus" (Schuster 2003, 513; Thompson 2003, 8). British tabloid newspapers such as the *Daily Mail* called for militaristic intervention, running headlines such as "Stop the invasion", "We can't take any more asylum seekers", "Asylum invasion reaches 12,000 a month", "Asylum: we're being invaded", and "Refugees, run for your life" (Schuster 2003, 511; Tempest 2002).

Schuster has described the popular response in Britain to Sangatte as a "migration crisis" marked by an "hysterical media campaign in which tabloid newspapers use the language of war" (Schuster 2003, 511). Such a perspective continues to inform the official statements relating to juxtaposed controls. The media release announcing the establishment of restrictive measures following the closure of Sangatte is interesting in this regard. Entitled "UK/French Cooperation Key to Combatting Terrorism and Illegal Immigration" the joint statement from the then-Home Secretary, David Blunkett and former Interior Minister, now President, Nicolas Sarkozy warns against the "threat of displacement" (of the refugee population) to other French ports and along the northern European coastline (Home Office 2003). This tone continues when the two politicians agree to maintain their "fight against global terrorism", and yet the initiatives wholly relate to "illegal immigration".

The three measures announced were the signing of an agreement for the UK immigration controls in Calais to be extended as needed; the "deployment" of technology to "spot illegal immigrants by their heartbeat or body heat" at Dunkirk and Cherbourg and proposals to increase the number of deportations for failed asylum seekers and immigrants from France (Home Office 2003). Search techniques such as manual searches, dog teams and CO_2 probes would also be used. "People will be refused entry to the UK," Blunkett said. "The latest technology will make it increasingly difficult to hide in lorries and trains." Throughout the document there is a constant slippage between "illegal" immigration and terrorism, with Blunkett at one point stating that "international terrorists have no respect for borders."

Conclusion

Uncertain legal frameworks and the perception that states are trying to evade their responsibilities are not confined to the policy of juxtaposed controls. Goodwin-Gill writing a little over two decades ago wrote of policies of "humane deterrence" under which refugees and asylum-seekers were "deliberately detained for indefinite periods, or simply as a result of the careless or wilful disregard of the refugee elements in individual cases" (Goodwin-Gill 1986, 193).

The apparent underlying motivation for this behaviour was to use the detained asylum applicants as an "example" for those who might be coming in the future. Much of the rhetoric of "humane deterrence" continues to inform contemporary asylum policy within the European Union. Statements are made about the need to "stem the tide", as Goodwin-Gill phrased it, and deal summarily with unfounded cases through accelerated, or "fast-track" processing where asylum applicants are routinely detained at the beginning of their claim.

None of the people detained at Coquelles Freight terminal, according to the 2005 records, entered Britain. What is unknown is whether among those in the so-called "dog kennels" there were people with protection claims that in another context might have had a chance to succeed.

References

ANAFE. 2005a. *Coquelles: le juge de libertés et de la détention cautionne une justice d'exception pour les étrangers*, 17 June 2005.
—. 2005b, Les enfants ont droit à un avocat, ils ne l'ont jamais, *l'Humanité*, 6 January 2005.
BBC. 2007. New visas "exporting the borders", Wednesday 8 August 2007.
Byrne, M. 2007. Fortifying Europe: Poland and Slovakia under the Dublin system, *The Contemporary Europe Research Centre*, April.
Cimade. 2005. *Centres et locaux de détention administrative*, Paris.
Conseil National des Barreaux. 2005. *Rapport sur l'avocat et retention administrative des étrangers*, Paris.
Fassin, D. 2005. Compassion and repression: The moral economy of immigration policies in France. *Cultural Anthropology*, vol. 20, no. 3, 362–87.
Flautre, H. 2005. *Justice d'exception pour étrangers: Hélène Flautre se rendra lundi à l'audience "décoalisée" de Coquelles*. Friday 10 June 2005.

Gil-Robles, A. 2006. *Report by Mr Alvaro Gil-Robles, Commissioner for Human Rights, on the effective respect for human rights in France following his visit from 5 to 21 September, 2005*. 15 February 2006, Strasbourg: Council of Europe.

Goodwin-Gill, G. 1986. International law and the detention of refugees and asylum seekers. *International Migration Review*, vol. 20, no. 2, Special Issue: *Refugees: Issues and Directions*, Summer, 193–219.

Guardian, The. 2002. Sangatte refugee camp, 23 May 2002.

HM Chief Inspector of Prisons. 2006a. *Annual report 2004/2005*. London.

—. 2006b. *Report on the unannounced inspections of three short-term non-residential immigration holding facilities—Calais seaport, France, Coquelles Freight, France, Coquelles Tourist, France*. London.

Home Office. 2007a. *Asylum statistics 1st quarter*. Surrey: National Statistics.

—. 2006a. *Asylum statistics 3rd quarter*. Surrey: National Statistics.

—. 2006b. *Operation enforcement manual*.

—. 2006c. *Nationality, Immigration and Asylum Act 2002* (Juxtaposed Controls) (Amendment) Order 2006.

—. 2006d. *Private Freight Searching and Fingerprinting at Juxtaposed Controls April 2006*. Consultation Document.

—. 2006e. Speeches and Statements. Inspection reports on short-term holding centres in Calais and Heathrow: Government response, http://press.homeoffice.gov.uk/Speeches/005-06-calais-heathrow (accessed 31 July 2007).

—. 2004. Explanatory Memorandum to the Channel Tunnel (Miscellaneous Provisions) (Amendment) Order 2004, no. 2589.

—. 2003. Statutory Instrument 2003, *The* Nationality, Immigration and Asylum Act 2002 *(Juxtaposed Controls) Order 2003*. Treaty between the Government of the United Kingdom and Northern Ireland and the Government of the French Republic concerning the implementation of frontier controls at the sea ports of both countries on the Channel and North Sea.

—. press releases

—. 2007b. GB £1.2 billion to strengthen "off-shore" border, 1 August 2007.

—. 2007c. Strengthening Britain's borders through international cooperation, 18 June 2007.

—. 2007d. Government to strengthen "off-shore" border, 28 March 2007.

—. 2003. UK/French cooperation key to combatting terrorism and illegal immigration, 4 February 2003.

—. 2007. Juxtaposed controls. http://www.ind.homeoffice.gov.uk/lawandpolicy/civilpenalty/juxtaposedcontrols (accessed 31 July 2007).

Home Office Border and Immigration Agency. 2007. Juxtaposed controls. http://www.bia.homeoffice.gov.uk/lawandpolicy/civilpenalty/juxtaposedcontrols (accessed 24 May 2007).

House of Commons, Home Affairs Committee. 2006. *Immigration control*. London.

House of Lords. 2006. Select Committee on Home Affairs 5th Report, *Border controls*.

ILPA. 2006. Response by the Immigration Law Practitioners' Association, 28 July 2006 Consultation document: Private freight searching and fingerprinting at Juxtaposed Controls.

Les Invisibles. Coquelles, c'est un peu la vitrine. http://www.lesinvisibles.net/spip.php?article31 (accessed 1 June 2007).

Ofpra. 2006. *Les demandes d'admission sur le territoire au titre de l'asile*, Rapport d'activité, 2006.

Oxfam with Refugee Council. 2005. *The internationalisation of EU asylum policy*, Joint Refugee Council and Oxfam Great Britain response to the Home Affairs Committee Inquiry into Immigration Control, 2 December 2005. Oxford.

Raulin, N. 2005. Associations et syndicates indignés, *Libération*, 14 June 2005.

Refugee Council. 2002. *Refugee Council's response to Home Office consultation on juxtaposed controls implementation, Dover–Calais*, November 2002.

République française. 2005. *Code de l'entrée et du séjour des étrangers et du droit d'asile*, 22 February 2005.

Rigo, Enrica. 2005. Implications of EU enlargement for border management and citizenship in Europe. *EUI–RSCAS Working Papers*, no. 21, 2005.

Saberan, H. 2005. Coquelles, tribunal "clandestin pour les clandestins". *Libération*, 14 June 2005.

Securicor G4S website http://www.g4s.com/uk/uk-justice/uk-justice-detention_escorting/uk-justice-detention.htm (accessed 25 May 2007).

Schuster, L. 2005. A sledgehammer to crack a nut: Deportation, detention and dispersal in Europe. *Social Policy & Administration*, vol. 39, no. 6, December 2005, 606–21.

—. 2003. *Asylum seekers: Sangatte and the Tunnel*. Hansard Society for Parliamentary Government, *Parliamentary Affairs*, 56, 506–22.

Tempest M. 2002. "Duncan Smith: Keep Sangatte refugees out," *The Guardian,* 24 May 2002.
Thompson, M. 2003. *Images of Sangatte: Political representations of asylum seeking in France and the United Kingdom,* Sussex: Migration Working Paper, No. 18.
United Kingdom Parliament. 2006. *Select Committee on Home Affairs, Fifth Report,* 2006.
Zappi, S. 2003. Sangatte shutdown signals new Anglo-French cooperation, *Le Monde,* Saturday 1 February 2003.

CHAPTER FIVE

AUSTRALIA'S BORDER CONTROL AND REFUGEE PROTECTION CAPACITY-BUILDING ACTIVITIES IN THE ASIA–PACIFIC REGION

SAVITRI TAYLOR

Introduction

Australia and other developed countries regard irregular migration as a threat to national security (widely conceived) against which defence is required. One defensive strategy which Australia, in common with other developed countries, is increasingly adopting is that of attempting to create an "offshore" border for itself in the countries of origin and transit of potential irregular entrants. The problem from a human rights perspective is that some of the irregular migrants who are being kept away from Australia's territorial borders are asylum seekers (i.e. individuals whose human rights are under such threat in their country of origin that they have no option but to seek in another country the protection they cannot find at home).

Most of Australia's offshore border control measures do not actually distinguish between asylum seekers who are trying to flee their country of origin (primary movers) and asylum seekers who are trying to move to Australia from a country in which they had or could have sought protection (secondary movers). In Australian government rhetoric, however, these measures have been justified largely in terms of the role they play in preventing secondary movement. Australia's position is that onward movement from a country of first asylum is voluntary rather than forced migration for which no exception to ordinary immigration rules need be made. At the same time, though, Australia has to take account of the reality that, if asylum seekers cannot, in fact, obtain effective protection in a so-called country of first asylum, they will feel compelled to move onward to a country better able to provide protection and that the country of first asylum, if it feels overburdened by the protection role thrust upon it, will have little interest in preventing such onward movement even if able to do so. Australia, therefore, recognises that it is sometimes in its interest to assist in building the refugee protection capacity of countries which asylum seekers presently simply transit en route to its own shores.

Since the early 1990s Australia has, with great success, pursued the objective of off-shoring border control through a huge array of Asian, Pacific and Asia–Pacific regional dialogue processes some of which will be mentioned in the course of this chapter. It also has a very active program of negotiating border control cooperation on a bilateral basis with countries of origin and transit of irregular migrants. Some of the bilateral agreements which Australia has negotiated deal with aspects of border control cooperation as part of more general cooperation on combating terrorism and/or transnational crime, but other agreements focus specifically on irregular movement of people. The rest of this chapter sets out the findings of a preliminary investigation into the border control and refugee protection capacity-building activities which Australia has undertaken in the Asia–Pacific region on the back of the program of regional and bilateral engagement just mentioned, considering in particular the implications of those activities for asylum seekers.

Export of legislation

Pacific island states

In the 2002 Nasonini Declaration on Regional Security, Pacific Island Forum[1] leaders:

> underlined the importance to Members of introducing legislation and developing national strategies to combat serious crime including money laundering, drug trafficking, terrorism and terrorist financing, people smuggling, and people trafficking in accordance with international requirements in these areas.

---

[1] The PIF (known as the South Pacific Forum until 2000) was established in 1971 to facilitate political and economic cooperation. The members of the PIF are Australia, Cook Islands, Federated States of Micronesia, Fiji, Kiribati, Nauru, New Zealand, Niue, Palau, PNG, Republic of the Marshall Islands, Samoa, Solomon Islands, Tonga, Tuvalu and Vanuatu.

The impetus for the Nasonini Declaration was probably Security Council Resolution 1373 of 28 September 2001 in which the Security Council, acting under Chapter VII of the United Nations Charter called upon all states to take a variety of anti-terrorism measures. Australia and New Zealand had, in fact, been attempting to get Pacific island states to introduce legislation dealing with various transnational crimes for at least a decade beforehand, but even after 9/11 legislative reform by Pacific island states probably remained more of a priority for Australia and New Zealand than for those states themselves (Boister 2005, 75–8; Fletcher, 2004, 14–15). Part of the reason for this is that Pacific island states have more pressing things than law-making on which to expend their very limited resources (Boister 2005, 76; Fletcher 2004, 14–15). Australia and New Zealand have tried to deal with this problem by providing funding, technical assistance and other support for Pacific island state law-making both directly and through mechanisms such as the Forum Secretariat (Boister 2005, 76).

For example, Australia, New Zealand and the Forum Secretariat, with input from the United States and the Commonwealth Secretariat,[2] discussed amongst themselves how they could achieve implementation of the Nasonini Declaration, and came up with a program of action which included the convening of an expert working group to draft model legislation to address terrorism and transnational crime (including people-smuggling and trafficking) and the provision by Australia and New Zealand of in-country drafting assistance to Forum members for the purpose of adapting the model legislation to their own legal systems (Fletcher 2004, 14–15; New Zealand Ministry of Justice 2005). The members of the Expert Working Group to Coordinate the Development of a Regional Framework including Model Legislative Provisions to Address Terrorism and Transnational Crime included representatives of New Zealand, Kiribati, Marshall Islands, Samoa, Vanuatu, the Oceania Customs Organisation (OCO), the Pacific Immigration Directors'

---

[2] The main intergovernmental agency of the association of 53 states known as the Commonwealth.

Conference (PIDC),[3] the Pacific Islands Chiefs of Police (PICP),[4] the International Monetary Fund (IMF), the Commonwealth Secretariat and also two expert legal drafters (Pacific Islands Forum Secretariat 2003; OCO 2003, 3). One of the expert legal drafters was provided by New Zealand (Goff 2003) and the other was provided by Australia (Secretariat of the Conference of the Parties to the United Nations Convention against Transnational Organized Crime 2005, para. 45).

In relation to immigration legislation specifically, a PIDC working group[5] comprised of Australia, the Cook Islands, Fiji, Nauru, New Zealand, Norfolk Island, PNG, Samoa and the Forum Secretariat which had been set up at the Fifth PIDC Conference in November 2001 had developed a framework for review of immigration legislation which some PIDC members were already using to assess their existing immigration legislation. However, it was noted by PIDC members at its Sixth Conference in September 2002 that "the framework did not detail the requirements for legislation dealing with asylum seekers and refugees" and they asked for this aspect of the framework to be "further developed" (Sixth Pacific Immigration Directors Conference Communiqué, 19 September 2002). The PIDC subsequently did draft model refugee status determination provisions for incorporation into the immigration laws of Pacific Island states. Unfortunately, PIDC's model refugee legislation is not nearly as comprehensive as UNHCR model refugee legislation. In UNHCR's *2006 Country Operations Plan for Papua New Guinea*, that agency lamented:

> Since November 2002, UNHCR has assisted GoPNG to develop draft domestic refugee legislation. It was hoped the legislation would be passed in 2004. However, the PNG Director-General recently informed UNHCR that the draft PNG *Refugee Law Act* would be abandoned in favour of

---

[3] PIDC was established in 1996 to "foster multilateral cooperation and mutual assistance aimed at strengthening participants" territorial borders and the integrity of their entry systems': PIDC, *Pacific Immigration Directors' Conference Home*, retrieved 22 August 2006 from http://www.pidcsec.org. The territorial entities eligible to participate in PIDC are American Samoa, Australia, Commonwealth of Northern Mariana Islands, Cook Islands, Federated States of Micronesia, Fiji, French Polynesia, Guam, Kiribati, Marshall Islands, Nauru, New Zealand, New Caledonia, Niue, Norfolk Island, Palau, PNG, Samoa, Solomon Islands, Tonga, Tuvalu, Vanuatu, Wallis and Futuna Islands.
[4] Formerly called the South Pacific Chiefs of Police Conference.
[5] PIDC Working Group on Development of a Strategic Plan, Repatriation of Illegal Immigrants, Regional Legislative Framework to Assist Members and Strategies and Action with UNSCR 1373 and TNOC.

simplified, basic refugee legislation, based on the Pacific Immigration Directors Conference (PIDC) model, to be included into a newly drafted *Immigration Act*.

It is worth noting that Australia worked very closely with PNG in drafting the amendments to its immigration laws (Downer 2002, 9444; Senate Foreign Affairs Defence and Trade References Committee 2003, paras 7.112–13).

PNG's new immigration laws (including refugee provisions thereof) are not actually in place yet. In fact, Fiji is the only Pacific island state that does have refugee laws in place so far, though even these are not yet fully implemented. In the circumstances, UNHCR is contenting itself with simply urging Pacific island states to put refugee laws in place whether based on its model, the PIDC model or both (Wright 2005).

The rest of the Asia–Pacific region

In 2002 Australia and Indonesia initiated the Bali Process on People Smuggling, Trafficking in Persons and Related Transnational Crime in which over fifty countries and several international organisations participate. One objective that Bali Process countries have agreed to pursue is the enactment of national legislation criminalising people-smuggling and trafficking. The Australian Attorney-General's Department co-facilitated a regional workshop which was held in Malaysia in September 2002 to promote the development of such legislation. The workshop, which was attended by 27 countries, agreed on the elements that national legislation needed to contain (Blackburn 2002, 143). The Australian Attorney-General's Department followed up by developing model anti–people-smuggling and model anti-trafficking legislation in cooperation with China (Bali Process, 2006). Nowhere in the model legislation is there any mention of refugees and asylum seekers let alone any provision made for their protection. For example, the model legislation includes "carrier sanctions", i.e. a provision imposing penalties on carriers bringing into a country a person who does not have the travel documents required for lawful entry into that country. Some countries which already have carrier sanctions in place actually waive the imposition of sanctions in the case of improperly documented passengers who make successful asylum claims (Brouwer and Kumin 2003, 10). Australia's own carrier sanction provisions make no such concession. Not surprisingly, the carrier sanction provisions in model legislation it has drafted do not make such a concession either. Of course, the deficiencies of the model legislation will only impact on asylum seekers if regional countries make use of it. By November 2003, seventeen regional countries already had (Bali Process 2006).

Export of border management and control systems

In recent years, the Australian Government has funded the International Organization for Migration (IOM) to conduct assessments of the border management and control systems of countries in the Asia–Pacific region, including Fiji, Indonesia, Laos, Pakistan and PNG (Department of Immigration 2005, 85; Department of Immigration 2004, 65; Department of Immigration 2003a; IOM 2007). Once the assessment process has identified what needs to be done to strengthen border security, Australia may well fund capacity-building in those areas. The following are some examples of border management and control systems.

Advance Passenger Processing systems

Australia requires Advance Passenger Processing to be undertaken by the forty-seven airlines which have regular flights to Australia (Department of Immigration 2006a, 124). When a passenger checks in at an international airport for any Australia-bound flight, airline personnel must (*Migration Act 1958* (Cth), ss. 245I–245N; Migration Regulations 1994 (Cth), reg 3.13A) feed certain information about the passenger into the APP system which automatically checks whether the passenger holds a valid Australian visa or valid Australian or New Zealand passport. Depending on the outcome of the check, the check-in operator is issued with a passenger boarding directive such as "OK TO BOARD" or "DO NOT BOARD" which the operator is expected to act upon (Department of Immigration 2006b).[6] Nowhere in the booklet setting out APP operating instructions for service providers is any mention made of the particular issues relating to asylum seekers.

Not content with relying on its own APP system to intercept potential unauthorised arrivals to Australia, the Australian government wants to go the logical next step and ensure that they are intercepted or at least identified before they even get to another country in the Asia–Pacific region (Department of Immigration 2005, 107). It is therefore encouraging

---

[6] The APP system has also been in place since January 2004 for all cruise ships travelling to Australia and since March 2006 is being progressively implemented in the cargo ship sector (Department of Immigration 2006a, 135).

regional countries to also adopt an APP system (or at least an Advance Passenger Information system) as part of their own border management (DFAT 2004, 91). The Australian Department of Immigration is assisting a number of PIDC members to develop and implement API/APP systems (PIDC 2006). It is also providing "continued leadership in Asia–Pacific Economic Cooperation (APEC)[7] initiatives for Advanced Passenger Information (API) processing" (Department of Immigration 2005, 85). For example, since 2002 it has done API feasibility studies for eleven APEC economies (Department of Immigration 2006a, 124).

Movement alert systems

Another border control device that Australia uses is its Movement Alert List (MAL). MAL is basically a computer database which contains details of "people and travel documents of immigration concern" (Department of Immigration 2007). These details have been obtained by the Department of Immigration as a result of "liaison with law enforcement agencies and departmental offices in Australia and overseas" (Department of Immigration 2007). MAL presently contains the details of about 450,000 people who, for example, have criminal records or debts to the Commonwealth and of about 2.3 million lost, stolen or fraudulently altered passports and other such documents. MAL is checked when visa applications are being processed (Department of Immigration 2007).

The Australian Department of Immigration is now involved in the development an APEC Regional Movement Alert List (RMAL) passports system which allows lost and stolen passports data of all participating countries to be accessed at airline check-in for the purpose of preventing use of such passports (Department of Immigration 2006a, 123). The Australian Budget handed down in May 2006 included $10.9 million additional funding to support the Department of Immigration in this endeavour (Downer 2006a). A pilot involving Australia, New Zealand and USA has already been conducted and extension to other APEC economies is expected to follow (Department of Immigration 2006a, 124).

---

[7] APEC was established in 1989. Its member economies are Australia, Brunei, Canada, Chile, People's Republic of China, Hong Kong, Indonesia, Japan, Malaysia, Mexico, New Zealand, Papua New Guinea, Peru, Philippines, Russia, Singapore, South Korea, Taiwan, Thailand, United States and Vietnam.

Provision of infrastructure, equipment, technical assistance and training

Every year, the Australian Department of Immigration provides document fraud detection training to hundreds of officials of regional countries (Department of Immigration 2006a, 144–5). The Department of Immigration and the Australian Federal Police working together also deliver more wide-ranging border control training to immigration, customs and law enforcement agencies in Pacific island states (Senate Foreign Affairs, Defence and Trade References Committee 2003, para. 7.119). In addition, Australia engages in more ambitious capacity-building projects such as the following.

Three Australian Department of Immigration officials seconded under the Enhanced Cooperation Program (ECP) package of assistance to PNG are presently putting in place a new border-management system in that country (Department of Immigration 2006a, 97). Somewhat less hands-on, part of Australia's aid to the Federated States of Micronesia (FSM) has been allocated to the FSM Improved Border Management System project (AusAID 2007). The project involves such matters as the provision of computer hardware (for example, passport scanners) and specialised border-management software (Australian Parliamentary Delegation to Palau and FSM 2006, para. 2.67). Australia's aid budget has funded similar border management systems projects in the Cook Islands (DFAT 2006), Marshall Islands, Palau (AusAID 2007), and Samoa (AusAID 2005).

In the past Australia has funded IOM to undertake an Enhanced Migration Management project in Cambodia which has involved the provision of advice, the design of migration legislation, the development of a computerised border processing and visa issue system, and so on (Department of Immigration 2003a). At present, Australia is funding IOM to undertake a Border Management project in Bangladesh which involves providing border-management training to Bangladeshi officials as well as the provision of equipment and so on (Australian High Commission Bangladesh 2006; IOM 2006).

The national security expenditure in the 2006/07 Australian Budget includes $7.1 million over three years for the Australian Customs Service to work with border control agencies in Indonesia, Malaysia and the Philippines to improve border control management in the Sulu and Celebes Seas region which is a very busy area of sea and, therefore, very difficult to monitor and secure (Attorney-General's Department 2006; Downer 2006b).

In addition to the funding of the Australian Customs Service–led project just mentioned, Australian border control capacity-building assistance to the Philippines includes the provision of two document fraud laboratories (and related training) by the Department of Immigration and the provision of maritime security training to the Philippines Navy and Coastguard by the Department of Defence (Downer 2006b).

On 28 June 2006 the Minister for Immigration announced that Australia would be equipping staff at two Thai airports with document examination equipment and would be working together with Thailand on a pilot to strengthen its border management at key land border checkpoints. The reason given was that such cooperation between Australia and Thailand was "important for Australia's border security" (Vanstone 2006b).

The country which receives the lion's share of Australian border control capacity building assistance, however, is Indonesia. Probably because about 85 per cent of past unauthorised arrivals to Australia have in fact come here via Indonesia (Mares 2002, 238–9), Australia considers Indonesia to be a "priority country for cooperation in enhanced migration management" (Department of Immigration 2003a). As well as providing Indonesian officials with training related to border control, Australia also provides Indonesia with infrastructure (for example, a document fraud laboratory (Department of Immigration 2003a)), equipment (for example, patrol boats (Australian Government 2002)) and various kinds of technical assistance to strengthen its border control capacity. Most notably, the Budget handed down in May 2006 included an allocation of $9.8 million over four years to be absorbed by the Department of Immigration for improving Indonesia's CEKAL border alert system, which is its version of Australia's MAL (Downer 2006a; Vanstone 2006a). The expenditure of the money, which is paying for hardware and software associated with the system, is being justified on the basis that "the stronger the border security arrangements that exist across the region, the better it is for Australia's border security interests" (Correll 2007, 90–1).

What about refugee protection?

At the end of 2005, there were 8,394,373 recognised refugees (excluding Palestinian refugees) and 773,492 asylum seekers worldwide. 9.8 per cent (825,599) of the refugees and 6.4 per cent (49,391) of the asylum seekers were located in the Asia–Pacific region (UNHCR 2006a, Table 1). However, the distribution of refugees and asylum seekers within the Asia–Pacific region was not necessarily reflective of the relative protection capacities of the countries in the region. The table below extracted from the *UNHCR Statistical Yearbook 2005* (UNHCR 2005, table V.1) shows the refugees 2001–05 to GDP (current) per capita protection contribution of countries in the Asia–Pacific region.[8] It can be seen that Australia's offshore border control measures ensured that its protection contribution as a host country to refugees was nowhere near as great as that of some other countries in the region. The question is whether it bore an equitable share of the region's total refugee burden by contributing in other ways.

Country of asylum	Refugees 2001–05 to GDP (current) per capita
Australia	1.9
Bangladesh	52.9
Cambodia	0.5
China	203.3
India	257.1
Indonesia	17.8
Japan	0.1
Malaysia	7.2
Nepal	516.5
New Zealand	0.2
PNG	10.5
Philippines	0.1
Sri Lanka	0.1
Thailand	46.1
Vietnam	19.4

In 2000, following more than three years of negotiations (Joint Standing Committee on Foreign Affairs, Defence and Trade, Foreign Affairs Sub-Committee 2004, para. 3.88), Australia, Indonesia and IOM commenced an unwritten (Killesteyn 2003, 26; Farmer 2003, 29), "semi-formal" (IOM Indonesia 2006), "regional cooperation arrangement" providing for the interception and care of irregular migrants. Under this

---

[8] The remaining countries (Bhutan, Brunei, Burma, East Timor, Federated States of Micronesia, Fiji, Kiribati, Laos, Maldives, Marshall Islands, Mongolia, Nauru, North Korea, Palau, Samoa, Singapore, Solomon Islands, South Korea, Taiwan, Tonga, Tuvalu, Vanuatu) and French, New Zealand and USA associates and territories were omitted from the UNHCR table or made a contribution which was rounded to zero.

arrangement, Indonesian police and immigration authorities, drawing on intelligence gathered by the Australian Federal Police (AFP) and other Australian authorities (Mares 2001, 13), intercept irregular migrants who appear to be headed toward Australia but allow them to remain in Indonesia pending determination of any asylum claims they may make (Killesteyn 2003, 26). The reason that the Indonesian authorities are prepared to do this is that, pursuant to the same arrangement, intercepted individuals are provided accommodation, food and emergency medical assistance by IOM at Australia's expense (Department of Immigration 2006c; IOM Indonesia 2006). Prior to the 2007/08 Budget, the Australian Budget allocation for these arrangements with IOM was about $3.5 million per year (Department of Immigration 2002; Department of Immigration 2006c).

Individuals who indicate that they are asylum seekers are referred by IOM to the Office of the United Nations High Commissioner for Refugees (UNHCR) for determination of their protection claims (Department of Immigration 2003b). Rejected asylum seekers who are willing to return to their countries of origin are assisted to do so by IOM at Australia's expense (Human Rights Watch 2002, 61) and UNHCR endeavours to find durable solutions for those found to be refugees. According to UNHCR, "authorities in Indonesia ... have come to expect that only resettlement can be considered as a solution for recognized refugees" (UNHCR 2006b, 4). Australia's formal position on those found to be refugees by UNHCR in Indonesia is that it will only take "its fair share", but political exigencies have resulted in it being thus far "the largest single country of resettlement" for those found to be refugees and having also to take others found to be in humanitarian need (Hughes 2007, 84).

The 2007/08 Budget included funding for a "new initiative" under which IOM would receive one-off funding of $7.7 million to improve Indonesia's immigration detention facilities and also to "develop guidelines with associated training for the management and care of intercepted people in accordance with international human rights standards and relevant international obligations" (Andrews 2007a). The Budget also included $450,000 in funding for UNHCR "to employ more staff and conduct more refugee status determinations in Indonesia" (Andrews 2007b). The rationale of the new initiative is to reduce the incentive for asylum seekers to travel onward from Indonesia to Australia by improving their situation in Indonesia (Topsfield 2007).

In December 2005 Australia entered a Memorandum of Understanding with PNG and with the International Organization for Migration on the Care, Protection and Voluntary Return of Certain Irregular Migrants from

PNG. As at 22 May 2006, the 2005 MOU had not yet been specifically utilised (Department of Immigration 2006d) but presumably the arrangement was negotiated because Australia believes that it will be of use in the future. According to the press release issued by the Minister for Immigration upon the signing of the 2005 MOU, it sets out an arrangement under which:

> PNG, Australia and IOM will co-operate in the areas of identification and processing of irregular immigrants transiting PNG *who might attempt to enter Australia unlawfully* as well as counselling, care and voluntary return (Vanstone 2005, emphasis added).

Similarly, a Department of Immigration official at an estimates hearing in February 2006 emphasised that the MOU related to people who *might be Australia bound*. Interestingly, the official suggested that such individuals were more likely to be entering PNG by air at Port Moresby than making their way across the land border with Indonesia (Hughes 2006a, 63).

If Australia-bound individuals are intercepted "and there is no way of funding their subsistence until their cases are looked into" (Hughes 2006a, 62), the MOU provides that Australia will fund IOM to meet those subsistence needs including accommodation and basic healthcare (Vanstone 2005). The MOU provides that PNG will consider any claims for refugee status made by such individuals (Vanstone 2005), with IOM, funded by Australia, continuing to meet their subsistence needs through that process (Hughes 2006a, 62). In selected cases, Australia will also pay the subsistence costs of individuals found to be refugees while they were awaiting resettlement to a third country (Hughes 2006a, 62). Finally, if intercepted individuals wish to return home but do not have the funds to do so and the PNG government does not have the funds to assist them either, Australia will fund IOM to arrange for their return (Hughes 2006a, 62), and care for them pending return (Hughes 2006b, 148).

Since 2000, Australia has entered into an arrangement similar to those described above with IOM and Cambodia (Okely 2002, 460) and another with IOM and East Timor (Killesteyn 2003, 26), in both cases relying, as above, on UNHCR's cooperation in conducting refugee status determinations. The available evidence suggests that both arrangements were ad hoc responses by the Australian government to particular incidents of attempted irregular movement to Australia and have not survived to the present day. However, the common theme running through all four regional cooperation arrangements mentioned is that Australia decided to invest in refugee protection activities in the Asia–Pacific countries concerned only because that investment was perceived to be the price which had to paid in exchange for border control cooperation from those countries.

On 8 May 2007, the Minister for Immigration announced that the 2007/08 Budget would include an "increase of $1.2 million over that provided in 2006/07 to meet the increased numbers of people cared for under the [Prospective Illegal Arrangements in Transit Countries (PIATC)] programme" (Andrews 2007c). Since he also stated that the PIATC program was the new name for the regional cooperation arrangements established in 2000, the extra funding may simply be for the existing arrangements with Indonesia and PNG. However, the failure to name the transit countries concerned could be read as indicative of the intention or fact of the program being expanded to other transit countries.

On 8 May 2007, the Minister for Immigration also announced an additional $2 million funding in 2007/08 for "providing effective protection to refugees and displaced people" and promoting "durable solutions for those in protracted situations throughout the world, particularly in source and transit countries". Again the rationale was to "reduce incentives for refugees and displaced people to utilise the services of people smugglers and lower the risk of irregular migration to Australia" (Andrews 2007d). According to the minister, the "total projected expenditure in 2007/08 for the care and management of irregular migrants and to address the situation of refugees and displaced people" was "more than $20 million" (Andrews 2007e). It is likely, however, that he was speaking only of the Immigration portfolio budget.

Australia also funds what could be described as refugee protection capacity building through the AusAID budget. The 2002/03 Australian Budget saw the introduction into the Overseas Aid Program of the International Refugee Fund through which Australia allocates about $15 million per year to projects assisting refugees and host communities in the Asia–Pacific region (ACFID 2004, 9; ACFID 2006, 3; ACFOA 2003, 8; Downer 2007; RCOA 2006). However, the same Budget saw Australia's core allocation to UNHCR drop from $14.3 million to $7.3 million and it remained at approximately that amount until the 2007/08 Budget which increased the allocation to $8.3 million (RCOA 2002; RCOA 2007). Although the UNHCR, as well as receiving its core allocation, is given the opportunity to access the International Refugee Fund and has been successful in doing so (Downer 2007), Australia has basically robbed Peter to pay Paul.

Conclusion

In summary, a preliminary investigation into Australia's border control and refugee protection capacity-building cooperation with countries in the Asia–Pacific region suggests that, although the situation may slowly be changing for the better, Australia presently puts far greater effort and resources into border control cooperation than refugee protection cooperation, with necessarily negative implications for asylum seekers. In other words, Australia is choosing to exert influence beyond its own territory in pursuit of its border control objective without taking a commensurate degree of responsibility for safeguarding the rights of those affected by its actions. The fact that Australia's behaviour is in line with that of other developed countries (Vedsted-Hansen 1999; Oxfam 2005, 43) does not make it any more palatable.

References

ACFID (Australian Council for International Development). 2004. *Aid budget 2004/05 overview and analysis*, 7 July.
—. 2006. *Aid budget 2006/07 overview and analysis*, 16 May.
ACFOA (Australian Council for Overseas Aid). 2003. *Aid budget 2003/04 overview and analysis*, May.
Andrews, K., Minister for Immigration. 2007a. *Strengthening Australia's border, budget media release fact sheet: assistance for management and care of irregular immigrants in Indonesia*, 8 May, http://www.minister.immi.gov.au/media/mediareleases/2007/budget07 08/budget0708-immigration_management_facilities.pdf.
—. 2007b. *Cooperation with Indonesia makes life harder for people smugglers, media release*, 3 May, http://www.minister.immi.gov.au/media/mediareleases/2007/ka07033.htm.
—. 2007c. *Strengthening Australia's border, budget media release fact sheet: prospective illegal immigrants—improved arrangements in transit countries*, 8 May, http://www.minister.immi.gov.au/media/mediareleases/2007/budget07 08/budget0708-prospective_illegal_immigrants.pdf.
—. 2007d. *Strengthening Australia's border, budget media release fact sheet: stabilising displaced populations*, 8 May, http://www.minister.immi.gov.au/media/mediareleases/2007/budget07 08/budget0708-address_refugees_worldwide.pdf.

—. 2007e. *Strengthening Australia's border, budget media release*, 8 May, http://www.minister.immi.gov.au/media/mediareleases/2007/ka07038.htm

Attorney-General's Department. 2006. *Budget 2006/07: Security environment update*, 9 May, http://www.ag.gov.au/www/agd/agd.nsf/Page/PublicationsBudgetsBudget_2006Information_Sheets.

AusAID. 2005. *Annual report 2004/05*, http://www.ausaid.gov.au/anrep05/s2b.html.

—. 2007. *Australian aid to Micronesia*, May, http://www.ausaid.gov.au/country/country.cfm?CountryID=7578636&Region=SouthPacific&CFID=2481220&CFTOKEN=68665129.

Australian Government. 2002. *Australian government budget 2002/03, budget paper no. 2 part ii, expense measures immigration and multicultural and indigenous affairs*, http://www.budget.gov.au/2002-03/bp2/html/03_bp2expense_3.html#P3305_119859.

Australian High Commission Bangladesh. 2006. *Australia provides funds to combat irregular migration in Bangladesh*, http://www.bangladesh.embassy.gov.au/daca/0605_IOM_Ph2.html.

Australian Parliamentary Delegation to Palau and FSM. 2006. *Report*, http://www.aph.gov.au/house/info/pro/41P_reports/Palau%20and%20FSM.pdf.

Bali Process. 2006. *Bali process on people smuggling, trafficking in persons and related transnational crime summary of activities*, http://www.baliprocess.net/files/Activities/SummaryofActivites.pdf.

Blackburn, J., Attorney-General's Department. 2002, *Official committee Hansard: Senate Foreign Affairs and Trade References Committee, Australia's relationship with Papua New Guinea and Pacific Island Nations*, 25 October.

Boister, N. 2005. Regional cooperation in the suppression of transnational crimes in the South Pacific. In *International law issues in the South Pacific*, ed. G. Leane and B. von Tigerstrom. Aldershot and Burlington: Ashgate.

Brouwer, A. and J. Kumin. 2003. Interception and asylum: when migration control and human rights collide. *Refuge: Canada's Periodical on Refugees*, vol. 21, no. 4, 6–24.

Correll, B., Department of Immigration. 2007. *Proof Committee Hansard: Senate Standing Committee on Legal and Constitutional Affairs, budget estimates*, 21 May.

Department of Immigration. 2007. *Fact sheet 77. The Movement Alert List*, 2 April, http://www.immi.gov.au/media/fact-sheets/77mal.htm.
—. 2006a. *Annual report 2005/06*. Canberra: Commonwealth of Australia.
—. 2006b. *Australia's APP Check-In Guide: An information booklet containing operating instructions for service providers*, November, http://www.immi.gov.au/managing-australias-orders/border-security/APP-check-in-htm.
—. 2006c. *Answer to question 156 taken on notice Budget Estimates Hearing*, 22 May, http://www.aph.gov.au/senate/committee/legcon_ctte/estimates/bud_0607/dimia/qon_156.pdf.
—. 2006d. *Answer to question 137 taken on notice Budget Estimates Hearing*, 22 May, http://www.aph.gov.au/senate/committee/legcon_ctte/estimates/bud_0607/dimia/qon_137.pdf.
—. 2005. *Annual report 2004/05*. Canberra: Commonwealth of Australia.
—. 2004. *Annual report 2003/04*. Canberra: Commonwealth of Australia.
—. 2003a. *Annual report 2002/03*.
http://www.immi.gov.au/about/reports/annual/2002-03/report26.htm
—. 2003b. *Answer to question 4 taken on notice supplementary Budget Estimates Hearing*, 25 November, http://www.aph.gov.au/senate/committee/legcon_ctte/estimates/sup_0304/dimia/DIMIA%201%20-%206.pdf.
—. 2002. *Answer to question 9 taken on notice, Senate Legal and Constitutional Committee Inquiry into the Migration Legislation Amendment (Further Border Protection) Bill 2002 and Related Matters*, http://www.aph.gov.au/senate/committee/legcon_ctte/completed_inquiries/2002-04/mig_bp/qon/dimia.doc.
DFAT (Department of Foreign Affairs and Trade). 2006. *Cook Islands country brief—July 2006*.
—. 2004. *Transnational terrorism: The threat to Australia*. Canberra: Commonwealth of Australia.
Downer, A., Minister for Foreign Affairs. 2007. *Australia provides support for the displaced in the Asia Pacific, media release AA 07 013*, 7 March, http://www.ausaid.gov.au/media/release.cfm?BC=Media&ID=8914_6617_5246_8028_3812.
—. 2006a. *Regional counter-terrorism package, media release FA046*, 9 May, http://www.foreignminister.gov.au/releases/2006/fa046_06.html.

—. 2006b. *Inaugural lecture on national and international security*, Wollongong: University of Wollongong Centre for Transnational Crime Prevention, http://www.foreignminister.gov.au/speeches/2006/060516_national_international_security.html.

—. 2002. *Parliamentary Debates: House of Representatives Official Hansard*, 3 December.

Farmer, B., Department of Immigration. 2003. *Official Committee Hansard: Senate Legal and Constitutional Legislation Committee, Budget Estimates Supplementary Hearings*, 25 November.

Fletcher, G. 2004. Terrorism and security issues in the Pacific. In *The eye of the cyclone: Issues in Pacific security*. ed. I. Molloy, Sippy Downs: PIPSA and University of the Sunshine Coast.

Goff, P., New Zealand Minister of Foreign Affairs. 2003. *NZ expertise to help draft PI counter-terrorism legislation*, 27 February, http://www.beehive.govt.nz/ViewDocument.aspx?DocumentID=16125

Hughes, P., Department of Immigration. 2007. *Proof Committee Hansard: Senate Standing Committee on Legal and Constitutional Affairs, budget estimates*, 21 May.

—. 2006a. *Official Committee Hansard: Senate Legal and Constitutional Legislation Committee, Additional Budget Estimates*, 13 February.

—. 2006b. *Official Committee Hansard: Senate Legal and Constitutional Legislation Committee, budget estimates*, 22 May.

Human Rights Watch. 2002. *By invitation only: Australian asylum policy*. http://hrw.org/reports/2002/australia/.

International Organization for Migration. 2006. *Australian and Bangladeshi governments extend border management project*, 10 March, http://www.iom.int/jahia/Jahia/pbnAS/cache/offonce?entryId=4706.

—. 2007. *Australia*, http://www.iom.int/jahia/page511.html.

IOM Indonesia. 2006. *Irregular Migrants Assistance Program*, May, http://www.iom.or.id/programmes.jsp?lang=eng&code=2&dcode=6.

Joint Standing Committee on Foreign Affairs Defence and Trade, Foreign Affairs Sub-Committee. 2004. *Near neighbours—good neighbours: An inquiry into Australia's relationship with Indonesia*. Canberra: Commonwealth of Australia.

Killesteyn, E., Department of Immigration. 2003. *Official Committee Hansard: Senate Legal and Constitutional Legislation Committee, Budget Estimates Supplementary Hearings*, 25 November.

Mares, P. 2002. *Borderline: Australia's response to refugees and asylum seekers in the wake of the Tampa*. Sydney: UNSW Press.

—. 2001. Canberra funds Jakarta's efforts to stem the tide, *The Age*, 29 August.
New Zealand Ministry of Justice. 2005. *Anti-money laundering and countering the financing of terrorism APG annual meeting 2005 Jurisdiction report: New Zealand*, http://www.justice.govt.nz/fatf/jurisdiction-report.html.
Oceania Customs Organisation. 2003. *The Quarterly News*. Edition 12.
Okely, J., Department of Immigration. 2002. *Official Committee Hansard: Senate Legal and Constitutional Legislation Committee, Consideration of Budget Estimates*, 29 May.
Oxfam. 2005. *Foreign territory: The internationalisation of EU asylum policy*, http://oxfamgb.org/ukpp/resources/downloads/foreign_territory_english.pdf.
Pacific Islands Forum Secretariat. 2003. *Press statement 51/03: Expert working group to coordinate the development of a regional framework including model legislation to address terrorism and transnational organised crime*, http://www.sidsnet.org/pacific/forumsec/Home.htm.
Pacific Immigration Directors' Conference. 2006. *Fact sheet*, July, http://www.pidcsec.org/files/PIDC_Newsletters/pidcfactsheet_july2006.pdf.
RCOA (Refugee Council of Australia). 2007. *2007/08 Australian government budget: Spending on programs related to refugees*, http://www.refugeecouncil.org.au/docs/current/0708%20Budget%20Response.pdf.
—. 2006. *2005/06 federal budget summary of refugee related issues*, http://www.refugeecouncil.org.au/docs/current/2005fedbudget.pdf.
—. 2002. *RCOA's reflections on the 2002/2003 federal budget*, May, http://www.refugeecouncil.org.au/docs/resources/ppapers/pp-budget2002-3.pdf.
Secretariat of the Conference of the Parties to the United Nations Convention against Transnational Organized Crime. 2005. *Implementation of the Protocol against the Smuggling of Migrants by Land, Sea and Air, supplementing the United Nations Convention against Transnational Organized Crime—Analytical report of the secretariat*, 2 September, http://www.unodc.org/pdf/ctoccop_2005/V0587652e.pdf.
Senate Foreign Affairs, Defence and Trade References Committee. 2003. *A Pacific engaged: Australia's relations with Papua New Guinea and the island states of the south-west Pacific*. Canberra: Commonwealth of Australia.

Topsfield, J. 2007. Crackdown planned on people smugglers, *The Age*, 4 May, http://www.theage.com.au/news/national/crackdown-on-smugglers/2007/05/03/1177788310417.html.

UNHCR. 2007. *Statistical yearbook 2005: trends in displacement, protection and solutions*. Geneva: UNHCR.

—. 2006a. *2005 global refugee trends*. Geneva: UNHCR.

—. 2006b. *Regional Operations Plan 2007 covering Indonesia, Brunei Darussalam, the Philippines, Singapore, and Timor-Leste*, http://www.indonesia-ottawa.org/UN/files/Regional%20Operation%20Plan%202007.pdf.

Vanstone, A., Minister for Immigration. 2006a. *Greater security from enhanced border management system, media release*, 28 June, http://www.minister.immi.gov.au/media/media-releases/2006/v06153.htm.

—. 2006b. *Immigration cooperation to improve regional security, media release*, 23 June, http://www.minister.immi.gov.au/media/media-releases/2006/v06156.htm.

—. 2005. *Strong teamwork key to migration management, media release*, 16 December, http://www.minister.immi.gov.au/media/media-releases/2005/v05157.htm.

Vedsted-Hansen, J. 1999. *Europe's response to the arrival of asylum seekers: Refugee protection and immigration control (New issues in refugee research working paper no. 6)*, Geneva: UNHCR.

Wright, N., UNHCR Regional Representative. 2005. *Statement, 9th Pacific immigration director conference's annual meeting*, Nadi.

Chapter Six

Out of Sight, Out of Right? Who Can Be Held Accountable for Detainees Harmed on Nauru?

Azadeh Dastyari

In September 2001, a few weeks before the 2001 Federal election, a raft of legislation pertaining to the rights of asylum seekers and amending the *Migration Act 1958* was passed with bipartisan support through Australia's Federal parliament.[1] The changes in the law created the legal framework for the "Pacific Solution".

Under the "Pacific Solution", certain asylum seekers are not processed in Australia but are transported to Nauru or Papua New Guinea (PNG) for their refugee determination. The Australian government ceased detaining asylum seekers in PNG in 2004 and the new Labor government, elected in December 2007, vowed to end the detention of asylum seekers in Nauru. Immigration detention in offshore processing centres, interception of boats and the use of facilities in other countries for the processing of refugees by Australia have left many individuals psychologically and physically damaged.

This chapter argues that people subjected to offshore processing in Nauru who have been harmed by the actions or omissions of the Australian government may have a right to compensation under tort law.[2]

---

[1] *Migration Amendment (Excision from Migration Zone) (Consequential Provisions) Act 2001*; *Border Protection (Validation and Enforcement Powers) Act 2001*; *Migration Legislation Amendment Act (No. 5) 2001*; *Migration Legislation Amendment Act (No. 6) 2001*; *Migration Legislation Amendment Act (No. 1) 2001*; *Migration Amendment (Excision from Migration Zone) Act 2001* and the *Migration Legislation Amendment (Judicial Review) Act 2001*.

[2] Under the law of tort, a person who has been injured or suffered property damage as a result of someone else's negligence may be able to claim compensation for that injury or damage.

Although the arrangements in Nauru are complicated and involve the International Organization for Migration (IOM), the government of Nauru, private contractors such as Chubb Security and Eurest as well as the Australian government, this paper contends that Australia cannot escape its obligation to care for asylum seekers in offshore facilities. Recent case law involving immigration detainees in Australia suggests that Australia has a non-delegable duty of care to asylum seekers and this may extend to asylum seekers Australia has transferred to Nauru for processing.

Arrangements in Nauru

Under the "Pacific Solution", certain Australian territory can be "excised" from the migration zone (s. 5 *Migration Act 1958*), that is, many of the rights enjoyed by asylum seekers in Australia under the *Migration Act 1958* will not apply to asylum seekers who enter Australia at excised places. Any asylum seekers who land in an excised place can be taken to a "declared country" (s198A *Migration Act 1958*) for refugee status determination.

Nauru is a small Pacific island of only 21 square kilometres with a population of 13,500 people. The country was a protectorate of Australia until 1968 and retains close connections with Australia, including the use of the High Court of Australia as its final appellate court. Nauru has serious economic problems and in 2001 agreed to host a processing centre on its shores in exchange for a pledge of $30 million in aid and development programs from Australia and is currently a "declared country" for the purposes of the *Migration Act 1958*. Since agreeing to the detention of asylum seekers on its territory, Nauru has been granted further aid of $41.5m for 2001–03, $22.5m for 2003–05 and $16.9m for 2005–06. Prior to housing Australia's asylum seekers Nauru had been scheduled to receive a mere $3.4 million in aid from Australia in 2001–02 (Oxfam 2002, 3). An administrative agreement was initially signed for the accommodation of asylum seekers on Nauru on 19 September 2001. This was replaced by a Memorandum of Understanding (MOU) on 11 December 2001. Foreign Ministers Alexander Downer and David Adeang signed a further four-year MOU between Australia and Nauru on 20 September 2005. The detention facility at Nauru consists of two camps: Topside and State House both located in the Meneng District.

Detainees in Nauru are provided with a visa which stipulates that they are only permitted to reside at the detention facilities. As was confirmed in the case of *Ruhani v Director of Police* (No. 2) (2005) 219 ALR 270, the asylum seekers on Nauru do not apply for the special purpose visas and need not consent to them.

The Australian government has attempted to argue that there is no detention in Nauru as asylum seekers on Nauru are residing under conditions established under special visa arrangements with the Nauru government (Senate Legal And Constitutional Legislation Committee 2006, 53). This argument has been rejected by the Senate Legal and Constitutional Legislation Committee and a number of human rights organisations in Australia (Senate Legal and Constitutional Legislation Committee 2006).

The arrangements in Nauru are highly complicated. The Australian government has signed a confidential Memorandum of Understanding (MOU) with the government of Nauru. Under the agreement Nauru accommodates asylum seekers in two processing centres, which are funded by Australia in return for foreign aid. The Australian government is present and offers assistance in the camps through the Australian Protective Services, Department of Immigration and Citizenship (DIAC) officers and the Australian Consulate (Republic of Nauru Permanent Mission to the United Nations 2004).

There is a further confidential agreement with the International Organization for Migration, with the IOM contracted to administer the offshore processing centres in Nauru. IOM responsibilities include arranging for the provision of food and water, power, sanitation, medicine and healthcare (IOM 2007). The catering services and security at the Nauru camps are further subcontracted to Eurest and Chubb Security Group respectively (Republic of Nauru Permanent Mission to the United Nations 2004). United Nations High Commissioner for Refugees (UNHCR) and DIAC have been responsible for the processing of asylum seekers on Nauru (Crock et al. 2006).

Harms suffered by detainees in Nauru

Long-term detainees on Nauru have suffered deteriorating health and mental illness in detention. There have been several hunger strikes and protests leading to hospitalisation of asylum seekers (Crock et al. 2006, 122–3). There has also been one death, that of Mohammed Sarwar, a 26-year-old Afghan refugee who died on Nauru on 23 September 2003. There are allegations that the drug Vioxx, which was prescribed for pain relief and was recalled in October 2004, continued to be prescribed to detainees on Nauru (Jackson 2005). This allegation has been denied by the Department of Immigration (DIAC 2005). Furthermore, there have been allegations that mental health services on the island have been inadequate (Penovic et al. 2006). In a report to Nauru camp managers in October 2002, Dr Dormaar, a Dutch psychologist employed by the IOM to work in Nauru in mid-2002 reported:

> I seldom or never encounter an asylum seeker who still sleeps soundly and is able to enjoy life. Mental health, or psychiatry for that matter, is basically not equipped to improve their situation in any essential respect (McKenzie 2003).

Dr Dormaar resigned from his role in 2002 because of claims that he provided many reports on the severity of mental illness of detainees on Nauru which were ignored by IOM officials. The Australian government has rejected the claims that Dr Dormaar's concerns were not addressed, arguing that Nauru has "comprehensive mental health services in the centres to improve the residents' psychological well-being" (McKenzie 2003).

DIAC has conceded that the detainee population in Nauru has suffered high rates of mental illness. Statistics revealed by DIAC indicate numerous acts of self-harm, suicide attempts, moderate and severe depression, acute stress reaction, adjustment disorder and anxiety disorder among the asylum seeker population (DIAC 2005). Although asylum seekers are a vulnerable group and can come to a country with pre-existing mental health issues, there is strong evidence that detention exacerbates mental health problems for asylum seekers and refugees. For example, refugees who have spent time in Australian detention centres have twice the risk of depression and three times the risk of post-traumatic stress disorder when compared with refugees who have not been in detention (Centre for Population Mental Health Research 2004).

Recent case law involving immigration detainees in Australia

Under the common law legal system which Australia has inherited from the UK, a person who is harmed physically or mentally because of the negligence of someone who owed them a duty of care may be entitled to compensation under the tort of negligence. The general principle underlying the tort is that a person or institution may be legally liable for failing to prevent a harm that was foreseeable. More and more asylum seekers are now claiming that they suffered psychological and physical harm as a result of Australia's interdiction policies, that the government owed them a duty of care and that the harms they suffered were foreseeable.

A 2005 decision by Justice Paul Finn of the Federal Court of Australia, *S v Secretary, Department of Immigration Multicultural and Indigenous Affairs* (2005) 216 ALR 252, confirmed the right of asylum seekers to seek compensation in some circumstances if they were harmed in immigration detention centres in Australia. In that case, Justice Finn found that the Commonwealth had breached its duty to ensure that reasonable care was taken of two Iranian asylum seekers. The asylum seekers in question were found to have received inadequate treatment for their respective mental health problems. More importantly, Justice Finn found that the Australian government could not simply relinquish their duty of care by claiming that they delegated the duty to the private company which ran the detention centre. The duty owed by the Commonwealth was found to be "non-delegable". Therefore, a person who has been harmed in detention in Australia because of the negligence of the Australian government may be able to sue the government for any physical or mental illness without the government claiming that the operators of the detention centres and not they were responsible for the wellbeing of the detainees.

In the case of *Badraie v Commonwealth* (2005) 195 FLR 119, another former asylum seeker, Shayan Badraie, a child who was irrevocably damaged by his time in immigration detention, settled a court case for $400,000 compensation plus costs to be paid by the Commonwealth on 3 May 2006. There is another case of an Iranian refugee, Mr Parvis Yousefi, before the Supreme Court of NSW. Mr Yousefi alleged that his time in immigration detention was responsible for his declining mental health and that the Commonwealth and the detention centre operators were negligent in his care. These cases indicate that the Commonwealth government can be and has successfully been sued for breaching its duty of care in detention centres in Australia.

The Australian legal system will compensate physical harm to a person more readily than mental harm caused by immigration detention. This is because of a general ambivalence in tort law to mental harm. Some reasons for this include the difficulty of proving mental harm, the difficulty of diagnosis, the difficulty of foreseeing mental harm and the fear of opening the floodgates to an unlimited number of litigants (Ipp et al. 2002). However, in most Australian States, people who have acquired a mental illness because of the time they have spent in detention may still be compensated for their mental illness if they can prove that they suffer from a recognised mental illness and that it was foreseeable that a person of normal fortitude would come to suffer that mental illness in the conditions under which they were detained.[3]

What law and where?

Detainees who were held in Nauru may also be compensated if their mental or physical health deteriorated while they were in detention in IOM-run facilities on the island. In a recent Senate Inquiry, Senator Kerry Nettle asked the Department of Immigration whether asylum seekers who were harmed in Nauru could seek compensation for the harms they had suffered. The Department representative suggested that asylum seekers who were harmed in Nauru could seek compensation under the law of Nauru (Official Committee Hansard 2006, 54). When Senator Nettle asked for further clarification, the Department of Immigration also agreed that people harmed by Commonwealth officers may have access to the Australian legal system for making a compensation claim against the Australian government (Official Committee Hansard 2006, 54).

According to the ruling in *Gosper v Sawyer* (1985) 160 CLR 548, an Australian court has jurisdiction to hear a case if a defendant is in its territory. It is very likely that any compensation claim against the Australian government or anyone else who is in Australia at the time a compensation case is brought can be heard before an Australian court. Therefore, there may be no need to resort to the courts of Nauru in most cases.

The second question that arises is whether a court will order a stay of proceedings on the grounds that Australia is not an appropriate forum. In the 1990 case of *Voth v Manildra Flour Mills* (1990) 171 CLR 538, the High Court of Australia accepted a "clearly inappropriate" test for determining whether a stay of proceedings should be granted on the grounds that the forum in which a proceeding is being brought is an inappropriate forum. This test was originally put forward by Justice Dean in *Oceanic Sun Line Special Shipping Co v Fay* (1988) 165 CLR 197.

Under the test, where any significant connection between the action and the forum exists, such as that the defendant resides there or the law of the forum applies to the action, then it would be difficult to describe the forum as clearly inappropriate. The court will also look at advantages to the plaintiff in bringing the action in the forum.

---

[3] *Civil Liability Act 2002* (NSW); *Civil Law (Wrongs) Act 2002* (ACT); *Civil Liability Act 2002* (WA); *Civil Liability Act 2002* (Tas); *Wrongs Act 1958* (Vic); *Civil Liability Act 1936* (SA).

The difficulty comes when determining which law the court should apply. An Australian court hearing a negligence claim may have to apply the laws of Nauru. In the case of *Regie National des Usines Renault SA v Zhang* (2002) 210 CLR 491, it was found that the applicable law is generally the law of the place where the wrong occurred. Unfortunately, Nauruan tort law is not as developed as the complex tort law in Australia and it is not clear what the law of Nauru actually is today with regard to negligence.

Nauruans adopted the English common law system as at 31 January 1968 (s. 4 *Customs and Adopted Laws Act 1971*). The 1968 cut-off date specifies exactly the stage of development of the common law and equity that was introduced in to the law of Nauru. It also allows Nauru to develop its own laws after the given date without being bound to developments in English law (Paterson 1997). There have been no published compensation cases under negligence in a Nauruan court since 1968. There has therefore been no development in negligence law in Nauru since independence and the law of negligence in Nauru today is the same as the law of negligence in England as at 31 January 1968.

Any court attempting to apply Nauruan tort law may need to update the Nauruan common law to be in line with modern times. To do this a court can look to developments in other common law countries. According to Sue Farran and Jennifer Corrin Care, the courts of the Pacific will often look to developments in the English courts or to developments in the laws of Australia (Farran and Corrin Care 2000).

Given Nauru's particularly close connection to Australia, including the use of the Australian High Court as a final appellate court, it is very likely that the law of Nauru applied will be influenced by the laws of Australia. However, it is open to the court to develop the law of Nauru according to what is deemed appropriate for Nauru.

In any case, when faced with a question governed by foreign law, Australian courts start, as a general principle, with the presumption that the foreign law is the same as Australian law unless proven otherwise. This was confirmed in the 2005 High Court case of *Neilson v Overseas Projects Corporations of Victoria Ltd* (2005) 223 CLR 331. The assumption is that "Australian courts know no foreign law" and so must have the foreign law proven to them by evidence. Therefore, given the lack of clarity regarding Nauruan law in this area, it is likely that a court will apply Australian tort law.

Liability of the Republic of Nauru

It is possible for a plaintiff to bring an action against a number of parties in a joint compensation claim and this is tactically advisable. However, certain parties are more likely to be found to be liable for harms suffered by detainees in Nauru than others.

Any compensation claim in an Australian court against Nauru would be defeated by the fact that Nauru enjoys immunity from any litigation in Australian courts. Traditionally, international law has recognised that states have absolute immunity from suits in the jurisdiction of other states. This right is recognised in Australia under s. 9 of the *Foreign States Immunities Act 1985* (Cth). Under s. 13 of the same Act a foreign state is not immune in a proceeding insofar as the proceeding concerns the death of or personal injury to a person but this exception to immunity only applies if the foreign state or its representative did an act or omission in Australia. As any compensation claim against the Nauruan government would be for acts or omissions committed in Nauru, the State of Nauru could not be sued in an Australian court.

The State of Nauru could be sued in a Nauruan court as the *Republic Proceedings Act 1972* makes the country liable in tort as if it were a private citizen (Ntumy 1993, 156). Under s. 48 of the Nauruan *Civil Procedures Act 1972*, a non-citizen can only seek compensation in a Nauruan court if they resided in Nauru with the permission of the cabinet. Under s. 88(2) of the Nauruan *Civil Procedures Act 1972*, it would not be possible for a person who is not a citizen of Nauru to sue the Republic of Nauru in a Nauruan court if they are residing in a foreign country. Therefore, while it may be possible for detainees to seek compensation against the Republic of Nauru while they are on Nauru, it would not be possible for them to seek damages in a Nauruan court once they have been resettled to a third country such as Australia or New Zealand or have been returned to the country from which they originally fled.

Liability of the International Organization for Migration

The IOM currently operates offshore processing facilities in PNG, Nauru and Indonesia. In Nauru, IOM provides security, water, sanitation, power generation, health and medical services for the duration of the stay of the asylum seekers at these centres and coordinates the return of asylum seekers to their home countries (IOM 2001). As the organisation responsible for the care of asylum seekers, it may be found to owe a duty of care to those who are held in their camps.

IOM was founded on a United States initiative in 1951. IOM is not and has never been part of the United Nations system. The IOM's role is dictated by its 120 member states. An additional nineteen states have observer status within IOM. According to the IOM constitution only the member states and the sponsors control the work of the IOM and therefore IOM is only accountable to its member states and not accountable to any democratically elected body. The UNHCR, United Nations Children Fund, World Health Organization, international trade union, religious and welfare organisations have observer status but have no voting power within the IOM. The majority of the organisation's funds have traditionally been borne by the United States and IOM's Director-General has always been a US State Department appointee.

There is reason to be concerned about IOM's caretaker role of asylum seekers on Nauru (Penovic et al. 2006). Unlike UNHCR, the IOM has no protection function and has no mandate to monitor human rights abuses. IOM's policy on "Effective Respect for Migrants' Rights" found on their website states:

> international law protection is based on a mandate, conferred by treaty or custom, which authorizes an organization to ensure respect of rights by states. These rights may include human rights, workers' rights or the rights of refugees, and can be found in various international instruments such as United Nations conventions and declarations. IOM has no such mandate, and thus is not concerned with legal protection per se (IOM 2006).

Human Rights Watch, the International Catholic Migration Committee, and the World Council of Churches have been highly vocal in their criticism of IOM activities with regard to refugees and asylum seekers stating that they are concerned that:

> Given IOM's active involvement in interception programmes—often in situations where UNHCR is not present—it does not have an explicit mandate nor the expertise to identify and protect those in need of international protection. Neither are there adequate safeguards in place to ensure that those in need of refugee protection have access to UNHCR, or the appropriate authorities, and to full and fair refugee status determination procedures (Human Rights Watch 2001).

Human Rights Watch and Amnesty International issued a joint statement in December 2002 to voice their concern about the IOM's activities:

As organizations committed to the promotion and protection of human rights, we come to this meeting with concerns about the human rights impact of certain IOM operations. In particular, we are concerned that IOM's work in certain contexts is adversely impacting upon basic human rights of migrants, refugees and asylum seekers, including for example the right to be free from arbitrary detention and the fundamental right to seek asylum (Amnesty International and Human Rights Watch 2002).

Asylum seekers and refugees in the care of IOM do not have any formal internal base for complaint or redress should IOM breach their human rights. Refugees seeking to gain compensation from IOM for any harm they may have suffered while in the care of IOM may also have difficulty accessing compensation.

IOM, as an international, treaty-based organisation, is treated differently by Australian law from corporations within Australia. It is possible for domestic courts in a country such as Australia to find that international organisations such as IOM have acted in a negligent way and owe compensation to anyone who has been harmed in their care (Triggs 2006, 179). However, in many cases, international organisations are immune from being taken to court for anything that arises in respect of their operational activities (Jens 1961,79).

Under Australian law, an international organisation enjoys immunity from legal process in respect of acts and things done in participating in the work or performing the mission of the international organisation (Fifth Schedule Section 6, Part I (2) *International Organisations (Privileges and Immunities) Act 1963*). This immunity is also recognised in the constitution of many international organisations. Article 28 of the IOM constitution states:

> 1. The Organization shall enjoy such privileges and immunities as are necessary for the exercise of its functions and the fulfilment of its purposes.
> 2. Representatives of Member States, the Director General, the Deputy Director General and the staff of the Administration shall likewise enjoy such privileges and immunities as are necessary for the independent exercise of their functions in connection with the Organization.
> 3. These privileges and immunities shall be defined in agreements between the Organization and the States concerned or through other measures taken by these States.

Unfortunately the agreements between Nauru, Australia and IOM are confidential. It is therefore difficult to speculate how IOM's "function" in Nauru or its "purposes" are actually defined.

IOM will not be able to enjoy immunity for any practice that falls outside of its "function" or "purpose" as it may be defined in its agreements with Australia and/or Nauru. IOM can waive immunity in any particular case. However, domestic courts cannot review an international organisation's decisions not to waive immunity (Wellens 2002, 115).

A domestic court will ultimately have to decide whether any particular practice does or does not fall in to its "function" or "purpose" as defined under the agreements with IOM. In a comprehensive study of domestic jurisdictions, August Reinisch has found that it is rare for findings of immunity to be controversial in domestic courts (Reinisch 2000, 134). Therefore, if a plaintiff is able to establish that they suffered harm that was foreseeable because of the negligence of IOM and that IOM owed them a duty of care, they may still face the additional barrier of proving that any actions or omissions that led to them being harmed was not part of IOM's function or purpose.

Liability of Australia

According to IOM's own website, IOM's work in the region is done on behalf of Australia. However, the Australian government claims that IOM is in Nauru and PNG on the invitation of the two Pacific countries (DIAC 2005a). Significantly, for the 2005 calendar year alone, Australia paid IOM US$42,466,082 towards operational costs and 659,651 Swiss francs towards administrative costs of the organisation (IOM 2006a). Nauru has not made any financial contributions to IOM and is not a member state.

It is difficult to gauge the Australian government's level of responsibility for asylum seekers in Nauru without access to the agreements between Nauru and Australia or Australia and IOM. However, there is strong indication that Australia may be able to be held liable for harms suffered by detainees on Nauru.

Australia has a strong presence in the detention centres on Nauru. According to the Department of Immigration this presence is "to facilitate management interactions on the ground and to enable quick coordinated responses to operational matters, such as medical evacuations" (DIAC 2005). There is also some suggestion that in the MOU with Nauru, Australia remains responsible for the care of asylum seekers. According to a press release from the Republic of Nauru the duty to care for asylum seekers transferred to Nauru by Australia does not rest on Nauru but on the Australian government. Nauru's minister of finance, Kinza Clodumar has in the past condemned the Australian government's inaction and dismissal of its responsibility to asylum seekers stating:

The M.O.U. signed when Nauru first accepted asylum seekers, underlines Australia's responsibility to ensure the day-to-day management of asylum seeker facilities including medical treatment and further clarifies that, "health and medical services, personnel, supplies and equipment will be provided by Australia at the facilities. Where medical cases cannot be treated at the facilities, Australia may seek the assistance of Nauru's Health Services." (Republic of Nauru Permanent Mission to the United Nations 2004).

That statement was made in January 2004 and thus pre-dates the most recently signed MOU. It is not clear whether the responsibility of the Australian government for detainees on Nauru has been updated by a subsequent MOU or whether the statements by Mr Clodumar in fact reflect the agreement signed with Australia.

As discussed above, the Australian government has been found to owe a non-delegable duty of care to asylum seekers who have been detained in Australia. Australia may be found to owe a duty of care to asylum seekers it moved from Australia to Nauru or refused to allow entry to Australia. It will then need to be established whether this duty of care was non-delegable for detainees in Nauru analogous to the non-delegable duty of care for detention centres in Australia. Australia may, in fact, be found to be ultimately responsible for any acts or omissions that led to physical or mental illness in detainees held in IOM camps in the Republic of Nauru.

Conclusion

The use of offshore facilities by the Australian government does make it much more difficult for asylum seekers who were harmed on Nauru to seek compensation for physical or mental injury they suffered in detention. The International Organization for Migration and the Republic of Nauru may enjoy immunity in Australian courts. Furthermore, lack of access to legal assistance by detainees on Nauru may make it difficult for detainees and former detainees to access justice. However, the detention of asylum seekers on Nauru rather than in Australia does not make it impossible for people to be compensated.

The Australian government may be found to owe a duty of care to asylum seekers moved from Australia to Nauru. It may be the case that Australia will not be able to escape its duty to asylum seekers simply by delegating the duty of care to the IOM or the republic of Nauru. Australian courts have found that the duty to take adequate care of asylum seekers is a non-delegable duty in Australia. It would be surprising if the same was not found for detainees offshore.

Australia's interdiction policies, including offshore detention in Nauru, affect a group that is largely powerless and without voice. Tort law may offer some individuals an avenue for redress for the wrongs they suffered. While tort law cannot change a system that has harmed and may continue to harm many others in the future, it may offer decision-makers an incentive to avoid costly compensation claims. Tort law can only offer compensation for a small number of people among many who deserve better. However, for those few who may receive compensation, it is a small step forward in achieving justice.

References

Amnesty International and Human Rights Watch. 2002. *Statement*. Geneva: The Governing Council, International Organization for Migration.

Centre for Population Mental Health Research. 2004. *Media release: Temporary protection visas compromise refugees' health: new research*, http://www.unsw.edu.au/news/pad/articles/2004/jan/TPV_Health.html (accessed 5 October 2007).

Crock, M., B. Saul and A. Dastyari. 2006. *Future seekers II : Refugees and irregular migration in Australia*. Sydney: Federation Press.

DIAC. 2005. *Media release: Setting record straight about Vioxx*, http://www.dimia.gov.au/media/media-releases/2005/d05011.htm (accessed 5 October 2007).

—. 2005a. *Annual report 2004/05*. Canberra: Commonwealth of Australia.

Farran, S. and J. Corrin Care. 2000. Towards a pragmatic approach to the contract or tort debate in the South Pacific. *Journal of South Pacific Law*. vol. 4, no. 8, 1–27.

Human Rights Watch. 2001. *NGO background paper on the refugee and migration interface*, http://www.hrw.org/campaigns/refugees/ngo-document (accessed 5 October 2007).

International Organization for Migration. 2001. *Off-shore processing of Australia-bound irregular migrants*, http://www.old.iom.int/iomwebsite/Project/ServletSearchProject?event=detail&id=AU1Z001 (accessed 5 October 2007).

—. 2006a. *Policies*, http://www.old.iom.int/en/who/main_policies_effrespect.shtml (accessed 5 October 2007).

—. 2006b. *Amendments to the International Organization for Migration (IOM) Constitution*, Geneva: IOM.

—. 2007. *Projects*, www.iom.int/australia/projects.html (accessed 5 October 2007).

Ipp, A., P. Cane, D. Sheldon and I. Macintosh. 2002. *Review of the law of negligence: final report*. Canberra: Commonwealth of Australia.

Jackson, A. 2005. Detainees given banned drug, say refugee groups, *The Age*, 12 April 2005.

Jens, W. 1961. *International immunities*. London: Stevens & Sons.

McKenzie, N. 2003. High rates of mental illness among detainees. In *7:30 Report*. Australia: ABC Television, broadcast 15 May 2003.

Ntumy, M. 1993. *South Pacific islands legal systems*. Honolulu: University of Hawaii Press.

Official Committee Hansard, Senate Legal and Constitutional Legislation Committee. *Migration Amendment (Designated Unauthorised Arrivals) Bill*, 6 June 2006, http://www.aph.gov.au/hansard/senate/committee/s9421.pdf#search%22hansard%20nettle%20nauruan%20law%20dima%22 (accessed 20 November 2007).

Oxfam Community Aid Abroad. 2002. *Adrift in the Pacific: The implications of Australia's Pacific refugee solution*, http://www.oxfam.org.au/campaigns/refugees/pacificsolution/. (accessed 20 November 2007).

Paterson, D. 1997. The application of common law and equity in countries of the South Pacific, *The Journal of Pacific Studies*. vol. 21, 1–20.

Penovic, T., A. Dastyari and J. Taylor. 2006. *Castan Centre submission to the Inquiry into the Provisions of the Migration Amendment (Designated Unauthorised Arrivals) Bill 2006*, http://www.law.monash.edu.au/castancentre/publications/migrationamend-bill-06-sub1.pdf (accessed 20 November 2007).

Phillips, J. and A. Millbank. 2006. *Protecting Australia's borders*. Canberra: Parliament of Australia Parliamentary Library.

Reinisch, A. 2000. *International organizations before national courts*. Cambridge: Cambridge University Press.

Republic of Nauru Permanent Mission to the United Nations. 2006. *Press release, Nauru calls for responsibility from Australian government as hunger strike worsens*, & January 2004, http//:www.un.int/nauru/government.html (accessed 20 November 2007).

Senate Legal and Constitutional Legislation Committee. 2006. *Report into the Provisions of the Migration Amendment (Designated Unauthorised Arrivals) Bill 2006*. Canberra: Commonwealth of Australia.

Triggs, G. 2006. *International law: Contemporary principles and practices*. Sydney: Lexis Nexus Butterworths.

Wellens, K. 2002. *Remedies against international organisations.* Cambridge: Cambridge University Press.

CHAPTER SEVEN

BEYOND THE CLINICAL CONTRACT: RESTORING ASYLUM SEEKER HEALTH THROUGH ADVOCACY AND CARE

DEBORAH ZION AND BEBE LOFF[1]

Our system is one of detachment: to keep silenced people from asking questions, to keep the judged from judging, to keep solitary people from joining together, and the soul from putting together its pieces.
—Eduardo Galeano, "Divorces." (Farmer, 2003, 1)

Introduction

The policies of the Australian Coalition government, led by John Howard concerning asylum seekers (unauthorised non-citizens) have used the misfortune and suffering of vulnerable people, the majority of whom are escaping torture, war and political instability to deter others in similar situations from risking such journeys. Part of this propagandised process of deterrence has been the incarceration of those seeking refuge, and the denial of such persons many of their fundamental human rights. In what follows, we will discuss how this population has been scapegoated and their suffering exploited to further a political agenda. We will then go on to discuss how healthcare professionals, individually and collectively, can restore to asylum seekers certain of their rights, and through so doing, draw them back into the human circle.

The experience of statelessness is often a conduit to the de facto loss of all human rights. Being deprived of citizenship is therefore a negation of "the right to have rights" (Benhabib 2004, 49–50). In Australia, asylum

---

[1] The research documented in this chapter is part of an Australian Research Council (ARC) funded project titled Caring for Asylum Seekers in Australia: Bioethics and Human Rights.

seekers have been deprived of the protection afforded by international rights treaties. The government believes that the strategy has proved to be an effective deterrent, although there are many complex reasons why so-called "boat-people" have stopped arriving in Australia.

Scapegoating—the act of ascribing unreasonable blame for social ills to an "innocent, weak and distinctive group" (Gibson and Howard 2007, 193), has paid a fundamental part in the fate of asylum seekers. As James Gibson and Marc Morje Howard suggest "[f]inding a scapegoat when times go bad is often a task of utmost importance, for political leaders and ordinary citizens alike" (Gibson and Howard 2007, 193). Strangely, however, the act of scapegoating asylum seekers took place when Australia was at peace and times were relatively good. While Australia was engaged in the war in Afghanistan, and later Iraq, there was little social or economic effect on the general population. Nonetheless, the Australian government continued with the use of selective media images, such as those concerning the "children overboard" event, and continued to equate those seeking refuge with terrorism.

The Prime Minister John Howard suggested that there were potential links between those seeking refuge and terrorist activity:

> I choose my language carefully ... I am not saying that in particular cases people on these boats are terrorists or have terrorist links ... What I am saying is that I have no way and unless you have a proper processing system nobody has any way of determining whether or not they are.
> (Transcript of the Prime Minister 2001)

Rights deprivation and scapegoating

As a population branded as potential terrorists, hidden from the gaze of the general public, and denied the automatic protection of administrative systems of accountability, asylum seekers were especially vulnerable to illness, both physical and mental. However, a lack of coherent and appropriate healthcare increased the suffering of already vulnerable and stigmatised people in detention. For example, a nurse who had worked at Baxter stated that:

> Five days a week a doctor would attend, but the doctors did not go into the compounds. You couldn't have people from one compound at medical with another compound, so they finally decided that each compound would have one day. There were six compounds so it was less than a day a week per compound, and because of this tedious process of driving people around and back before the next lot could come and much opening and

closing of gates through central command and only one gate open at a time, the number of people you could actually process at a medical centre diminished to about 8 or 10 in a day.

When a person came to the nurses in the compound medical centres you'd say, "Yes, you need to see the doctor," you'd look up the computer, "Your day is Tuesday, well there's not an appointment for another three Tuesdays." These were things like a foreign body in an eye, things that needed to be seen and so even though in theory there were doctors available, in practice there really weren't (Australian Council of Heads of Schools of Social Work 2006, 55).

Furthermore, inappropriate or non-treatment of illness is commonplace in detention. For example, depression and psychosis were often punished by solitary confinement in the "management" unit, rather than effective and compassionate treatment. However, even where healthcare was provided, many engaged in treatment of asylum seekers found themselves confronted by a "dual loyalty" conflict.

Dual loyalties

"Dual loyalty" has been defined as situations where physicians and other healthcare providers are required to subordinate the interests of patients to those of the state (International Dual Loyalty Working Group 2002). For example, forensic physicians and pathologists working under regimes where systems of justice may be in transition or in crisis might find themselves under pressure to find responses satisfactory to those in political power. The Report of the South African Truth and Reconciliation Commission revealed how far many medical practitioners worked to serve political ends rather than their patients. Mildred Solomon has identified four ways in which healthcare practitioners and the duty owed by them to patients may be compromised. First, medical judgment might be compromised; second, there might be an imposition of inappropriate medical procedures to serve state interests; third, the desired standard of care might be lower than it should be; and finally, healthcare practitioners might keep silent about abuses they observe (Solomon 2005).

Dual loyalty conflicts are manifest in asylum seeker detention. According to clinical psychologist Guy Coffey, clinicians external to detention (that is, those to whom detained patients are referred) face several problems. At the core of these is the problem that detention itself both causes and exacerbates mental disorders and damages physical health. Clinicians therefore face the dilemma as to whether to give recommendations based upon patients' genuine needs or whether to reduce the scope of the recommendation to that which might be implemented. More fundamentally the clinicians' role in treating detainees inherently conflicts with their role in providing assessments for the purposes of detention management, government departments or tribunals with power to determine the future of the detainee. In addition, therapeutic action taken by the clinician might have unintended consequences, or be limited scope in practice (Coffey 2006).

The following example illustrates the nature of these problems: A psychologist, one of the first to speak out, told a story about having to decide to put a fifteen-year-old in solitary, who was threatening suicide.

> I think there was a situation where I was unhappy about it as an option, like a boy who was fifteen. Now he didn't want to be in, but he didn't want to be in the compound either. I said, "I've got not choice." I just sat around with him and got him to agree not to threaten suicide ... He wanted a particular book from the school; this is how pathetic the whole thing was. It was a book that would be at a much younger level than he would be (he was fifteen going on sixteen). It was a book about a dog. A boy feels lonely and he wants a dog, and the closest thing he could come to was a picture book. Was there a hoo-ha to get this book! For starters they know how to get the key to this school. The school had nothing in it anyway. The fact is that there were no books for the kids in the compound. I still find it hard to keep explaining it because it's the meanness of it. It was so amazing to the extent that there is nothing for the kids. You'd say that and they would say "We had lots of stuff but they burnt it in the fire." That might be true but there were some computers destroyed. That doesn't mean you say we have lots of food so we stop giving them food. That is their problem, how to not let that happen. I tried very hard to get that boy admitted to the hospital. The hospital also wasn't a great option but it was better (Interview with Lyn).

Conflicts related to dual loyalties were further exacerbated by the administrative arrangements that determined the relationships between healthcare providers and the correctional system. For example, between February 1998 and August 2003 health services in detention were provided by Australasian Correctional Management (ACM). ACM entered into a detention services agreement with the Commonwealth of Australia to provide detention services. The Detention Services Agreement did not require a separation between the operating company and the health service. Furthermore, ACM directly employed the majority of healthcare professionals. External general practitioners were also engaged on a locum or contract basis by ACM (Singh 2007).

In detention, healthcare was provided by a Centre Health Manager, usually a senior nurse, general and psychiatric nurses and allied health professionals. All practitioners working with detainees in the detention setting, including general practitioners, were answerable to the Nurse Manager. She in turn reported to the ACM Operations Manager. All health-related reporting was also sent directly to the ACM Manager of Health Services Head Office in Sydney. Health-related incident reports of incidents such as attempted suicides were sent to the Department of Immigration and Multicultural and Indigenous Affairs (DIMIA) state and Canberra Offices through the ACM reporting mechanisms (Singh 2007).

How then can healthcare workers restore those in detention to the human circle, given the ambiguous nature of healthcare provision in such circumstances and the lack of openness and accountability? Moreover, on what basis do they have obligations to do so? In order to answer these questions we must examine the nature of the duty of care.

Duty of care

A "duty of care" is based upon several different premises. These include both law and different formulations based upon professional ethics. Insofar as the law is concerned, in Australia, legislation dealing with the registration of healthcare practitioners creates a standard to which it is expected practitioners will adhere. For example, the Victorian *Health Professions Registration Act 2005* defines "unprofessional conduct" as including:

> (a) conduct of a health practitioner occurring in connection with the practice of the practitioner's health profession that is of a lesser standard than a member of the public or the health practitioner's peers are entitled to expect of a reasonably competent health practitioner of that kind;
> (b) professional performance which is of a lesser standard than that which the registered health practitioner's peers might reasonably expect of a registered health practitioner;
> (c) infamous conduct in a professional respect;
> (d) providing a person with health services of a kind that are excessive, unnecessary or not reasonably required for that person's well-being;
> (e) influencing or attempting to influence the provision of health services in such a way that client care may be compromised;
> (f) a contravention of section 94 or the guidelines issued under section 95;
> (g) the failure to act as a health practitioner when required under an Act or regulations to do so …

In addition, there is a substantial body of case law in the field of medical negligence which leaves beyond doubt that services should be performed competently, respectful of patient privacy and confidentiality. Furthermore, the patient must be properly informed of the risks of any intervention that he or she would consider to be material and in a way that he or she is capable of understanding.

Overwhelmingly, in consideration of Australian states and Australian Federal privacy law, law dealing with healthcare practitioner registration and case law dealing with medical negligence, it would seem that a stronger duty is owed to the detainee/patient than the party contracting the services of the healthcare practitioner.

If we turn to considerations based upon professional ethics, we also see the relationship between responsibility and vulnerability, the social contract and virtue ethics. In the first instance, Robert Goodin describes the *moral* relationship between vulnerability and responsibility in his discussion of a passenger on a plane, and the duties owed to him by the pilot. We might think that a pilot has a professional duty to his passengers, or reciprocal duties based upon payment for his services. Goodin, however, suggests that the fact that the passenger is especially vulnerable to the pilot's actions also creates certain special responsibilities. Goodin's account also relies upon a generalisable duty to help others that intensifies as one party becomes more vulnerable to the other's acts, or failure to act (Goodin 1985, 111–13).

Co-existent with the argument from vulnerability is the idea of duty based upon the social contract whereby in "exchange for the performance of a vital and public service ... physicians as a group have monopolistic privileges over the practice of medicine" (Arras 1988, 24–9). Lynnette Reid adds that high social status and wealth are also part of the exchange between doctors and society (Reid 2005, 352–3).

Many have argued, however, that the social contract does not adequately explain the nature of duties that doctors and other healthcare workers hold towards those in their care. They point instead towards issues related to character. Central to virtue ethics is the claim that "(a)n action is right if and only if it is what an agent with a virtuous character would do in the circumstances" (Oakley 1996, 128). To be a good practitioner then requires cultivating virtues within the self, such as beneficence, kindness, trustworthiness and skill. Therefore, to *be* a doctor involves cultivating virtues (Oakley 1996, 128). Implicit in this way of thinking is that to be a good professional involves close identification between the role a person occupies, and his or her personal values. The question remains: how then do these three explanations—the virtue model, the social contract, and the argument from vulnerability—regarding professional obligations, relate to the duties that healthcare workers have to asylum seekers? Let us begin with vulnerability.

Vulnerability again

In the world of asylum seeker detention the vulnerability of patients is appalling. Their vulnerability is based not just upon their lack of citizenship, their stigmatisation and their incarceration, but also upon the lack of accountability and consistency within the provision of healthcare. In their submission to the Palmer Inquiry into the Detention of Cornelia Rau, the office of the public advocate of South Australia described four cases (Harley et al. 2005). In the first case, "Q", a Hazara Afghan was away from his village the day when the Taliban arrived and killed his entire family. Q arrived in Australia and developed severe post-traumatic stress disorder. He was moved back and forth between Glenside Psychiatric Hospital in Adelaide and Woomera Detention Centre, while those caring for him repeatedly stressed the urgency of his bridging visa claim (that is, his claim for a visa to live outside of the detention setting) to DIMIA. Despite his spiralling health status, DIMIA refused to respond to his application for a visa, and only responded after the legal action was taken on his behalf by the office of the Public Advocate of South Australia. He was, finally, awarded a permanent visa.

The other cases presented to the Palmer Inquiry bore disconcerting similarities regarding lack of systemised healthcare, total lack of accountability, and poor communication between healthcare providers and DIMIA. It was therefore, left to those providing healthcare to develop relationships with the Public Advocate's Office of South Australia to protect the health of those in their care from further deterioration. At this time, this involved more than simply providing clinical care. In order to reduce vulnerability and to access healthcare, those working with asylum seekers in detention had also to act as their advocates.

Despite a warning from the then South Australian Director of Mental Health Services and Programs, Margaret Tobin, that all reports should be vetted by her office, and that "clinicians [should be] mindful not to include comments on immigration matters in psychiatric reports," many who were engaged in the care of asylum seekers saw that their vulnerability could only be addressed though the refugee protection process. In short, it was detention that was making them ill, and hastening the process of refugee protection and release from places like Woomera was seen by many as the only path back to health. As Harold Bilboe, a psychologist who had worked in Woomera stated:

No matter how much I worked with the clients, I couldn't change the cause of the behaviour, the course of their stress, it's like having a patient coming into the hospital with a nail through the hand and you are giving them Pethidine injections for pain but you don't remove the nail. That's exactly what is happening in Woomera. You've got people down there with nails through their hands, we're holding them, we're not treating the cause. So, the trauma, the torture, the infection is growing (HREOC 2004, accessed 28 July 2007).

The case of Glenside Special Stay Unit

There came a time when it was recognised that some asylum seekers were so traumatised by the detention that they needed care that went beyond what was provided in general psychiatric facilities. A special unit was set up at Glenside psychiatric facility, the main psychiatric facility in Adelaide, for asylum seekers who had been detained for long periods at Baxter Detention Centre, and were experiencing severe mental illness. The unit was established as a result of the Palmer Inquiry (Palmer 2005). It was funded by DIMA and staffed by Glenside Hospital.

Care in the unit was highly specialised and involved the use of community advocates, psychiatric staff, volunteers and teachers. The unit achieved excellent results through their commitment to holistic healthcare practice, and adherence to high levels of professional ethics. Fifteen acutely mentally ill men improved enough to reside in the community without requiring acute care.

Despite its success, the unit was closed one year after it opened. The six men still residing there were sent back to Baxter. In permitting this to happen the Director of Glenside, Professor Norman James, overruled the advice of the consultant psychiatrists. He also went against the advice of the South Australian public advocate, who was the legal guardian of the men involved (ABC 2006).

In May 2006, the senior psychiatrist at Baxter, Dr Fiona Hawker, spoke out publicly concerning the fate of six asylum seekers who she had helped restore to health, who were returned to detention when the unit was closed, against her advice, and that of the treating team who believed that they should remain in community care, Hawker stated that:

> Going back to detention is a guaranteed trigger that will stir up high levels of anxiety, and for many of them, they will become psychotic ... The post-traumatic stress disorder, the depressive problems, the associated psychosis that a lot of them had would recur, given that they were going back to the situation that provoked their mental health difficulties in the first place (ABC 2006a).

Dr Fiona Hawker had never been politically involved, and put at risk a twenty-five-year career in psychiatry by speaking out. In other cases, healthcare professionals engaged the Office of the Public Advocate of South Australia in order to protect patients against a return to Baxter. Such action was, for example, undertaken for Mr B.

Mr B was admitted to Rural and Remote Inpatient Unit, Glenside Campus in October 2004. It was obvious upon admission that he was extremely unwell and he was assessed with a major depressive disorder. The consensus of the treating team was that his lengthy detention first at Woomera and then at Baxter had significantly contributed to, if not caused, his condition. The delay in transferring him to an acute psychiatric unit was also considered to have contributed to his condition.

Prior to being admitted to Glenside Campus, Mr B was held at Baxter in a room on his own in the Management Unit (that is, solitary confinement). He made several attempts on his life while at Baxter. Health professional staff working at Glenside Hospital applied for guardianship in early November 2004 and a full order was granted on 7 November 2004.

Reports from staff at Glenside Hospital suggest that communication with the DIMIA and GSL (Global Solutions Limited, the company then in control of detention centres) was difficult from the outset. It has been suggested to the Public Advocate by Glenside staff that this bordered on obstruction at times. Consequently this meant that it was very difficult to ascertain exactly how far in the process of application for a visa Mr B had progressed—a crucial fact in the formulation of a treatment plan.

There appeared to be no recognition by DIMIA or GSL of Glenside Hospital's role in treating Mr B, nor any understanding that cooperation was required if his condition was to improve. Steps taken by GSL to restrict and monitor visitors were considered extreme. On one occasion, the Public Advocate was told that he was required to complete a visitor's form and give 24-hours notice of his intention to visit Mr B.

At all times it was not clear whether the DIMIA would seek to return Mr B to Baxter even though the opinion of the treating team at Glenside Hospital was that any return would be non-therapeutic and extremely dangerous. Therefore Section 32 powers (of the South Australian *Guardianship and Administration Act 1993*) for residence were sought and granted in January 2005 in order for the Public Advocate to be able to direct where Mr B resided.

In late January 2005, the Public Advocate wrote to the Minister requesting that consideration be given to community detention. In effect, it took until late July to actually move Mr B into the community—six months of obstruction, non-communication and red tape. All this time Mr

B's mental state was extremely vulnerable and DIMIA was made well aware of this (Harley et al. 2005, 20).

The alliance formed between healthcare professionals like Dr Fiona Hawker and the South Australian Public Advocate's Office addresses the issue of vulnerability. As well, it highlights the significance of moving beyond the clinic in the care of this vulnerable and traumatised population. The Dutch psychiatrist Anne Miek Richters has stated that for asylum seekers, "…mental disorders characterised by standardised psychiatric diagnosis may often better be described as normal reactions to abnormal political situations." She continues, "…it is at the level of the political, social, and cultural that healing should occur" (Richters 2002, 312–13).

The social contract, role obligation and an argument from virtue

The significance of advocacy in order to restore asylum seekers to health raises ethical questions concerning the social contract and obligation. The necessity of advocacy, as well as clinical care, might be seen to be an example of non-voluntary obligation. That is, obligations that attach to professional roles that are neither foreseen nor explicitly agreed to.

The idea that we might be bound by obligations that we have not chosen causes many people a certain amount of disquiet. The volunteer principle—that is, the belief that we have control over our own lives to the degree that we can choose to whom we have duties—seems to be an integral part of a view of autonomy in which we are authors of our own lives (Hardimon 1994, 343). However, it is commonly accepted that we have non-voluntary duties, both as persons and as occupants of particular roles. The obligation not to harm others is, for example, a general duty that we owe others without entering into a voluntary contract (Hardimon 1994, 340). Moreover, we commonly accept that we owe particular duties to certain people by virtue of the roles we have in their lives. The most obvious case in question is that of roles within families. Many believe, for example, that they have particular duties towards elderly parents simply by virtue of being a son or a daughter. These are duties that we acquire through birth, rather than obligations we agree to when we join some kind of association, or enter into a profession.

How then do these ideas translate into professional life, and how can they illuminate the discussion about duties held by those who are treating asylum seekers? We consider that healthcare workers have duties to address the needs of patients within the clinic, even if these duties might put them at some degree of risk. This understanding is reinforced by law. If the only way that healthcare workers can actually restore asylum seekers to health is through advocacy, there is an argument to make that this is what they should do, especially if there is no one else in a more appropriate role to take up their cause.

Jennifer Radden gives a further reason that goes beyond role obligation. She argues that a psychiatrist should not only inhabit a professional role in which she exhibits caring and concern in the course of her work. Rather she suggests that a psychiatrist should also be an empathetic and caring person. Her premise is based upon three issues: namely, "(i) the relationship or therapeutic 'alliance' forged between treater and patient; (ii) certain characteristics of the psychiatric patient; and (iii) the goals and purposes of the therapeutic enterprise itself" (Radden 2002, 115–18).

Radden's work has application to other mental healthcare workers who cared for asylum seekers in detention. While several psychiatrists engaged in advocacy with external institutions, there were other examples of seemingly smaller acts of benevolence and compassion performed by social workers and mental health nurses that restored, at least temporarily, those seeking refuge back into the human circle.

"Hannah" was a psychiatric nurse who worked in Woomera for six weeks. In the course of her visits she handed out medication to those who needed it rather than making them stand in line in the sun. She stated:

> [A] ... main area that I was involved in (and everyone was involved in) was medication and giving that. That caused as much angst for me as a nurse and for other people, because of the rules that surrounded it and because the symbolism that that had for some of the detainees ... Medication giving was a big one. First of all, if you can imagine ... I don't know if someone has illustrated the layout of Woomera to you, so if you could imagine the different compounds separated by wire in no-man's-land and God knows what else, a locked gate which you had to speak through a radio to get an Officer to come and unlock for you if there was no officer standing there. Visualise that, remember that you have a huge number of people. The majority of people are frustrated by their predicament. One, they're frustrated; two, disturbed, profoundly disturbed or psychotics or incredibly depressed at the other end with the degrees between anger, despair and so on. So, imagine being told by nursing colleagues that you weren't allowed, but anyone who wanted medication, for example, like if they had a headache had to come to the medical centre to get it, If they had indigestion and wanted Mylanta, they had to come to the medical centre to get it. If they had back pain and wanted analgesic, they had to come to the medical centre and get it. Why shouldn't someone who is providing care

> go to that person and give them care? To me it was incredibly bizarre for someone who was prescribed medication that they were still supposed to come and get it. If they didn't get it when the nurse went to give out the medication at the allocated times during the day, if the person hadn't turned up for it, and all of us nurses were responsible for delivering the medication, if someone didn't turn up for their prescribed medication when the nurse was in the compound to give it and maybe an hour later and said, "You seem to forget my Zoloft," or "I didn't get my Mylanta," or "I didn't get my Digoxin and may I please have it?" I would be happy to take it to them but I was told time and time again that I was not to take it to them (Interview with Hannah).

Other healthcare workers also broke with the detention protocol in order to restore dignity and hope to those detained.

"Sarah" was a midwife, and both a general and psychiatric nurse. She worked in nearly all of the detention centres, and in so doing entered into the lives of her patients, befriending them and organising appropriate food and clothing for them. She also put them in contact with friends in the general community who wrote to them, and provided valuable contacts when visas were finally approved. In what follows we see a simple incident in which two detainees were returned to the circle of normal human relationships through her care.

> So I took with me one day a nurse who seemed amenable, intelligent and was keen to learn but was actually terrified of the detainees ... I said to her one day "Come with us. We'll go and have a cup of tea with a couple of guys." There were two Afghans I knew really well. I was only working there as a general nurse so it was a bit of a long stretch to get permission to say "I'm just going to catch up with these guys, I'm a bit worried about one of them." We went into the compound and the difference was, the same two guys had shared a compound in Curtin and I had sat with them, just the two of them and me on two or three occasions for at least an hour each time ... One of them was corresponding with my sister and her family the other was corresponding with an old schoolmate and her friend who live in Melbourne ... They were excited to see me again when I arrived back in Baxter. "Mother Sarah or Aunty, we thought we'd never see you again. Come in, come in." I went to see them again and this other nurse and I said, "She wants to meet you, can I bring her and have a cup of tea with you?" "Oh yes, come at 4 pm." When I went there at 4 pm I had to convince the guards it was okay. "Oh no, it's too dangerous to go into their rooms. You don't know about these people." I said "I need to talk to them. I'm quite happy to go into the rooms. We'll sit in the room with the door open so you can see us but we will be in their room. They have invited us. We are having a cup of tea and I want to talk to them. Also, Sharon is going to be taking over this week when I leave so she's coming with me."

"Oh, I don't know that it's safe." When we got there it was one of the most interesting experiences in my life because she had worked there from the opening of Baxter, which was then some months, I had only been there a few days. When we got there one of them was running in and out and they sat us down on the floor and they put out a piece of cloth to make a nicer newer area to sit on. It was like a great big tablecloth—an embroidered tablecloth. I don't know where they got it—into the room. We took our shoes off and he kept running out to do things. She said, "Where's their fridge?" I said, "They haven't got a fridge." "I'm sure they have fridges. They all have fridges." I said, "No, they don't have fridges." What they learned to do in Curtin was to take the front off the air-conditioners and put their cartons of milk into the air-conditioners. She couldn't believe that. She said, "We were shown around the rooms, I'm sure they had fridges." She said, "They have to have a fridge. I don't believe that." I said, "Well, they don't have a fridge." "They're now three to four years in detention, they've never had a fridge. That's unbelievable." I said, "Isn't it funny the things you learn when you spend five minutes in their room rather than being told about it or reading about it?" ... I have never been greeted with such formality and manners. If I had been at the Windsor Hotel or dining with the Queen it couldn't have been finer. They had beaten up the milk to make the equivalent of cappuccino and it was an absolute blow-out. [One of the young men asked her] "Do you have any children?" She said, "Yes, I have two children." He said, "How old are they?" and she said, "One is 19 and one is 21." He said, "That is the same age as I am. What would you do if your children disappeared and you did not know where they were for five years?" She said, "I don't know." He said, "I am telling you, your heart would be broken." He said, "It is five years." For the Afghans in detention, more so than any other group, I think, they had the hardest time of all, because during the time of the detention September 11 happened, then America rushed in and bombed all sorts of parts of Afghanistan, then there was a major earthquake which wiped out many of the areas where some of these people came from. There was no telephone service and no postal service. The Iranians could phone home, a lot of other people had people who got out and they were in Syria and Pakistan, so for a lot of these Afghans they had no knowledge whether they were alive or dead. For many of them, they were last surviving male. That's why they were here, because when it got to the stage where the last brother was taken by the Taliban or disappeared: the whole idea of keeping the genealogy and the keeping the family going. I did a lot of talking to them about the need for them to start rebuilding the family. They must find a partner and marry and start again, and this is the beginning. That's what I did: a lot of talk. Is it medical? Is it nursing? I don't know whether it's any of those things. It's just the need, the need for me to understand where they were coming from and what was happening in their lives. Also, for somebody to validate that their situation was as grim as it was (Interview with Sarah).

Why is the story so significant in terms of the ethics of healthcare provision and duty of care? There are several aspects that are significant. Firstly, Sarah acted as an advocate for asylum seekers within the detention system in some small way mitigating the ongoing deterrent effect of incarceration by negotiating with the prison management and with the guards. More fundamentally, her story exemplifies the way in which care can restore to people dignity, hope and the right to be heard.

Conclusion

The health of asylum seekers in Australia has demonstrated clearly that the right to health cannot be separated from other fundamental human rights. Therefore the care of such highly vulnerable, stigmatised and traumatised people, to be effective had to move beyond the world of the clinic and embrace both care and advocacy outside it. In so doing, healthcare providers had to move beyond the usual duties incumbent upon them in providing treatment and protection from further harm.

References

ABC. 2006a. *7.30 Report*, 22 May 2006, www.abc.net.au/7.30/content/2006/s1644678.htm.
—. 2006b. *AM*, Mental health of detainees under the spotlight, 23 May 2006, http://www.abc.net.au/am/content/2006/s1645004.htm (accessed 19 November 2007).
Arras, J. 1988. The fragile web of responsibility: AIDS and the duty to treat. *Hastings Center Report*, vol. 18, no. 2, 10–20.
Australian Council of Heads of Schools of Social Work. 2006. *We've boundless plains to share: The first report of the people's inquiry into detention*, http://www.peoplesinquiry.org.au/PIDFirstReportNov_2006F[1].pdf.
Benhabib, S. 2004. *The rights of others. Aliens, residents and citizens.* Cambridge: Cambridge University Press.
Coffey, G. 2006. Locked up without guilt or sin: The ethics of mental health service delivery in immigration detention, *Psychiatry, Psychology and Law*, vol. 13, no, 1, 67–91.
Farmer, P. 2003. *Pathologies of power: Health, human rights and the new war on the poor.* Berkeley: University of California Press.
Gibson, J. and M. Morje Howard. 2007. Russian anti-semitism and the scapegoating of Jews. *British Journal of Political Science*, vol. 37, 193–223.

Goodin, R. 1985. *Protecting the vulnerable*. Chicago: Chicago University Press.

Hardimon, M. 1994. Role obligations. *Journal of Philosophy*, vol. 91, no. 7, 333–63.

Harley, J., M. Allstrom and A. Phillips. 2005. *Submission to the Palmer Inquiry from the Office of the Public Advocate of South Australia*.

Human Rights and Equal Opportunity Commission. 2004. *A last resort? National inquiry into children in immigration detention*, http://www.hreoc.gov.au/Human_Rights/children_detention_report/index.html.

Interviews conducted by Deborah Zion for ARC Discovery Grant "Caring for asylum seekers in Australia: Bioethics and human rights". Investigators Deborah Zion, Linda Briskman and Bebe Loff, 2007–09.

International Dual Loyalty Working Group. 2002 *Dual loyalty & human rights in health professional practice: Proposed guidelines & institutional mechanisms*, http://physiciansforhumanrights.org/library/documents/reports/report-2002-duelloyalty.pdf.

Mellama, G. 2000. Scapegoats. *Criminal Justice Ethics*, vol. 19, no. 1, 3–9.

Oakley, J. 1996. Varieties of virtue ethics. *Ratio*, vol. 9, no. 2, 128–52.

Palmer, M. 2005. *Inquiry into the circumstances of the immigration detention of Cornelia Rau: Report*, www.immi.gov.au/media/publications/pdf/palmer-report.pdf.

Radden, J. 2002. Psychiatric Ethics. *Bioethics*, vol. 16, no. 5, 397–411.

Reid, L. 2005. Risk and the duty to care in the SARS epidemic. *Bioethics*, vol. 19, no. 4, 348–61.

Richters, A. 2002. When ethics, healthcare and human rights conflict: Mental healthcare for asylum seekers. *Cambridge Quarterly of Healthcare Ethics*, vol. 11, no. 3, 304–18.

Singh, C. 2007. Personal correspondence.

Solomon, M. 2005. Healthcare professionals and dual loyalty: Technical proficiency is not enough. *Medscape General Medicine*, vol. 7, no. 3, 1–14.

Transcript of the Prime Minister, The Hon John Howard MP, Press Conference, Melbourne, 7 November 2001, http://www.pm.gov.au/News/interviews/2001/interview1452.htm.

CHAPTER EIGHT

ENEMIES EVERYWHERE: (IN)SECURITY POLITICS, ASYLUM SEEKERS AND OTHER ENEMIES WITHIN

JUDE MCCULLOCH

Introduction

This chapter focuses on the genesis and dynamic of (in)security politics and the vested interests that seek to reap political profit from its deployment. It describes and analyses the federal "law and order" elections that took place at a national level in Australia in 2001 and 2004. It also looks at the lead up to the 2007 federal election where security and law and order issues have once again being used as a political tool in the quest for election success. It argues that in each of these election years the reigning conservative political party, led by Prime Minister John Howard, deliberately exploited fear by engendering a sense of national emergency surrounding a minority group demonised as the "dangerous other". The pattern was set in the lead-up to the 2001 election and is now well established. A social, economic or political problem is "discovered" and amplified through the rhetoric of law and order to the level of national crisis that requires firm action by a resolute leader in the name of national security. In 2001 it was "tough on border control", in 2004 it was "tough on terrorism" and in 2007 it is "tough on child abuse" in remote Indigenous communities.

In each of these cases the purported response to the contrived crisis is counter-productive in addressing underlying causes, reducing threats and assisting victims or potential victims. The human costs of security politics are high. It is almost inevitably people most in need of protection that are constructed and targeted as security threats and subjected to punitive counter-measures. Beyond analysing, documenting and witnessing the human costs associated with security politics, a task well advanced by progressive scholars and public intellectuals in the field of refugee studies, it is also important to understand who and what profits from these contrived national emergencies. This chapter argues that the political tactic mobilised around national emergencies has been politically successful in distracting attention from other problematic issues, eliminating the need for substantive policy, in creating a rhetorical platform for staging strong leadership and providing a context for progressing hidden agendas.

(In)security politics winners and losers

The political profits to be gained through the deployment of (in)security politics are particularly important in an era of neo-liberal globalisation when governments have increasingly less to offer on a whole range of issues closely tied to diverse forms of security related to income, employment, housing, education and health (McCulloch 2004a). The willing embrace of neo-liberalism by governments like the conservative government in Australia, facilitates social and economic *insecurity* for the majority of the population. The targeting of minority populations that seek asylum, who embody the stereotype of terrorists, and Indigenous Australians, creates or deepens the process of scapegoating providing a smokescreen for government's failure to deliver economic and social security.

In a collection that focuses primarily on asylum seekers and refugees it is nevertheless vital to recognise that the punitive politics of fear that has played out around asylum seekers in Australia and other parts of the globe is part of a broader political strategy readily transferable to other issues and other vulnerable populations. Indeed, many of the "threats" around which emergency and crisis are constructed are represented as overlapping and continuous Post 9/11, for example, asylum seekers have readily been conflated with terrorists by governments, effectively becoming "the interface between the war on terror and the war at home" (Perera 2007, 7).

Governments, government authorities and state agents like the police, have what might be thought of as a "defamation edge" when it comes to labelling and targeting asylum seekers and members of minority groups constructed as dangerous others more generally as "illegals", criminals, terrorists, and child abusers (see Herman 1993, 56 on "defamation edge"). Governments and state organisations have credibility, ready access to the media and a monopoly over key information, particularly as situations emerge. When governments invoke a state of emergency through a constructed crisis, national security is frequently declared to override the public's right to know and government deems itself obliged to act with great speed (see, for example, Marr 2007). In these circumstances, emergency time takes over from public time and the processes of democracy so that debate is strictly circumscribed and even shut down and significant government action is mandated ahead of any substantial public scrutiny of alleged facts (Giroux 2004). It frequently takes the media, public intellectuals, lawyers, community leaders and the concerned public some time to begin to unpack the distortions and misrepresentations behind the rhetoric of fear and emergency emanating from official sources. If, however, we are attentive to *patterns* and become informed about the way (in)security politics works, the tactic itself loses its potency. Often, in the first instance, the government is given the benefit of the doubt by many people because the political *motive* for deliberately creating anxiety and fear and the *methods* by which this are done are not fully understood and recognised.

The case studies set out in some detail here are confined to Australia but their relevance extends beyond this one jurisdiction to provide insights and lessons more generally. As Italian philosopher Agamben points out, there "is a continuing tendency in *all* of the Western democracies ... [towards] an unprecedented generalisation of the paradigm of security as the normal technique of government" (2005, 14, emphasis added). He observes that we are facing "extreme and most dangerous developments" as "[i]n the course of the gradual neutralisation of politics and the progressive surrender of traditional tasks of the state, security imposes itself as the basic principle of state activity" (Agamben 2001). Khaki is fast becoming the colour of choice for elections and budgets, as the major political parties in Western democracies fall over themselves to look strong in the face of what is marketed in the "fear economy" as pervasive threat, and defence and homeland security absorb an increasing proportion of national revenue (see Davis 2001 on the "fear economy"; on Australia's Khaki elections see Hogg 2002). The space of politics is in the process of being militarised as state-centred notions of national security drastically reduce what is understood to be the legitimate boundaries of debate. State repression of debate is expanded through repressive legislation, monitoring, withdrawal of government funding, censorship, intimidation, vilification and slander, and denial of information (Giroux 2004; Hamilton and Maddison 2007; Marr 2007). Beyond this, the right to political association and political speech are reconfigured as security threats (Lynch and Williams 2006). (In)security politics as manifest in states of emergency manufactured around asylum seekers, terrorists, and most recently Indigenous Australians living in remote communities, find their genesis in law and order politics.

Law and order elections and the state of emergency

Since the mid-1980s, consistent with trends in the United Kingdom and United States, law and order politics became an important ingredient in Australian state and territory elections. During the 1980s police used their industrial militancy, media influence and public legitimacy to push a "win back the streets" battle metaphor around crime. The focus on law and order and a "tough on crime" approach reflected both the police worldview and vested interests around police numbers, budgets and powers. The media amplified and mirrored the police vision. The prominence of crime as a news staple, the "if it bleeds it leads" news values, the rise and rise of radio news entertainers, and the emergence of a headkicking style of tabloid journalism that feeds and creates a sense of moral outrage around crime helped to create an exaggerated fear of crime. Politicians came to understand that this fear could be manipulated to deliver election success, leading to a convergence between the conservative and Labor parties on law and order. Consensus developed around an increasingly punitive agenda with parties disagreeing only on the details. In this context, elections often degenerate(d) into law and order "auctions" or "bidding wars", with each side vying to outdo the other with tough and tougher responses to crime and each accusing the other of being soft (McCulloch 2004a).

Law and order politics is a system in positive feedback gathering momentum as it goes. The crime fighting and crime control measures proposed and implemented by government serve only to highlight the threat. Security talk paradoxically leads inevitably to fear and insecurity. As Mike Davis observes "the quest for the bourgeois utopia of a totally calculable and safe environment has paradoxically generated radical insecurity" (2001, 41). As each election nears political parties come up with increasingly punitive measures justified on the basis that crime and violence are worse than ever, fuelling community fears to meet the political need to be seen to be taking tough measures. Law and order politics has proved politically profitable but frequently counter-productive in addressing crime. By channelling social wealth into coercive measures, such as police and prisons and away from services like education, health and social support, law and order politics deepens the inequality that fuels crime, exacerbating the cycle of fear, crime and punitiveness (Brake and Hale 1992, 48–51).

Significantly, law and order frameworks provide an effective mechanism for politicians to transmit race-based fears while maintaining credible deniability in the face of accusations of racism. Although formal racial equality is widely accepted, racial resentments, fears and prejudices—often unconscious—still hold sway amongst many. Since the 1980s (particularly conservative) politicians in the United States have used implicit messages to appeal to racial fears while managing to avoid the racist tag. Research demonstrates that the crime theme is one of the most effective in simultaneously conveying and concealing racial overtones (Mendelberg 2001). Political insiders call this tactic "dog whistle politics". It involves "pitching a message to a particular group of voters that other voters do not hear" (Laurie Oakes quoted in Marr and Wilkinson 2003, 280). In the case of an implicit race-based message it is a way of winking at a racially ambivalent or prejudiced audience without getting caught.

Prior to the 2001 *Tampa* election (see below) law and order politics in Australia were confined to the states and territories. This is because Australia is a federation and the Commonwealth constitution gives responsibility to the states for crime control and internal defence. The Commonwealth, on the other hand, has responsibility for external security and the military. This strict demarcation between state and Commonwealth responsibility for internal and external security began to break down in the mid-1970s when the Commonwealth became involved in policing transnational crime through its external affairs powers. This involvement grew around issues such as organised crime, drug trafficking, people-smuggling, sex trafficking and terrorism (see, for example, Hocking 1993). Under the auspices of these crimes the Australian Federal Police grew substantially in terms of numbers, powers, resources and prestige and the Commonwealth became involved in policing cross-border crimes (Pickering 2004).

Commonwealth involvement in law enforcement also opened the way for greater military involvement in policing crime, particularly cross-border crime but also, potentially, domestic crimes (Head 2006). The blurring of the lines between the police and military and thus military and civilian functions undermines basic tenets of democracy, including the rule of law (McCulloch 2001; Giroux 2004, 44). The use of the military to combat crime intensifies the punitive and "othering" potential of law and order politics. While police deal with citizens who have broken the law, the use of the military implies an external other who is an enemy. Criminals are vilified and punished, while enemies are understood to represent a heightened form of threat and thus may be eliminated or destroyed. Criminals, although precariously situated legally and culturally, are nevertheless part of society whereas enemies are necessarily outside and alien. Enemies, unlike those constructed as merely criminal, are not entitled to the type of due process protections generally available to citizens (McCulloch 2001, 15–31).

The hybrid of war and crime response used to respond to constructed emergencies facilitates the denial of both criminal justice due process protections and the universal human rights standards mandated in war. Domestically the threat is said to amount to one beyond crime, making traditional criminal justice due process protections unaffordable, while internationally the unconventional nature of the threat is said to render human rights unaffordable luxuries (McCulloch and Carlton 2006). In Agamben's formulation this creates a situation where internationally and domestically the "force of law" is reduced to simply a situation of "force" devoid of law (2005, ch. 2). In this space of force without law, law ceases to function as protective *and* punitive and becomes simply punitive, an exercise of arbitrary and seemingly unlimited sovereign power. (In)security politics succeeds in overcoming the limits to executive power that exist in domestic and international law. Pre-emptive punishments, indefinite detention, psychological and physical abuse and torture become possible and even normalised within this punitive (in)security context.

Asylum seekers and the state of emergency

This expansion of law and order politics at a state level created the context for the 2001 *Tampa* election. Polling done for the Liberal Party prior to that election indicated that playing to people's race-based anxieties was an effective way of capturing their vote. The challenging aspect of this was devising ways to exploit race-based fear while simultaneously avoiding the accusation of racism (Marr and Wilkinson 2003, 175–6). The government could set up credible deniability in relation to accusations of racism, and persuade people whose economic status predisposed them to voting Labor to vote conservative, if the race card was hidden in a deck labelled national security or law and order. The arrival of the *Tampa*, a Norwegian cargo ship carrying more than four hundred mainly Afghan and Iraqi rescued asylum seekers, off Australia's coast on 26 August 2001 provided Prime Minister John Howard with an issue that allowed him to do "something no federal leader had ever been able to do before: fight a law and order election and pitch it in terms of national survival" (Marr and Wilkinson 2003, 93). That asylum seekers are not criminals and in no way present a substantial risk to national security or Australia's sovereignty was irrelevant. The deployment of counter-measures, including the military and particularly the commando squad, the Special Air Service, to keep the *Tampa* from entering Australian waters assisted in painting those on board as enemies representing a serious threat. By labelling the asylum seekers "illegal" the government conflated them with people-smugglers and organised crime. After the 9/11 attacks on the United States, only a few weeks after the *Tampa* sailed into Australian waters, the vilification of asylum seekers was extended through suggestions that they might be terrorists (Manne 2004, 41–4; Marr and Wilkinson 2003, 198, 280–1). Language was deliberately deployed to create a "fog of deviancy" around the asylum seekers eclipsing from public view the humanitarian crisis they represented and their human identity as vulnerable people in need of safe harbour (Marr and Wilkinson 2003, 145, 198, 280–1; Pickering 2004).

Law and order politics at the state level created fertile soil for treating asylum seekers as dangerous others. Scott Poynting's analysis of the rhetoric surrounding the reporting of crime, immigration and security issues in Australia points to "striking parallels between ideological constructs of Middle-Eastern, crime-prone immigrants, of Middle Eastern queue-jumping, people-smuggler paying 'boat people" with no respect for orderly waiting lists and civilized rules, of violent Middle-Eastern Muslim rapists and terrorists' (Poynting 2002, 59; see also Poynting et al. 2004). The government's vilification of asylum seekers also built on Australia's longstanding invasion anxiety (Burke 2001). In contrast to landlocked countries most asylum seekers to Australia arrive by boat. The government's false claim that asylum seekers threw their children overboard in order to coerce the navy into rescuing them rather than towing them out of Australian waters, and the sense of moral indignation deliberately whipped up by the Immigration Minister and the Prime Minister in the immediate lead-up to the election about this added to the general picture of asylum seekers as dangerous others "not like us" (MacCallum 2002, 47–61; Manne 2004, 40–1).[1] Summing up the sea change in Australian politics heralded by the government's handling of the *Tampa*, Marr and Wilkinson conclude that "[n]ascent racism, ancient fears of invasion by immigrants and talkback radio ranting about Asian crime"

---

[1] Claims that children were thrown overboard received widespread publicity which fed popular sentiment that asylum seekers were deeply manipulative and morally repugnant. According to Marr and Wilkinson the impact on the electorate immediately before the election was "immense" (2003, 209). The claims that asylum seekers threw their children overboard were untrue. Pictures purportedly depicting these events in fact related to sea rescue of children from a sinking asylum-seeker boat. The truth was not revealed until after the election. The record of events makes it clear that the government manipulated the truth to support its political agenda and election success (Marr and Wilkinson 2003).

fused into a "new and extraordinarily potent political force" (Marr and Wilkinson 2003, 93).

The arrival of the *Tampa* and the manufactured state of emergency over what was depicted as a threat requiring intervention by the military boosted the electoral fortunes of the Howard government and substantially assisted in securing its victory in the 2001 election (Marr and Wilkinson 2003; Manne 2004, 42–4). The harsh treatment of asylum seekers, including a naval blockade of boats entering Australian waters, mandatory and indefinite detention in isolated "desert boot camps", and exile on offshore islands and third countries under the "Pacific Solution" continued to prove popular with the electorate for a number of years (Carrington 2006; Weber 2006). Eventually, however, as the government lost control of the story, and the human face and human costs of these policies became more widely known and understood, a popular backlash, including amongst government backbenchers, demanded and achieved an amelioration of the harshest of these policies (Carrington 2006). By this time, however, the government was opening up a new front line in its battle for continued electoral success.

Post 9/11 politics of fear

Although the 2001 federal election took place after the September 2001 attacks on the United States, the asylum seeker issue remained most significant in that poll. The government used the threat of terrorism to underline the importance of its border protection policy, suggesting that those seeking asylum could include terrorists (Manne 2004, 41–4; Marr and Wilkinson 2003, 198, 280–1). The criminalisation of asylum seekers deepened in the context of the "war on terror" For example, the Kurdistan Workers' Party (PKK) was listed by the Australian government as a proscribed terrorist organisation in 2006. This was done even though there is ample evidence that the actual and perceived members of this group are persecuted by the Turkish state on the basis of their political beliefs and ethnic identity, and no evidence that the group poses any threat to Australia. The same evidence of persecution and identity that would formerly have provided the basis for a claim for refugee status can now be used for criminal prosecution under anti-terrorism laws (Federation of Community Legal Centres 2006).

The declaration of the "war on terror" by the United States in 2001 and Australia's enthusiastic participation in its every aspect, including the invasion of Iraq in March 2003 expanded the opportunities for the domestic deployment of security politics for political gain. In the lead-up to the 2004 election the Prime Minister revealed that his strategy for the election would be "to attack Labor as weak and divided on national security and in the war against terrorism" (*Age* 9 June 2003, 4). Political commentator Michelle Grattan, noting the emerging pattern related to the manipulation of fear and threat, declared, prior to the 2004 election, that security is "a new *Tampa*" (2003). The government's resolute stand on national security was underlined by a raft of counter-terrorism legislation giving police and security agencies widely expanded powers (Lynch and Williams 2006). In addition to this the military was further integrated into policing frameworks and law enforcement given an expanded remit in terms of national security (Head 2006). That the threat was cast in terms of Arab/Muslim extremism deepened already widely circulating prejudices and fears (Poynting et al. 2004; Perera 2007). Australia's participation in the United States–led invasion of Iraq in 2003 worked to present Howard, like Bush, as a strong leader in uncertain times.

While talking and acting tough on terrorism may have provided political opportunities it is not apparent that repressive legislation and military action have led to greater security, domestically or globally. The invasion of Iraq has been a disaster for the Iraqi people and led to increased global insecurity (Cole 2006; Ali 2005). It is also increasingly clear that the public was thoroughly duped on the reasons for the invasion. The weapons of mass destruction that provided the original justification proved to be non-existent and the intelligence that was said to confirm their existence inaccurate and substantially manipulated for political advantage. Increasingly the evidence suggests that the invasion of Iraq was, as critics maintained, primarily motivated by a desire to control Iraq's oil reserves (Kramer and Michalowski 2005). It is clear that Australia's domestic counter-terrorism laws have dramatically impacted upon individual freedoms and opened the door to miscarriages of justice as a result of the substantial erosion of the presumption of innocence (Lynch and Williams 2006). While the government claims it has the "balance right" there is no evidence that the trade-off of civil liberties will reduce the threat of terrorism, and a body of research suggests that repressive legislation may ultimately add to insecurity as a result of state terror and alienation and resistance in response to state terror (see, for example, Hillyard 2005; Pickering et al. 2007, 38–60).

Extending (in)security politics

More recently there are signs that the strong security credentials that were once an unambiguous advantage to the government may be becoming a political liability in the face of increased concern for individual liberties, human rights and a growing recognition of the way the government is deliberately creating a sense of crisis and fear aimed at securing political advantage. Just as the government eventually lost control of the story in relation to asylum seekers it appears that the government may have lost its ability to control the story in relation to national security and the "war on terror". After several years of indifference a groundswell of popular support for Australian citizen David Hicks, held by the United States at Guantanamo Bay without charge for five years, transformed the "tough on terrorism" posturing into a political liability for the government, with one poll indicating that seventy per cent of people believed that Hicks should be returned to Australia (ABC news online 2006). The concern for human rights generated in the Hicks case appears to have fed into the popular sympathy for Indian doctor Mohamed Haneef, whose second cousin was involved in the failed suicide bombing at Glasgow airport in Scotland in July 2007 (ABC 2007). Dr Haneef was detained without charge for nearly two weeks by the Australian Federal Police over suspicions of supporting terrorists, subject to bungled and ultimately withdrawn charges, vilified by authorities in the media, forced to stay in prison after a magistrate granted him bail when the Immigration Minister revoked his visa, and finally forced to leave the country, despite the withdrawal of all charges, when the Immigration Minister nevertheless refused to reinstate his visa. According to political commentator Michelle Grattan, Haneef:

> can probably be grateful to David Hicks. It took years for Australian public opinion to react against the lack of justice accorded to Hicks in the Guantanamo Bay process. But finally there was a backlash. The public's "fair go" syndrome has kicked in immediately in the case of the Indian doctor … (2007).

The extent to which the public expressed sympathy and support for the doctor and the degree to which the media and the public were prepared to question the government's motives in this case suggests that there is greater awareness of the way the dynamics of (in)security politics operates. Even extremely conservative media commentators considered that the government's invocation of national security in the Haneef case was not an adequate explanation or justification for the treatment of Dr Haneef (see, for example, Albrechtsen 2007). Indeed many people were quick to point to a pattern. Writers to major newspapers and callers to talkback radio questioned the government's motives with comments such as whether "the Government regarded Hicks and Haneef as puppets in useful political pantomimes to promote the image as being hard on terrorists and strong on national security?" capturing the emerging cynicism towards the government (see Pringle 2007).

In June 2007 the Howard government, in a replay of the insecurity politics circulating around asylum seekers in the lead-up to the 2001 election and the play on national security in relation to the "war on terror" in the lead-up to the 2004 election, "discovered" a crisis in relation to remote Indigenous communities in the Northern Territory. As peoples who have continuously occupied the country now called Australia for millennia, Indigenous Australians could be understood to embody a type of authentic Australian identity at the polar opposite of those "dangerous others", asylum seekers and Muslim and Arabs recently constructed as threats to national security. In reality, however, Indigenous Australians have long been represented as a threat to nationhood (Dodson 2004, 119). Criminalisation of Indigenous people through punitive law and order policies has worked to maintain them as a dispossessed minority and an evil social element, eclipsing their status as peoples with legitimate political claims on the nation state (Cunneen 2001). After a report on the issue of child sexual abuse in Indigenous communities the federal government announced an emergency plan, involving the non-negotiated and thus coercive intervention of police and military in Indigenous communities. Such a response, similar to the use of the military against asylum seekers in the 2001 *Tampa* election, works to construct Indigenous people as enemies representing a real and substantial threat to national security. The ostensible reason for Commonwealth government intervention is to protect Indigenous children from sexual abuse. The report which purportedly triggered the government's response, made 97 recommendations, largely directed at effecting long-term social change within Indigenous communities, with primary emphasis on education, support services and community involvement to address long-term disadvantage (Wild and Anderson 2007). The government's response addresses very few of these recommendations (Law Council of Australia 2007). According to Indigenous leader Patrick Dodson:

> [t]here continues to be a wide perception in the indigenous community, and considered opinion across the nation, that the "national emergency" intervention strategy is motivated by political factors in an election year. It lacks integrity (2007).

That political profit can be made from the opportunity to be seen to act resolutely on an emotive issue like child sexual abuse no doubt figures in the government's calculation. In addition, the extended and continuous construction of Indigenous Australians as criminals assists in masking the continual failure of the Federal government to provide basic and desperately needed resources in the areas of health, education and housing to Indigenous people (see, for example, Dodson 2004). The masking of the failure of mainstream political leadership on Indigenous issues through punitive "solutions" resonates with the way that the repressive "solutions" in relation to asylum seekers and in the "war on terror" not only fail to address but also divert attention from root causes such as gross global disparities in wealth and opportunities and divisive and aggressive foreign policy.

Conclusion

(In)security politics serves to obscure the social, economic and political forces, particularly mismanaged globalisation, that work to produce social chaos, violence, forced migration and terror by focusing attention exclusively and obsessively on individuals or types caricatured and constructed as embodiments of evil. This is no clearer than in the treatment of asylum seekers in Australia. The ultimate and overriding success of security politics lies in its vanguard role in relation to the expansion, consolidation and intensification of neo-liberal globalisation. National security has become the pre-eminent space upon which political leadership is staged in a time where the dominant economic paradigm of neo-liberalism dictates that governments have increasingly less to offer citizens in terms of substantive social wellbeing and economic security.

The central tenets of neo-liberalism: privatisation, deregulation and the reduction of the social safety net, all reduce and erode the willingness and ability of the state to engage to perform roles related to welfare and public enterprises Security politics has been successful in opening up a political project that maintains and projects the image of a strong state in a context where states' power is diminishing or eroding in a range of other significant spheres. With increasingly less to offer in terms of social security (a term that has disappeared from the political vocabulary altogether), national security is fast becoming the central focus of state activity and the primary basis for political legitimation. Historically and continuously the law and order/security framework operates to deny national and global citizenship to those groups constructed as crime problems and security threats.

It is important to understand the way that the "threats" around security politics are readily substitutable so that insights and responses gained from critical engagement in one arena are not always playing catch-up on the "front lines", as various states of emergency proliferate according to emerging political opportunities. This chapter focused on drawing out the patterns, motives and methods used by governments seeking to reap the political wages of fear. It attempts to contribute in some small way to taking the body politic beyond this cynical political tactic towards a sustainable future based on an inclusive vision of security.

References

ABC Newsonline. 2006. Poll finds most Australians want Hicks home, http://www.abc.net.au/news/newsitems/200612/s1811171.htm (accessed 2 August 2007).
ABC. 2007. Glasgow attackers intent on suicide, http://www.abc.net.au/news/stories/2007/07/06/1971295.htm (accessed 10 August 2007).
Agamben, G. 2001. Security and terror. *Theory and Event* 5 (4) trans. Carolin Emcke (see: http://muse.jhu.edu/journals/theory_and_event/v005/5.4agamben.html, accessed 10 January 2003)
—. 2004 No to bio-political tattooing, *Le Monde*, www.ratical.org/ratville/CAH/totalControl.pdf (accessed 4 August 2006).
—. 2005. *State of exception*. Chicago: The University of Chicago Press.
Albrechtsen, J. 2007. Bungles have undermined laws. *The Australian*, 25 July 2007, http://www.theaustralian.news.com.au/story/0,25197,221291305013450,00.html (accessed 10 August 2007).
Ali, T. 2005. *Rough music: Blair, bombs, Baghdad, London, terror*. London: Verso.
Brake, M. and C. Hale. 1992. *Public order and private lives: The politics of law and order*. London: Routledge. 48–51.
Burke, T. 2001. *In fear of security: Australia's invasion anxiety*. Annandale, New South Wales: Pluto Press.
Carrington, K. 2006. Law and order on the border in the neo-colonial antipodes. In *Borders, mobility and the technologies of control*. ed. S. Pickering and L. Weber. Dordrecht, Netherlands: Springer.
Cole, D. 2006. Are we safer? *New York Review of Books*, vol. LIII (4) 15, 17.
Cunneen, C. 2001. *Conflict politics and crime: Aboriginal communities and the police*. Crows Nest, NSW: Allen and Unwin.

Davis, M. 2001. The flames of New York. *New Left Review*, no. 12, 34–50.
Dodson, M. 2004. Indigenous Australian. In *The Howard Years*. ed. R. Manne, 119–43. Melbourne: Black Inc Agenda.
Dodson, P. 2007. An entire culture is at stake. *The Age*, 14 July 2007, http://www.theage.com.au/news/opinion/an-entire-culture-is-at-stake/2007/07/13/1183833765256.html?page=fullpage (accessed 20 July 2007).
Federation of Community Legal Centres. 2006. *Submission of the Federation of Community Legal Centres (Vic) Inc to the Parliamentary Joint Committee on Intelligence and Security, review of the listing of the Kurdistan Workers Party (PKK) as a terrorist organisation under the Criminal Code Act 2004*. Carlton: Federation of Community Legal Centres.
Giroux, H. 2004. *The terror of neoliberalism: Authoritarianism and the eclipse of democracy*. Boulder: Paradigm Publishers.
Grattan, M. Plumbing the depths on Haneef. *The Age*, Melbourne, 27 July 2007.
—. Labor smells a new Tampa. *The Age*, 5 November 2003.
Hamilton, C. and S. Maddison, eds. 2007. *Silencing dissent: How the Australian government is controlling public opinion and stifling debate*. Crows Nest, New South Wales, Allen and Unwin.
Head, M. 2006 Military call-out powers expanded: Disturbing questions posed. *Alternative Law Journal*, vol 31, 83–7.
Herman, E. 1993. Terrorism: misrepresentations of power. In *The politics and imagery of terrorism*. ed. D. Brown and R. Merrill, 47–56. Seattle: Bay Press.
Hillyard, P. 2005. *The "war on terror": Lessons from Ireland*, http//www.ecln.org/essays/essays-1.pdf (accessed 15 December 2005).
Hocking, J. 1993. *Beyond terrorism: The development of the Australian security state*. St Leonards, New South Wales: Allen and Unwin.
Hogg, R. 2002. The khaki election. In *Beyond September 11: An anthology of dissent*. ed. P. Scraton, 135–42. London: Pluto Press.
Hogg, R. and D. Brown. 1998. *Rethinking law and order*. Sydney: Pluto Press.
Kramer, R. and R. Michalowski. 2005. War, aggression and state crime. *British Journal of Criminology*, vol. 45 no. 4, 446–69.
Law Council of Australia. 2007. *Law Council criticisms of NT emergency plan*, http://www.lawcouncil.asn.au/shared/2439777967.pdf (accessed 10 August 2007).

Lynch, A. and G. Williams. 2006. *What price security: Taking stock of Australia's anti-terror laws*. Sydney: UNSW Press.
MacCallum, M. 2002. Girt by sea: Australia, the refugees and the politics of fear. *Quarterly Essay*, no. 5.
Manne, R. 2004. The Howard years: A political interpretation. In *The Howard years*. ed. R. Manne, 3–53. Melbourne: Black Inc Agenda.
Marr, D. 2007. His master's voice: The corruption of public debate under Howard. *Quarterly Essay*, no. 26.
Marr, D. and M. Wilkinson. 2003. *Dark victory*. Crows Nest, New South Wales: Allen and Unwin.
McCulloch, J. 2001. *Blue army: Paramilitary policing in Australia*. Carlton: Melbourne University Press.
—. 2004a. National (in)security politics in Australia: fear and the federal election. *Alternative Law Journal*, vol. 29, 87–91.
—. 2004b. Blue armies, khaki police and the cavalry on the new American frontier: Critical criminology for the 21st Century. *Critical Criminology*, vol. 12, 309–26.
—. 2005a. (In)security in the age of globalisation: human precariousness in the move from welfare to warfare state. *Just Policy*, no. 37, 19–24.
—. 2005b. State of emergency: The militarization of civil society. *Dissent*, no. 19, Summer 2005/06, 7–9.
—. 2007. In the occupied territory, Howard targets the "enemy" within. *The Age*, 6 July 2007, http://www.theage.com.au/articles/2007/07/05/1183351371041.html (accessed 7 July 2007).
McCulloch, J. and B. Carlton. 2006. Pre-empting injustice: Suppression of financing of terrorism and the war on terror. *Current Issues in Criminal Justice*, vol. 17, no. 3, 397–412.
Mendelberg, T. 2001. *The race card: Campaign strategy, implicit messages, and the norm of equality*. Princeton: Princeton University Press.
Perera, S. 2007. Introduction: Acting sovereign. In *Our patch: Enacting sovereignty post-2001*. ed. S. Perera, 1–22. Curtin University, Perth: Network Books.
Pickering, S. 2004. The production of sovereignty and the rise of transversal policing: people-smuggling and federal policing. *Australian and New Zealand Journal of Criminology*, vol. 37, 362–79.
Pickering, S., D. Wright-Neville, J. McCulloch and P. Lentini. 2007. Counter terrorism policing and culturally diverse communities. Monash University and Victoria Police: Monash University, Arts.

Poynting, S. 2002. "Bin Laden in the suburbs": Attacks on Arab and Muslim Australians before and after 11 September, *Current Issues in Criminal Justice*, 14 (1) 2002, 43–64.

Poynting, S., G. Noble, P. Tabar and J. Collins. 2004. *Bin Laden in the suburbs: Criminalising the Arab other.* Sydney: Sydney Institute of Criminology.

Pringle, R. 2007. Why lock up Dr Haneef? *The Australian*, 26 July 2007.

Weber, L. 2006. The shifting frontiers of migration control. In *Borders, mobility and technologies of control.* ed. S. Pickering and L. Weber, Dordrecht, Netherlands: Springer.

Wild, R. and P. Anderson. 2007. *Little children are sacred*, http://www.partnerships.org.au/Library/littlechildrenaresacred.htm.

Chapter Nine

Detention as Deterrence

Linda Briskman

Introduction

The abhorrent policy of indefinite and mandatory immigration detention in Australia has been exposed by refugee advocates and academics and distorted through government declarations and media hyperbole. Political statements of the present and past illuminate the way in which entry restrictions, both at the border and within, enter the political arena and the public discourse. The policies are grounded in the concept of national sovereignty, a fundamental reasoning behind mandatory detention (Whyte 2003). These are illustrated in a variety of statements emanating from the political domain.

Australian Prime Minister John Howard has stated that "we and we alone will decide who comes to this country and the circumstances in which they come," (interview on 2GB radio 2001) and "I certainly don't want people like that here," in response to false allegations that asylum seekers had thrown their children overboard (ABC radio October 2001, cited in Mares 2002, 135). In 2004 the Liberal Party and the National Party of Australia, in their election plank of Stronger Border Protection, stated the three objectives of immigration detention. These were to protect the community from individuals who pose a health, criminal or national security threat; to ensure that non-citizens who are in Australia in breach of immigration laws are available for removal from this country; and to deter prospective unauthorised arrivals (cited in Taylor 2006, 49). Matthew Zagor (2007) explains that it is an old and macabre tradition to design punishments as deterrents to would-be offenders. For example, public executions were aimed at educating and terrifying the public as much as punishing the perpetrator. This tradition continues in Australia in the guise of mandatory detention.

The recent policy initiatives build on previous ideological standpoints. Pauline Hanson, founder of the controversial One Nation Party, told the federal parliament in 1996, "If I can invite people into my home, then I should have the right to have a say in who comes into my country" (cited in Dawson 2006). Years earlier T. W. White, Australia's delegate to the 1938 Evian conference in France in response to the "problem" of Jewish refugees, said, "It will appreciated that as we have no racial problem, we are not desirous of importing one" (cited in Kaldor 2002).

The critiques

Deterrence measures are enacted by the Australian government in a number of ways including the inability of many asylum seekers to access legal processes in Australia through the excision of islands from Australia's migration zone; Operation Relex, whereby the Australian Defence Forces actively push back would-be arrivals who are approaching Australian waters; offshore processing in neighbouring countries, the most controversial of which is Nauru; and mandatory detention. It is the issue of mandatory detention that has arguably provoked the greatest sense of controversy and outrage. It is with mandatory detention that the inter-disciplinarity of law, ethics and politics converge to challenge the basic premises on which the policy is constructed and implemented.

Imagery and language created by government has allowed sections of the community to be convinced that mandatory detention is necessary. The terminology includes invoking the fraudulent concepts of queue jumpers, illegals and floodgates, a form of textual abuse[1] (Goddard and Saunders 2001, 29). Although most attention has been on the policies of the current decade, as Brennan states (2003, 10) Australians are sensitive to the unauthorised arrival of persons by boat and has gradually tightened laws and policies since the end of the Vietnam War. The fact that mandatory detention is an over-reaction to a modest challenge (Crock, Saul and Dastyari 2006) is irrelevant in populist discourse and community prejudice.

When legislation to introduce mandatory detention was proposed by the Federal Labor Government in 1992 in response to the arrival of Cambodians, the Immigration Minister at that time, Gerry Hand, stated in parliament that:

---

[1] Goddard and Saunders use of the term textual abuse in relation to the discourse on child abuse is relevant to the depiction of asylum seekers.

The government is determined that a clear signal be sent that migration to Australia may not be achieved by simply arriving in this country and expecting to be allowed into the community (cited in Brennan, p. 87).

That "clear signal" continues unabated and, notwithstanding the endeavours of advocates from all walks of life and despite parliamentary pressure that introduced some policy changes,[2] it remained a fundamental policy principle of the conservative coalition federal government and unopposed by the Labor Party which came to power in December 2007.

On Radio National on 1 August 2002, the then Minister for Immigration, Philip Ruddock, made the government's deterrence position undeniably evident, emphasising the importance of detention arrangements as "a very important deterrent in preventing people from getting into boats". The emphasis on the deterrence component of the policy has been particularly unsettling for refugee advocates and has resulted in legal commentary that argues that the deterrence factor is in breach of Guideline 3 of the United Nation High Commission for Refugees:

> The detention of asylum seekers as part of a policy to deter future asylum seekers, or to dissuade those who have commenced their claims from pursuing them, is contrary to the norms of refugee law.

In emphasising that incarcerating people for the purposes of deterrence is not legitimate under international law, Savitri Taylor (2006, 50) points out that detaining unauthorised arrivals for the purposes of deterring others from following in their footsteps is illegitimate for one very simple reason. It involves treating human beings as mere means to an end and is, therefore, a repudiation of the fundamental premise of international human rights law, which is the equal worth of every human being. Other critiques abound from a range of commentators and these illustrate deep concern, legally and ethically. Crock et al. (2006) assert that detention cannot be justified to deter other unlawful arrivals. At the most basic level, they say, it is improper to use the pain and discomfort of some asylum seekers to deter others. For Fiske (2006) it is not ethical to punish one group of people to deter another, particularly when this group has not broken any law and is a vulnerable group in society. Former Human Rights and Equal Opportunity Commissioner, Sev Odowski (2003) suggests that even if it

---

[2] A 2005 challenge to the Howard government by federal Liberal backbencher Petro Georgiou and colleagues, resulted in some changes to immigration detention practices, including the release of children and long-term detainees.

could be proved that mandatory detention stopped the boats, it remains a flagrant breach of human rights obligations. Here the concept of proportionality is paramount where the policy response should be proportional to what it aspires to achieve.

Frank Brennan (2003, x) states that although it may be convenient for a government to keep people in detention while their asylum claims are being processed, the deprivation of liberty and the harm, especially to children, are disproportionate to the convenience. He says that the government has no problem in justifying initial detention of an unlawful entrant in order to satisfy health and security concerns, nor those awaiting removal who are deemed not to be refugees; the government's problem has been in establishing that ongoing detention is necessary to enable the government to process a refugee claim more fairly and more quickly, whereas the evidence reveals that detention in fact hinders quick and fair decision-making rather than assisting processing (Brennan 2003, 38).

Even the seemingly benign underpinnings of the purposes of detention have been debated, particularly the credence given to the necessity for detention for health and security checks, the need to contain people while their claims are processed and to prevent absconding. The length of time in which many people have been detained far exceeds the brief time needed for checks and there is no evidence that people need to held for processing for fear of absconding as most asylum seekers (those arriving with a valid travel document) live in the community without posing health and security threats and without absconding. The pursuit of goals of deterrence clearly sits alongside the concept of detention as punishment for those who have had the audacity to arrive on Australian shores without permission.

Moral breaches

Even if the spurious arguments of the necessity of strong deterrence measures have some essence of justification, there are questions of morality that need to be answered by the whole of society. Does it work? Does the perceived threat provide justification for the enormous financial costs of operating and maintaining the mandatory detention system? For Nauru, Manus Island (Papua New Guinea) and Christmas Island alone, the financial tally adds up to at least $1 billion since 2001. (Oxfam 2007). And what of the impact on the lives of those who have been detained? The detention of children is perhaps the worst insult to the deterrence rationale. Children arrive through no fault of their own. Even though they arrive because adults bring them here, they are held accountable and this reflects how Australia treats those who are innocent (Rogalla 2003). Former Federal Court judge, Marcus Einfeld (2006) asks "by what cruel standards of thinking do we empower ourselves to abuse and mistreat children who have already arrived here as a weapon to deter others who have not?"

Taking a broader view, Matthew Gibney (2004, 2) describes a kind of contradictory response that pervades Western responses to asylum seekers and refugees. He speaks of how all Western states have implemented over the last three decades an array of restrictions on those seeking asylum. Paradoxically, he points out, the measures adopted operate in a context where the states involved publicly speak of responsibilities to refugees. This applies within the Australian context where there are two competing traditions—one of generosity towards refugees and migrants, and one of xenophobia (Purcell 2001). Australia effectively divides refugees into categories of "good" and "bad" (Mares 2002, 25), rewarding the "deserving" (Pratt 2000). Good refugees are selected through an orderly humanitarian process and have entitlements. Those deemed unworthy undertake perilous journeys and are detained in the abomination of desert detention facilities as they proceed through the lengthy, arduous, confusing and unjust refugee determination system. Those successful at the end of this process are still punished through the granting of the limited category of temporary protection, described by some commentators as detention in the community (Marston 2003). It is the so-called boat people who "trigger the paranoia about defending our borders" (Steketee 2007). Although other countries use detention, Australia's policy of mandatory and indefinite detention is far more severe and inflexible than the measures imposed in countries with comparable legal and political systems (Mares 2002, 69).

Does detention deter?

There is little evidence that detention has, in fact, deterred asylum seekers. Unlawful arrivals to Australia have dropped dramatically (Crock, Saul and Dastyari 2006). This cannot be explained by the mandatory detention laws but is more the result of a global reduction in refugee outflows and asylum claims, as documented by the United Nations High Commission for Refugees. Combined with this has been increased border protection measures and surveillance (Crock, Saul and Dastyari 2006). In addition, the tyranny of geography (Gibney 2004, 195) is a key factor, as is disruption of smuggling rings (Gauthier 2005). Despite these facts, government policy continues unchanged, ignoring the oft-quoted words of

John Maynard Keynes who asked: "When the facts change, I change my mind—what do you do, sir?" (cited in Duffy 2005).

The stark reality is that those fleeing persecution are not deterred by mandatory detention. Generally they do not know of its existence and often know little of Australia before embarking on a journey to a destiny not usually of their own choosing. Testimony to the People's Inquiry into Immigration Detention—a citizen-driven inquiry—reveals little or inaccurate knowledge of what would happen on arrival. Fiske (2006) points out an even more disturbing way in which the deterrence argument is flawed including post-detention release on a temporary protection visa. With lawful means of family reunion unavailable to them, refugee families have attempted to be reunited through desperation. This saw an increase in the numbers of women and children undertaking the perilous boat crossing from Indonesia.

Duping the public

The Australian government's resolve is evident in a statement to the federal parliament in 2001 by Prime Minister Howard who shamelessly proposes the need to send:

> a message to people smugglers and others around the world that, whilst this is a humanitarian, decent country, we are not a soft touch and we are not a nation whose sovereign rights in relation to who comes here are going to be trampled on (cited in Brennan 2003, 43).

Conveniently for the government, asylum seeking and terrorism converge in the public view, particularly since the events in New York of September 11, 2001. It is in these "anxious times" that sovereignty is jealously guarded through the wielding of an iron fist against those who cross borders without seeking permission (Zagor 2007). We are led to believe that people arriving on leaky boats are, at worst, a threat to national security, or at best people we 'don't want in this country'. They are demonised when engaging in desperate practices of self-harm in immigration detention that are portrayed as primitive, aggressive and dangerous to us all. The term "not genuine refugees" has been twisted by the government and some sections of the media as an attempt to further discredit asylum seekers. As Hannah Arendt (1986, 269) tells us, refugees have been considered to be "the scum of the earth". There is no statement more telling than the following by Peter Reith (2001) at the time he was the Minister for Defence:

...I shouldn't make assumptions about that and I don't want to refer to any particular group of people by their ethnic background. But there is a simpler, broader point to make and it was in fact made by Jim Kelly the Assistant Secretary of State, the number two bloke to Colin Powell[3] responsible for our region, when he was in Jakarta only ten days ago and he said, the press reports were that he said, look you've got to be able to manage people coming into your country, you've got to be able to control that otherwise it can be a pipeline for terrorists to come in and use your country as a staging post for terrorist activities. Now that's in no reference to anybody's background, ethnic background, the Middle East or anything else. But you know that you couldn't get a clearer message and that is that if you can't control who comes into your country then that is a security issue. And that is one of the reasons why the Government is so determined to ensure that we can within the law manage the right of people to come into Australia.

Politicians and sections of the media successfully collude in portraying the myth that on-shore arrivals are "illegals" and that the only people truly deserving our compassion are those who have waited in a mythical queue and suffered in refugee camps while awaiting the outreached hand of compassion from the welcoming state, a hand that is only selectively forthcoming. Hence a picture of "order" is given as opposed to chaos that is engendered by unauthorised boat arrivals, who have little choice about the means by which they leave their countries and the manner in which they arrive. In this discourse a Politics of Fear pervades and harsh political leadership is seen to offer safety and security against unknown threats in what the public are cunningly convinced is a war on terror. As some of the excesses of the immigration detention regime have disappeared, such as the release of children and many long-term detainees, we are told that the so called war on terror could last for fifty years, hence preparing us to be fearful of strangers and to accept whatever policies the federal government has in store.

Unlike the criminology literature that extensively theorises the place of sentencing in deterring crime, the field of detention and deterrence is still embryonic. Critical theories of whiteness go some way to explaining the way "other" is constructed as deviant, dangerous and are applied in the current political context to those not wanting to assimilate and adopt Australian values. Hence locking people up who "we don't want here" keeps more of the unwelcome "other" away. Drawing on rational choice theory, Anna Pratt (2000) has undertaken a detailed analysis of the Canadian immigration and refugee policy regime including deterrence

---

[3] At that time, Colin Powell was the United States Secretary of State.

measures, an analysis that can be transposed to the Australian policy regime. She says (170) that by increasing the "costs" of coming to Canada through punitive crackdowns, even tougher legislation, more rigorous enforcement, interdiction initiatives and increased sanctions, the rational decision-maker will be dissuaded from choosing to come to Canada to abuse the system and endanger the public.

In her research on asylum seekers and deterrence in Australia, Lauren Gradstein (2006), also dispels the notion of rational choice in interviews with eighteen asylum seekers. She states that the assumptions underlying their detainment is that they are rational actors who choose to commit a criminal offence and that mandatory detention will deter other potential asylum seekers from coming to Australia unlawfully. The majority of her participants indicated that on leaving their country of origin they had not identified a particular country as their final destination. Their objective was to reach any safe country. Often they relied on the smuggler to transport them to a "safe" country, with no choice of destination. Stories were conveyed of false information on the likely outcomes being given to them by smugglers. The narratives revealed lack of awareness of the existence of detention camps before coming to Australia. As one said (106) "They didn't say they will put us in detention centres with barbed wire around us."

Stories told to the People's Inquiry reveal similar patterns. Many participants spoke of their reactions of shock at being detained, and especially for such a lengthy period. They had believed they would be quickly processed and afforded some rights, including reunification with family members they had left behind in their countries of origin. In hurriedly fleeing, there was little opportunity to contemplate what would happen on arrival. Fiske's analysis of why people came to Australia reinforces that it was the "push" factors rather than the pull factors of migration that were influential (Fiske 2006). She reinforces that asylum seeker decision-making was primarily driven by fear and the need to escape from a situation rather than looking at the repercussions, generally unknown, at destination. Decisions were made on the basis of immediate options available, often at the direction of a smuggler. Few people had anything other than a superficial knowledge of Australia and certainly very little information about its immigration and detention policies and practices.

Pratt speaks of a policy discourse framed in Canada around a numerical threat needing to be limited particularly in the name of "bogus" claims, the threat to national security and a criminal threat to public safety. Quoting a Canadian immigration authority:

An immigration program that is not properly controlled is vulnerable to abuses by criminals, terrorists and others who might jeopardize the safety and well-being of Canadians. In recent years we have seen the development of more organized, highly professional criminal networks intent on circumventing international and national laws ... (statement by Immigration Canada in 1992, cited in Pratt 2000, 144–55).

As in Australia, a culture of disbelief about the legitimacy of claims to asylum has been effectively created in Canada. This stands in stark contrast to the so-called genuine refugees who are acted upon socially, legally and political as deserving victims in need of protection and deserving of assistance (Pratt 2000). This pitting of one group against another is a deeply disturbing consequence of law, policy and practice. It remain baffling why, given the distrust that many Australians have of "truth in government,"[4] that the voices of dominant groups prevail over those who have experienced the reality of seeking asylum. Asylum seekers and their advocates face an uphill battle to convey the hardships faced.

Deterrence within detention and post-detention

The *threat* of detention is not only the only means of deterring asylum seekers. There are other ways in which detention has a deterrence framework by pressuring arrivals to return to the countries from which they fled. The first of these deterrence measures is through the acts people are subjected to in detention facilities and the second through the post-detention limitations imposed. These examples are further evidenced through the testimonies to the People's Inquiry and through compelling stories of refugee advocates (Mares and Newman 2007).

Within detention

The humiliation, abuses, rejection and uncertainty experienced by people in detention are increasingly reaching the public domain. One of the key deterrence methods used was to convince immigration detainees that Australians despised them and would never accept them. These tactics of fear and the subsequent breaking of the will of some people was too

---

[4] There have been many examples where federal government credibility has been challenged. These include the detaining of Australians in immigration detention facilities and the "children overboard" scandal whereby photographs were released that scurrilously depicted asylum seekers throwing their children overboard to achieve their ends.

much to endure, and they accepted meagre packages to return home, despairing, often ill and facing danger in their own countries. For those who refused such coercion, the gradual awareness of many Australians who became aware of what was happening inside detention facilities and extended the hand of friendship, mitigated the pressure to return.

Other tactics used in detention broke the spirit of many. Slight misdemeanours or acts of resistance could result in people being placed in "management". In these separate facilities, detainees were isolated from contact with others and were under constant surveillance. In the main compounds, wakenings at night through room checks caused exhaustion and fear. Immigration detainees speak of footsteps in the night that give rise to a belief that they could be on the "selection" for deportation, a practice that occurred at irregular hours.

The effect of detention on their children made people question remaining in detention to pursue their claims. Inadequacy of education, the witnessing of violence and self-harm and the loss of childhood effectively combined as deterrence factors.

The high rate of medication prescription, including anti-depressants and sleeping tablets, dulled the capacity of many to think rationally, a capacity that was already diminished by the experiences of detention which were triggers to severe depression and anxiety.

A story conveyed by a refugee supporter about a family arriving in Perth from the detention centre in Derby, in the far north of Western Australia, illustrates what they were now fortunate enough to leave behind. The story revolves around the simple act of sharing a meal of fish and chips in newspaper. The woman told her friend:

> This is the most important meal of my life. In the camp the guards said Australians hated us and we believed them. They said we would never belong here. But now sharing this meal with you, I see they were lying and I have hope for our future here (cited in Fiske 2006).

Post-release

Upon release from detention a raft of exclusionary provisions are put in place that can only be interpreted as ongoing punishment and a message of deterrence, with the underlying connotation of telling asylum seekers not too feel too comfortable or confident in their newly found freedom.

The difficult-to-obtain Bridging Visa E was sometimes provided for people who could demonstrate that they were so ill that they were being further harmed by the detention regime. These were among the cruellest of visa provisions for, on release, asylum seekers were excluded from the most basic of entitlements. They were not allowed to work and not entitled to social security provision; hence they were forced to rely on charity or from help from their Australian supporters, something that many found humiliating and that also placed them well below the poverty line. A denial of access to the universal health cover of Medicare was particularly devastating for those released with physical or mental illnesses. It resulted in asylum seekers and their advocates having to "shop around" for practitioners who would offer free treatment.

Temporary protection visas (TPVs) are considered by many as a policy scourge. Prior to October 1999 successful refugee claimants were granted permanent protection. After that date asylum seekers who arrived without authorisation or on false documentation were only entitled to a TPV (Fiske 2006), which was granted to the majority of those released from detention. One of the key hardships created by this visa is the denial of family reunion without the humanity of recognising that refugee families are frequently separated during flight (Fiske 2006). Years of separation from spouses and children resulted in some refugees being deterred from remaining in Australia, such was the pain of the suffering through this policy.

The Return Pending Bridging Visa that came into effect in August 2004 creates even greater uncertainty. Granted at the discretion of the Minister, this visa allows a person to remain in the community when all other channels have been exhausted while awaiting deportation or another determination (Mares and Newman 2007).

Building on what went before

It would be remiss not to locate the policies of the present in past constructions that sought to deter those of non-British origin from entry to Australia and to briefly examine how Australia has reached such a point where it can engage in the illegitimate act of locking away people in inhumane conditions. Australia's endeavours to be quintessentially British are evident in a history that saw Indigenous people not only excluded from society but hidden from public view on missions and reserves or in children's homes that were designed to assimilate. Throughout its post-colonial history a Politics of Fear has pervaded, whether directed at people from communist regimes in Asia (the "yellow peril") or Middle Eastern asylum seekers. Negative attitudes towards humanitarian refugees in some rural communities continue a discourse where newly arrived people from non-Western cultures are seen as problematic, usually framed as law-breakers, a discourse that creates hesitant communities and obstructs refugees from acceptance. Examples of non-British exclusion in recent times include offering only temporary shelter to Kosovars, with those who tried to stay being transferred from safe haven to immigration detention, and endeavours to return East Timorese to their country once it had been deemed safe, including children who had been born in Australia (Briskman 2007). The trajectory of exclusion continues. Adopting an increasingly ruthless stance, new provisions make conditions for citizenship more stringent, including the introduction of a nonsensical values test. Such measures will affect many refugees and continue to convey a monocultural message in what in composition has become a multicultural country.

British writer Arun Kundnani (2007, 3) offers some explanations. He suggests that the aggressively promoted stereotypes about asylum seekers reflect the West's anxieties and instead of understanding forced migration there is a fear that we are being overrun by people from other nations, with a silence on what the West inflicts on other countries. The persistence of these stereotypes depends on hiding from view the reality of what people are fleeing from.

Conclusion

Journalist Mike Steketee (2007) states that deterrence is all about politics and is not about policy. This was clearly exemplified in 2007 when the governments of Australia and the United States signed an unconscionable exchange deal, a Memorandum of Understanding, whereby asylum seekers incarcerated by the United States on Guantanamo Bay, Cuba could be exchanged for asylum seekers on Nauru. America and Australia were interested in this arrangement as it could have served the purpose of deterring people from seeking protection in their respective countries (Dastyari 2007). This policy was however, not implemented.

I conclude by again revisiting the question of the morality of a harsh regime that destroys people. Deterrence equates with exclusion, a phenomenon that pervades the Australian public policy discourse in terms of the unwanted who sit outside the citizenry and are not afforded the rights offered to "the deserving". Disturbingly, it is a component of what Richard Falk (2005, 225) describes as the descending spiral of human rights.

Furthermore, the policies of mandatory detention fly in the face of a reality that demonstrates that the benefits of granting refuge are significant for the nation (Legrain 2006; De Lorenzo 2007).

Considering that the vast majority of people detained in Australia are eventually granted refugee status, the question remains as to why detention is so strongly entwined in the nation's psyche and then overturned at a point where significant damage has been caused to the individual and the reputation of the country. There is little doubt that Australia will remain diminished as a nation until the policy of mandatory detention is eliminated.

References

Arendt, H. 1986. *The origins of totalitarianism*. London: Andre Deutsch.
Australian Council of Heads of Schools of Social Work (ACHSSW). 2006. *We've boundless plains to share: First report of the people's inquiry into detention*, Melbourne: ACHSSW.
Brennan, F. 2003. *Tampering with asylum: A universal humanitarian problem*. St Lucia: University of Queensland Press.
Briskman, L. 2007. Continuing exclusion: Asylum seekers and refugees in Australia. Paper presented at conference on Refugees and Empire, De Montfort University, Leicester.
Crock, M., B. Saul and A. Dastyari. 2006, *Future seekers II: Refugees and irregular migration in Australia*. Sydney: The Federation Press.
Dastyari, A. 2007. Trading in refugees. *On Line Opinion*, 28 May, http://www.onlineopinion.com.au/print.asp?article=5896, (accessed 1 June 2007).
Dawson, E. 2006. What the PM owes to Hansonism. *The Age*, 8 September.
De Lorenzo, M. 2007. The accountability gap in refugee protection. Keynote address at the National Network Conference of the US Committee for Refugees and Immigrants, Washington, 23 May.
Duffy, M. 2005. Policy where facts are foreign. *Sydney Morning Herald*, 20 August.
Einfeld, M. 2006. *Address to the ACT launch of the People's Inquiry into Immigration Detention*, Australian Catholic University, 4 May.
Falk, R. 2005. Human rights: A descending spiral. In *Human rights in the war on terror*. ed. R. A. Wilson, New York: Cambridge University Press, 2005.
Fiske, L. 2006. Australia's TPV policy: Inhumane, exclusionary and unnecessary, unpublished paper, Perth: Curtin University Centre for Human Rights Education.

Gauthier, K. 2005. *Presentation to the People's Inquiry into Immigration Detention*, Sydney: Australian Council of Heads of Schools of Social Work.

Gibney, M. J. 2004. *The ethics and politics of asylum: Liberal democracy and the response to refugees*. Cambridge: Cambridge University Press.

Goddard, C. and B. Saunders. 2001. Journalists as agents and language as an instrument of social control, *Children Australia*, vol. 26, no. 2, 26–30.

Gradstein, L. 2006. Questioning deterrence policies in the mandatory detainment of asylum seekers, unpublished Doctor of Psychology (Forensic) thesis, Deakin University, January.

Howard, J. 2001. Statement to the House of Representatives, August 2001, cited in Brennan, F. 2003. *Tampering with asylum: A universal humanitarian problem*. St Lucia: University of Queensland Press.

Kaldor, A. 2002. A pragmatic approach to immigration. *Quadrant*, vol. xlvi, no. 3, March, http://quadrant.org.au/php/archive_details_list.php?article_id=677, (accessed 17 August 2007).

Kundnani, A. 2007. *The end of tolerance: Racism in 21st century Britain*. London: Pluto Press.

Legrain, P. 2006. *Immigrants: Your country needs them*. London: Little, Brown.

Mares, P. 2002. *Borderline: Australia's response to refugees and asylum seekers in the wake of the Tampa*, second edn, Sydney: UNSW Press.

Mares, P. and L. Newman. 2007. *Acting from the heart: Australian refugee advocates for asylum seekers tell their stories*. Sydney: Finch Publishing.

Marston, G. 2003. *Temporary Protection Permanent Uncertainty: The experience of refugees living on temporary protection visas*. Melbourne: Centre for Applied Social Research, RMIT University.

Odowski, S. 2003. Immigration detention—The current position. Speech delivered at the Monash Institute for the Study of Global Movements, Monash University, Clayton, 10 October. http://www.humanrights.gov.au/speeches/human_rights/immdetention.htm, (accessed 8 October 2006).

Oxfam. 2007. *A price too high: The cost of Australia's approach to asylum seekers*, August, Carlton and Glebe: Oxfam and A Just Australia.

Pratt, A. 2000. A political anatomy of detention and deportation in Canada, PhD thesis. Graduate Centre of Criminology, University of Toronto.

Purcell, M. 2001. Xenophobia fuels Australia refugee problem, *Anglican Media*, October.

Reith, P. 2001. *Transcript of the Hon Peter Reith MP radio interview with Derryn Hinch—3AK*, http://www.minister.defence.gov.au/ReithSpeechtpl.cfm?CurrentId=999 (accessed 16 August 2007).

Rogalla, B. 2003. Modern-day torture: Government-sponsored neglect of asylum seeker children under the Australian mandatory immigration detention regime. *Journal of South Pacific Law*, vol. 7, no. 1, http://www.paclii.org/journals/fJSPL/vol07no1/11.shtml (accessed 17 September 2007).

Steketee, M. 2007. Return to sender, *The Australian*, 1 March.

Taylor, S. 2006. Immigration detention reforms: A small gain in human rights. *Agenda*, vol. 13, no. 1, 49–62.

Whyte, J. 2003. Life in the camp: Giorgio Agamben and Australia's mandatory detention of asylum seekers, unpublished Bachelor of Social Science (Hons) thesis, RMIT University, Melbourne.

Zagor, M. 2007. The Dark Age art of punitive detention. *Canberra Times*, 19 March. http://law.anu.edu.au/cipl/Expert%20Opinion/2007/M%20Zagor_19Mar07_The%20Canberra%20Times.pdf (accessed 10 December 2007).

Chapter Ten

New Racisms and Asylum Seekers in Australia

Hurriyet Babacan and Narayan Gopalkrishnan

Introduction

This chapter focuses on new racisms that have emerged in Australia and their negative impact on asylum seekers. After broadly defining new racisms, the characteristics of new racisms will be discussed in the context of impacting upon asylum seekers. These characteristics include the close linking of new racisms to the promotion of fear of the "other", Islamophobia, the promotion of new forms of citizenship rights and new definitions of Australian identity. It is argued that the negative portrayal of asylum seekers to justify the Australian government's policies relating to border control and the war on terror has resulted in the racialisation of asylum seeker issues and has resulted in their victimisation, demonisation and social exclusion and has contributed to increased levels of fear and insecurity at the broader community level. In the meantime, there has been a total silence on issues of racism and an official denial that racism exists.

New racisms

Racism is a set of beliefs and behaviours that presumes that "races" are inherently different and so excludes certain groups from equal access to social goods. In the past, those differences were often linked to assumed genetic or physical difference. In many cases today, the differences are expressed in terms of supposedly incompatible lifestyles or cultural or religious values. Racism changes its forms and meanings in different historical contexts. These forms are multiple, historically specific, situationally variable and often contradictory. They also are gendered, and interconnect with nationalist and religious identities in complex ways (Hollinsworth 2006).

Racism defines the way in which social relations between people are structured and operates through a range of personal, relational, systemic and institutional practices that serve to devalue, exclude, oppress or exploit people. It is an act of power and is a tool for maintaining privilege. It involves the process of categorising certain groups or individuals as inferior through the use of economic, social or political power that legitimates exploitation or exclusion (Mac an Ghaill 1999).

The adoption of multiculturalism as policy in Australia in 1973 led to the recognition of the ethnicity, culture, religion and language of ethnic minorities. Over time, the "old racism" in which ethnic communities were viewed as inferior was largely replaced by "new racism". New racisms are concerned with a broader understanding of race issues as they relate to:

- cultural dimensions of racism;
- linkages with identity, ethnic signifiers or markers;
- construction of whiteness, invisibility of white majority;
- racism's treatment of subgroups, e.g. asylum seekers;
- interconnections between race, nationhood, patriotism and nationalism;
- changing language and discourses of racism (Solomos & Back 1996).

In common with old racism, the new racism still maintains the relationship of power based on constructing "others" as different in order to exclude, ignore or exploit them. The power to represent others, to negatively evaluate others and to make these representations and evaluations prevail in public domains are still key features of new racisms.

With the advent of this form of racism, ethnic communities are differentiated as being a threat to the cultural integrity of the Anglo-Celtic host society (Dunn et al. 2004). Questions as to who does or does not "belong" to Australian society, and who or what is not "Australian" are integral aspects of the intolerance to some groups and the new racism in Australia (Dunn et al. 2004). Racism has been located in different settings such as individual, institutional, informal, formal, direct and indirect. A number of writers note that racism now is often not demonstrated by direct acts of hostility but rather by more covert comments relating to moral character, alien cultural values and lifestyles (Pedersen et al. 2004; Fraser and Islam 2000). Racism is not only reflected in events such as the "race riots" which took place in Cronulla in 2005 (Babacan 2006) but includes the ordinary "everyday" racisms, silently experienced by individuals and communities (Essed 1991).

While racism can permeate social structures, the invisibility of racism makes it seem normal and neutral. Thus by saying, "It is their culture," there is the creation of the chain of equivalence to substitute "race" with "culture". This leads to new forms of racisms—cultural racisms with arguments that cultural differences are insurmountable. There is the normal and the ones that do not fit into the norm, creating categories of new "others". This often leads to public or popular anxieties about "alien" cultures or cultural practices and concerns about "integration" and threat to lifestyles. "Rednecks" are viewed as the extreme end of society, and to have nothing to do with us. Messages about particular groups are hidden or coded, which results in the failure to see the racialised practices of "everyday racism" (Essed 1991).

Aspects of new racisms and asylum seekers

The new racisms in Australia not only encompass a changing definition of race, but are also closely linked to the promotion of fear of the "other" and Islamophobia. It is characterised by new forms of citizenship rights and new definitions of Australian identity. The official denial of the existence of racism has meant that there is a general absence of victim support.

Changing definitions of "race" and resort to fear of the "other"

As noted above, the concept of "race" has expanded to incorporate "culture" and "religion". There is evidence of discrimination and prejudice occurring on the basis of difference in culture and religion (Gopalkrishnan and Babacan 2007). The government has portrayed asylum seekers as a "threat" to be "feared".

An important aspect of the new racism is that it is often closely linked to fear of the "other". The use of fear to bring people together against a real or imagined enemy is not a new tool in the hands of the elite. It is not restricted to use by governments and many political and religious leaders over the centuries and across the world have used fear to draw their in-groups together (Gopalkrishnan 2003). Wars are a manifestation of this and the anthropologist, Desmond Morris, describes this as:

> ...one could say that nothing helps a leader like a good war. It gives him his only chance of being a tyrant and being loved for it at the same time. He can introduce the most ruthless forms of control and send thousands of

his followers to their deaths and still be hailed as a great protector. Nothing ties tighter the in-group bonds than an out-group threat (Morris 1969, 33).

The "war on terror" in the post–September 11 environment can be viewed in this context as a never-ending engagement with a threat that is invisible and yet always present. The role of the media in creating an atmosphere of fear is crucial and is well facilitated by the highly concentrated ownership of the media and the global nature of media networks (Appadurai 1990). The messages of fear become even more ominous when they are targeted on racial lines that frequently occur in the media (Stratton 1998).

Gopalkrishnan (2005) developed the word *Infeartainment* as one that represents the use of fear, as spectacle and narrative, by the powerful, to contain the population while also providing them with entertainment as a form of distraction. In today's world, infeartainment can be seen in numerous media circuses, including the invasions of Iraq and Afghanistan, as well as the September 11 attacks on the Twin Towers (Gopalkrishnan and Babacan 2007; Kellner 2003a). At another level, infeartainment presents as a grand narrative of fear of the "other", where it provides a simple and easily understood view of an increasingly complex world involving sub-narratives of "Good" versus "Evil", "Civilisation" versus the "Savage" (Kellner 2003b).

The narratives are clearly visible in the Australian government's negative portrayal of asylum seekers to justify its asylum policies. The fall of communism and economic restructuring in Australia between the 1980s and into the post-2000 period resulted in migration and asylum becoming highly politicised through respective Australian governments' deliberate exaggeration of the arrival of asylum seekers. This period witnessed the enactment of harsh legislative measures designed to deter and prevent asylum seekers from arriving on Australia's shores. These measures included mandatory detention, new offences for migrant trafficking, the Temporary Protection Visa and the Pacific Solution which excised certain islands from Australia's immigration law (Human Rights Watch 2002; Brennan 2003; Manne and Corlett 2004). The blocking of the asylum route through comprehensive border control policies together with the Australian government's resort to the politics of fear, achieved largely by the conjoining of security matters with asylum policy through discursive labelling, has served to recast asylum seekers in the public mind. The government discourses have been presented in binary form: "good" versus "evil", "legal" versus "illegal" or "genuine" versus "non-genuine". By the post-2000 period, the status of asylum seekers has been lowered from a person worthy of respect and therefore assistance, to people who "associate" with people smugglers, criminals and even terrorists in the post–September 11 climate.

Islamophobia

Since the events of September 11 and the London and Bali bombings, racial violence and discrimination have increased against Muslim communities. This is referred to as *Islamophobia*. Over the last ten years, the climate for refugees, asylum seekers and particular groups of immigrants has become more and more unwelcoming. In pushing its harsh asylum and counter-terrorism policies the Howard government has deliberately and persistently negatively portrayed Arabs and Muslims as the "other" with the effect of demonising and dehumanising them (Poynting and Noble 2004; Howie 2005). This has been accompanied by the portrayal of this group to appear "responsible" for "threatening" Australian values and Australian identity.

There is considerable evidence in Australia that fear and hatred against Muslims has also increased. Collins (2006) notes that there is a strong correlation between the social construction of ethnic crime and a fear of the stranger or the "other". Immigrants and asylum seekers from "Middle Eastern" backgrounds have been the victims of "criminalisation discourse", with a central role being played by both the media and opportunistic politicians in the perpetuation of such discourses. The construction of the "Middle Eastern" as "other" results in the criminalisation of cultural difference that is portrayed as a threat to not only the legal order but also the moral and social order. This in turn created prejudicial stereotypes, fear of ethnic minorities and a concern for safety (Collins 2006). The report by HREOC (2004) documents instances of attacks on "Muslim/Middle Eastern" communities since the events of September 11 across Australia.

The Australian government's strong anti-Muslim sentiments were not accidental. Former prime minister Howard, in talking about Muslims, stated that:

> I do think there is this particular fragment which is utterly antagonistic to our kind of society and that is a difficulty and … I think some of the associated attitudes towards women are a problem (*The Australian*, 20 February 2006, 1).

He repeatedly warned "sections of the Islamic community" that they must learn English and Australian core values, assimilate, stop abusing "their" women and supporting "terrorist" groups (ABC 2006, The

Australian 2006). The government was greatly assisted by the media in this.

In creating the "Muslim" or "Middle Eastern" other, the "perpetrators" involved and their perceived communities, depend on the racist imagining of a supposedly homogeneous category that includes those of Arab or Middle Eastern or Muslim background. The discourse takes no account of the fact that the singular descriptions used such as Middle Eastern or Muslim includes people of diverse ancestries, countries and very distinct histories. Furthermore, whole communities are blamed for criminal acts. Many from minority communities are made to "stand for" or represent the whole group.

The flipside of this burden of representativeness is the common linking of the criminal behaviour of an individual to the "essential nature" of the community or group to which that individual belongs. This extrapolation is almost never made when the individual is Anglo-Celtic, but is very common for 'pariah groups' (ADB 2003; Poynting and Noble 2004). Additionally, by labelling as "deviant" certain actions—such as seeking asylum, wearing veils or scarves—there is a reinforcement of the fear of certain groups (Collins 2006; Hage 2002; Poynting and Noble 2004). Particularly since September 11, the so-called unmanageability and undesirability of people from the Middle East has been common in populist media discourses (Saniotis 2004; Koo 2005). These discourses have also adversely impacted on asylum seekers from the Middle East. Most of the boat people arriving in Australia during the 1990s and into 2001 were of Islamic backgrounds (mainly from Afghanistan, Iran, Iraq, Bangladesh and Pakistan). A convenient connection was made by the Australian government between asylum seekers and terrorists in public discourse. Muslims asylum seekers were portrayed as a collective group, to be feared and treated with suspicion and not deserving of assistance that should be granted to refugees selected by the Australian government as part of its offshore refugee program.

New forms of citizenship rights

Citizenship rights are the civil, political and social rights of individuals living within a nation state. The new forms of institutional racisms are hidden and subtle and divide people based on strict criteria linked to definitions of immigration categories. These are driven by particular philosophies that determine who are "deserving" and who are "not deserving" of rights and who "belong" and who "do not belong" within the nation. McCulloch (2004) points out that the reduction of services and programs has been replaced by the promotion of security and/or safety. Governments now seek to implement a new kind of security and identity bargain to substitute for the insecurities and anxieties created by the erosion of government programs and services. Groups or individuals (e.g. youth, asylum seekers, refugees) who were once considered as being "at risk" and considered as requiring the support of the state are now portrayed as groups or individuals who are a "risk" to society (McCulloch 2004). Citizenship and belonging are portrayed as a privilege rather than a right. The social consequence is that a sense of anxiety and insecurity is created among the community (McCulloch 2004). Solutions to this anxiety are presented in the form of coercive legislation and a powerful political campaign that "emphasises a return through cultural renewal to a more secure—often mythical—idea of community" (Jayasuriya 2006, 3).

Moreover, the debates on citizenship have been reduced to attempts at defining and tightening the legal elements of being a citizen. This has meant a move towards legalistic definitions of citizenship and less emphasis on normative definitions. The normative notion of citizenship not only deals with legal citizenship rights, but also how less advantaged people in a given community should be treated. Thus, increasingly citizenship is a tool with which people assert their sovereignty and restrict certain peoples' access to social and economic resources (Weekley 1999).

Australia has been at the forefront in curtailing the settlement services, entitlements and social rights available to asylum seekers. Asylum seekers who have been portrayed as "unworthy" of Australia's assistance have been denied numerous rights which should have been granted to them. For example, Temporary Protection Visa (TPV) holders (Subclass 785) were not entitled to many of the settlement services which were provided to refugees who entered Australia with "authorisation", such as English classes, the full range of health services and extensive range of employment assistance programs. They were not eligible for assistance with orientation, accommodation and household formation and had to pay full fees if they wished to study at university (Manne and Corlett 2004; Corlett 2002). Similarly, the two new temporary visa categories which were created in 2001 (the Secondary Movement Offshore Entry (Temporary) Subclass XB447 and the Secondary Movement Relocation (Temporary) Subclass 451) (DIMIA 2002) provide for differential treatment by encouraging asylum seekers to remain in their own countries and provide for a hierarchy of benefits depending on where the asylum seeker made their application and whether they moved from a country of first asylum (DIMIA 2002).

New definitions of Australian identity

Identity gives us an idea of who we are and how we relate to others who share a particular position and those who are different. Identities are constructed on the back of recognition of common origins, shared characteristics with another person or group and the natural formation of solidarity and allegiance established on this foundation (Woodward 1997). The process of globalisation and the trans-nationalisation of economic and cultural life have broken the old structures of national states and communities (Beck 2000). Disposable products designed for immediate obsolescence have replaced the world of durable objects. In such a world identities are also utilised, adopted and discarded. The processes of globalisation have caused fragmentation and dislocation of individuals. Thus contemporary society is characterised by a move away from class-based political allegiances such as trade unions, to the rise of other arenas of social conflict such as those of gender, "race", ethnicity or sexuality (Laclau 1990). The cultural homogeneity promoted by global marketing leads to different and contradictory outcomes:

a) detachment of identity from community and place;
b) reaffirmation of national or local ethnic identities; and
c) the emergence of new identity positions
(Westwood and Phizacklea 2000; Du Gay et al. 2000).

Today the stereotypical images of the stranger as asylum seeker, migrant or refugee often precede the arrival of migrants through the media and other networks. This sets the scene in context for negotiating identity.

In contemporary post-colonial societies such as Australia, both the colonisers and the colonised peoples have responded by a renewed search for ethnic certainties. Some previously marginalised ethnic groups have resisted their exclusion within their host societies by reasserting their identities of origin. On the other hand, among dominant groups in these societies there is also an ongoing search for old ethnic identities and the nostalgia for more culturally homogenous states such as "Englishness" or "Irishness" and for a return to "good old family values" (Woodward 1997). The search for identity has created contestations that seek justification for the forging of new and future identities. Often these justifications take the form of bringing up past origins, traditions, mythologies and boundaries and create new forms of *patriotisms* that exclude anyone who does not conform to them. The boundaries are particularly contested at the level of national identity and the desperate production of a unique and homogenous national identity. *Fear* (of difference, of loss) is at the heart of the question of identity and results in the nationalist affirmation of one group over another.

There is a unilateral debate happening, driven mainly by the nation state and aided by the media, on what constitutes Australian values. The Federal government mainly drives these discourses without appropriate processes for public participation. There is an attempt to construct Australian identity in particular ways. National identity is constructed as a particular "way of life", a particular set of values represented by those who are white and of Anglo-Saxon or Celtic backgrounds (Markus 2001), excluding ethnic or Indigenous identities based on a set of values and imagery. For example, the creation of Australian identity based on images, such as "Simpson and his donkey", build a particular image of what it means to be Australian—mainly white and masculine. The exotic appeals are through food, clothing, crafts, folk dancing and other cultural elements. These are non-threatening to social structures and provide token evidence of a pluralistic society (Rizvi 1994).

The depiction of asylum seekers as people abusing and threatening us shapes the discourse of nationalism ... "Un-Australian" draws lines of acceptability—delineating what is regarded as reasonable, proper and decent forms of public speech and behaviour. Who is an Australian, what are Australian values, what makes up the Aussie battler and what is "unAustralian" have been redefined. Regular pronouncements by the Prime Minister, other ministers and media celebrities "license" such abuses. Alongside statements that exclude or "other" minority racial or religious groups, powerful discourses invoke images of meritorious Aussie "battlers" or ordinary Australians who deserve more respect and more support. As Johnson observed, "ordinary Australians are not Aboriginal, Asian, homosexual, lesbian, feminist or migrant" (Johnson 2000, 64–5).

One month prior to the November 2001 federal election, the Australian government hit the electorate, through the media, with the electrifying information, backed up by blurred visual images, that a boatload of "illegal refugees" had threatened to throw, and in some cases had thrown, their children into the sea as a threat against interception by the Australian navy. It was dubbed the "Children Overboard" incident. The Minister for Foreign Affairs stated:

> These people had behaved abominably right from the start. The disgraceful way they treat their own children. Any civilised person would never dream of treating their own children that way (cited in Corlett 2002).

The prime minister added: "I tell you—I don't want people like that in Australia. Genuine refugees don't do that" (Markus 2002). The media circus that ensued continually presented the basic position of dehumanising the asylum seekers and presenting them as people without the core values of love and caring for family (Glover 2003). Although a Senate Select Committee later examined the entire incident and the accusations and found these to be incorrect, the narrative played its part in swaying the electorate during the 2001 Federal election (Gopalkrishnan 2005).

Denial of racism

Racism is often downplayed or explained as something else, less deliberate or oppressive, such as cultural misunderstanding by those who are not subject to its violence and belittling (Hollinsworth 2006, 40–5). Dunn et al. (2004) note that there is a privilege of whiteness that is associated with a way of life and a perspective where racism is unseen or is considered an exceptional aberration. Often, racism is couched in soft language, equating it with community relations or harmony. This fails to address fundamental issues about discriminatory behaviour and action (Stratton 1998). There has been a reluctance to engage with root causes of racism by government and political leaders as it is seen as touching a "sensitive nerve" in their electorates. The denial of racism is very obvious. In commenting on the Cronulla riots, the prime minister denied that there was any racism underlying the events. Poynting and Noble (2004) argue that Howard's purposeful refusal to accept race as a cause of the riots ignored the reality that racism played a central role in the incidents and that the state's refusal to act on this is a clear message that there is state "permission to hate".

Documenting racism has been a difficult task in Australia. Governments have been reluctant to fund research relating to racism. While there are bodies that record complaints of racism in Australia, many are reluctant to report complaints for a range of reasons including fear of authority, lack of information about rights, lack of English language skills, fear of the consequences of complaining, lack of support systems to assist with complaints and lack of belief in the efficacy of systems of redress and feeling that complaints will not change things (Babacan 1998; HREOC 2004).

The denial of racism fails to validate victims' experiences and blames the victim for their failure to "fit in". In the case of asylum seekers, they have little recourse for action. Taking legal proceedings in a court with federal jurisdiction is limited in terms of the outcomes and can be costly. Institutional processes are portrayed as fair and neutral for the "protection" of Australia. There is a denial by the Australian government that its asylum policies breach human rights, that it is acting in a manner which is discriminatory or that the processes employed in deterring and interdicting asylum seekers form institutional racism. This leaves asylum seekers as victims of institutional and silent racism. The power of silence or denial is often described as a form of oppression as noted by Stokes:

> A person or group of people can suffer real damage, real distortion if the people or society around them mirror back to them a confining or demeaning or contemptible picture of themselves. Non-recognition or mis-recognition can inflict harm, can be a form of oppression, imprisoning someone in a false, distorted and reduced mode of being (Stokes 1997, 19).

The denial and silence on racism ensure that there are no policy responses to address the consequences of racism. There is an absence of adequate processes to provide validation of the experiences of those who experienced racism on a daily basis and consequently, a lack of any attempt redress their suffering (Babacan 2006).

Service providers and policy makers often see racism as an aberration by the victim and its presence and occurrence are downplayed. This results in the lack of validation of suffering and damage caused to victims of racism and more importantly it results in the lack of support to victims of abuse caused by racism. This partially explains why there are no specialist support services for victims of racial abuse. Although Australia has victim-centred support services in many areas of abuse, such as child-centred child protection services and survivor-centred domestic and family violence services, there is a huge gap in victim-centred approaches to people who experience racism. Although there are legislative bodies that work against racism and victims can complain there, these processes are highly legalistic and many people do not have the confidence, skills or willingness to complain.

Conclusion

Government policies and public comments from key social figures signify a retreat from the spirit of multiculturalism and the Refugee Convention and provide tacit approval of racist behaviour. The treatment of asylum seekers in Australia is part of a large "race politics" that has burdened this country since its white colonisation. This ordinariness is because racism often goes unchallenged and becomes pervasive throughout our society and in our daily lives. Individual instances of racism are seen as unimportant or trivial or having occurred due to a lack of good manners, thereby ignoring the effects of their frequent reiteration. These ordinary and unremarked manifestations of racism need to named and emphasised (Hollinsworth 2006).

The Howard government's moving away from multiculturalism and cultural diversity has weakened the fabric of society. This, in turn, has led to racial and ethnic intolerance. As anthropologist Ghassan Hage observes:

> Violent racists are always a tiny minority. However, their breathing space is determined by the degree of "ordinary" non-violent racism a government and culture allow to flourish within it (Hage 2002, 247).

Racism needs to be tackled at the local, regional and national levels and the Commonwealth government's deliberate and negative portrayal of asylum seekers, and Muslims as the "other" needs to be replaced with policies that are more accommodating and inclusive. There is now, more than ever before, a need for Australia to adhere to its obligations under the Refugee Convention and for it to develop a more inclusive multiculturalism that is based on social justice, human rights and citizenship.

References

ABC (Australian Broadcasting Corporation). 2006. World after September 11, "Five Years",
http://www.abc.net.au/4corners/content/2006/s1738419.htm.
ADB (Anti-Discrimination Board). 2003. *Race for the headlines: Racism and media discourse.* Sydney: Anti-Discrimination Board of NSW.
Appadurai, A. 1990. Disjuncture and difference in the global cultural economy. In *Global culture: Nationalism, globalization and modernity.* ed. M. Featherstone. London: Sage Publications.
Australian, The. 2006. Opinion, 20 February 2006, 9.
Babacan, H. 1998. *I still call Australia home: An exploration of issues relating to settlement and racism.* Brisbane: Centre for Multicultural and Pastoral Care.
—. 2006. Racism and multiculturalism. In *Responding to Cronulla: Rethinking multiculturalism.* ed. N. Gopalkrishnan and S. H. Toh, 59–76. Brisbane: University of the Sunshine Coast and Griffith University. http://www.usc.edu.au/Research/Centres/CMCD/Responding+to+Cronulla.htm
Beck, U. 2000. *What is globalization?* Cambridge: Polity Press.

Brennan, F. 2003. *Tampering with asylum: A universal humanitarian problem*. Brisbane: University of Queensland Press.
Collins, J. 2006. Ethnic gangs, ethnic conflict and the Cronulla beach riots in Proceedings from the National Symposium Responding to Cronulla: Rethinking Multiculturalism, University of the Sunshine Coast and Griffith University, 59–76,
http://www.usc.edu.au/Research/Centres/CMCD/Responding+to+Cronulla.htm (accessed 5 April 2007).
Corlett, D. 2002. Asylum seekers and the new racism. *Dissent*, no. 8, Autumn–Winter, 46–7.
Department of Immigration Multicultural and Indigenous Affairs (DIMIA). 2002. *Fact sheet no. 65: The new humanitarian visa*, www.immi.gov.au/facts/65humanitarian.htm (accessed 29 September 2002).
Du Gay, P., J. Evans and P. Redman. 2000. *Identity: A reader*. London: Sage Publications.
Dunn, K., J. Forrest, I. Burnley and A. McDonald. 2004. Constructing racism in Australia. *Australian Journal of Social Issues*, November, vol. 39, no. 4, 409–30
Essed, P. 1991. *Understanding everyday racism: An interdisciplinary theory*. New York: Sage.
Fraser, C. and M. Islam. 2000. Social identification and political preferences for One Nation: The role of symbolic racism. *Australian Journal of Psychology*, vol. 52 (3), 131–7.
Ghosh, B. 2000. *Managing migration: The need for a new international regime*. Oxford: Oxford University Press.
Glover, D. 2003. *Orwell's Australia*. Victoria: Scribe Publications.
Gopalkrishnan, N. 2003. Fear, diversity and the globalisation paradigm. *International Journal of Diversity in Organisations, Communities and Nations*, vol. 3, 601–09.
—. 2005. In-Fear-Tainment: The convergence of fear, diversity and governance. *International Journal of Diversity in Organisations, Communities and Nations*, vol. 5, no. 2, 85–90.
Gopalkrishnan, N. and H. Babacan. 2007. *Racisms in the New World Order: Realities of culture, colour and identity*, Newcastle, UK: Cambridge Scholars Publishing.
Hage, G. 2002. *Arab-Australians: Citizenship and belonging today*. Melbourne: Melbourne University Press.
Hollinsworth, D. 2006. *Race and racism in Australia*, third edn, Melbourne: Thomson and Social Science Press.

Howie, L. 2005. The threat of terrorism and social change. *Human Rights Defender*, Special Issue, 2005.

Human Rights and Equal Opportunity Commission (HREOC). 2004. *Ismae—listen: National consultations on eliminating prejudice against Arab and Muslim Australians*. Sydney: Human Rights and Equal Opportunity Commission.

Human Rights Watch. 2002. *Not for export. Why the international community should reject Australia's refugee policies. Human Rights Watch briefing paper*, http://www.hrw.org/press/2002/09/ausbrf0926, (accessed 22 February 2007).

Jayasuriya, K. 2006. *Howard, Tampa and the politics of reactionary modernisation*, www.australianreview/2003/03/jayasuriya.html (accessed 23 March 2007).

Johnson, C. 2000 *Governing change: From Keating to Howard*. St Lucia: University of Queensland Press.

Kellner, D. 2003a. *Media spectacle*. New York: Routledge.

—. 2003b. *From 9/11 to terror war: Dangers of the Bush legacy*. Colorado: Rowman and Littlefield.

Koo, K. L. 2005. Terror Australis: Security, Australia and the "War on Terror" discourse. *Borderlands eJournal*, vol. 4, no. 1, 2005, (accessed 23 August 2007).

Laclau, E. 1990. *New reflections on the revolution of our time*. London: Verso.

Mac an Ghaill, M. 1999. *Contemporary racisms and ethnicities: Social and cultural transformations*. Buckingham: Open University Press.

Manne, R. and D. Corlett. 2004. Sending them home. Refugees and the new politics of indifference. *Quarterly Essay*. Melbourne: Black Inc.

Markus, A. 2001. *Race, John Howard and the remaking of Australia*. Crows Nest: Allen and Unwin.

—. 2002. Race politics. Paper presented at Beyond Tolerance: National Convention on Racism, http:www.hreoc.gov.au/racialdiscrimination/beyond_tolerance/speeches/markus.html.

McCulloch, J. 2004. *National insecurity politics in Australia: Fear and the federal election*, www.statewatch.org/analyses/no-30-jude-mcculloch.pdf, (accessed 27 April 2007).

Morris, D. 1969. *The human zoo*. London: Corgi Books.

Pedersen, A., J. Beven, I. Walker and B. Griffiths. 2004. Attitudes towards indigenous Australians: The role of empathy and guilt. *Journal of Community and Applied Social Psychology*, vol. 14, 233–49.

Poynting, S. and G. Noble. 2004. *The experience and reporting by Arab and Muslim Australians of discrimination, abuse and violence since September 2001*. Report to the Human Rights and Equal Opportunity Commission, 19 April 2004, www.hreoc.gov.au/racial_discrimination/isma/research/index.html, (accessed 17 March 2007).

Rizvi, F. 1994. The arts, education and the politics of multiculturalism. In *Culture, difference and the arts.* ed. S. Gunew and F. Rizvi. Sydney: Allen and Unwin.

Saniotis, A. 2004. Embodying ambivalence: Muslim Australians as other. *Journal of Australian Studies*, no. 82, 49–61.

Solomos, J. & L. Back. 1996. *Racism and society.* London: Macmillan.

Stokes, G., ed. 1997. *The politics of identity in Australia.* Cambridge: Cambridge University Press.

Stratton, J. 1998. *Race daze: Australia in identity crisis.* Annandale: Pluto Press.

Weekley, K. 1999. Introduction. In *Globalisation and citizenship in the Asia Pacific.* ed. A. Davidson and K. Weekley, 3–4. London: Macmillan.

Westwood, S. and A. Phizacklea. 2000. *Trans-nationalism and the politics of belonging.* London: Routledge.

Woodward, K. ed. 1997. *Culture, media and identities: Identity and difference.* London: Sage Publications.

CHAPTER ELEVEN

THE FUTURE FOR ASYLUM SEEKERS IN A CHANGING WORLD

ALPERHAN BABACAN AND LINDA BRISKMAN

Introduction

Although the Refugee Convention has been historically concerned with the persecutory actions of states, the preceding chapters have demonstrated that over the last decade, measures of surveillance, information sharing and deterrence of the "unauthorised" movement of people have increased across developed nations. Border security has come to dominate state preoccupation to deflect the protection needs of asylum seekers. Most Western states have implemented a raft of measures directed at deterring and keeping out asylum seekers who seek to invoke the states' protection obligations. These measures include carrier sanctions, detention, the imposition of visa requirements on refugee-producing states, the placement of immigration officials in overseas airports and ports, intercepting asylum seekers to prevent their entering into the territory of the state, forced deportation, rebuttal of the principle of refoulement through provision of inadequate avenues to apply for refugee status, extra-territorial determination systems and processing, safe third country determinations, and the removal of judicial review rights (Morris 2003; Sianni 2003; Tazreiter 2003). Further, in recent times, asylum seekers who arrive at the shores of industrially developed states are rendered as illegal and deviant through state discourses and subjected to law and order practices (Pickering 2005). This has been amply demonstrated throughout the book, in particular in the chapters written by Babacan and Gopalkrishnan, McCulloch and Briskman.

Interdiction and interception frequently result in arbitrary detention and the adoption of measures which do not leave asylum seekers with proper and adequate procedures to make an asylum claim or to seek civil remedies. As Dastyari and Taylor have, for example, demonstrated, extra-territorial protection in the form of third country processing centres (such as Australia's Pacific Solution) and regional protection areas work to de-territorialise the protection provided to asylum seekers. In the process, such measures not only constitute a retreat from the Refugee Convention, but also shift the burden to developing countries, come at a high economic cost to the state and leave asylum seekers in limbo both in terms of their human rights and their civil rights.

The Refugee Convention, sovereignty and interdiction

The Refugee Convention continues to be an important legal instrument to protect the rights of asylum seekers facing persecution. The Convention-based rights regime is significant as it sets a minimum standard for the treatment of refugees and provides a moral (although imperfect) obligation to which states subscribe (Haines 1995, 275). The combined force of international instruments is quite powerful by inclusion of a prohibition against returning people to a place where they fear persecution or torture, a prohibition against arbitrary detention and the right of access to courts (Stratton and McCann 2002, 142).

Although refugee status is grounded in the idea of loss of membership of a state, international refugee law fails to guarantee membership elsewhere. Recognising the fundamental international law norm that states have complete control over entrance into their territory, the Convention fails to place a duty upon states to admit refugees (Cronin 1994, 117). Accordingly, the Refugee Convention's shortcomings are used by states to deflect the very obligations which the Convention had intended to place upon them.

Hathaway points out that "the notion of refugee law as a rights based regime is largely illusory" (Hathaway 1991, 113). This is evident in several areas. Notwithstanding the Convention's definition of "who is a refugee" and the standards for treatment that must be accorded to refugees, both the Convention and Protocol remain silent on the procedures that are to be adopted in the determination of refugee status (Goodwin-Gill 1996, 74). The international instruments leave the means of implementation to each state. Before refugee status is confirmed, the Convention only assumes that there will be a process to regularise refugee status (Article 31(2) Refugee Convention). The fate of asylum seekers is left to states, as it is the states that determine the procedures to make an asylum claim and whether asylum will be granted or denied. All states consider these procedures to be part of their national sovereignty and have been unwilling to hand over this authority to the UNHCR or other international or inter-government bodies (Loescher 1999, 186).

The mistreatment of asylum seekers occurs as a result of the fundamental shortcomings of the Refugee Convention, which confers a right to apply for asylum on the one hand, but fails to impose corresponding obligations on governments to admit asylum seekers (Philpott 2002, 70). These deficiencies in international refugee law have allowed developed nations to increase their assertions of sovereignty rather than place restrictions on their ability to detain and/or interdict asylum seekers (Dauvergne 2000, 60).

The principle of state sovereignty has been surfacing in debates concerning asylum seekers. The right to control entry and exit into the borders of nation states is regarded as a cornerstone of state sovereignty. Refugee policy takes place against this reality. Asylum seekers who cross borders without the states' authority are subjected to state discourses rendering them as illegal and deviant (Pickering 2005).

This gives rise to a conflict between a general duty to the rights of refugees and asylum seekers on the one hand and to national interests on the other (Carter 2001, 75). Given such conflict, Kneebone states that in reality "the initial premise in considering their right is the sovereign right of the government to exclude aliens" (Kneebone 2002, 4). Harvey argues that expectation of a more humanistic approach to asylum on part of governments is largely illusory as the international community is still divided into states that in essence, are geared towards protecting their own economies and citizens (Harvey 2001, 96). The absence of an international enforcement mechanism means that in the reality, states only provide protection to refugees and asylum seekers if such protection suits their national and wider interests (Binzegger 1980). Economic restructuring and privatisation remain a central part of the agendas of many developed countries. The opening of their doors to asylum seekers, who often lack education or skills in high demand, or who do not possess a geo-political value, does not reconcile with state economic interests in this era of a knowledge economy.

Although the practices of many interdiction policies have met criticism from the UNHCR and human rights groups, they have been largely ignored by host states on the basis that state obligations under the Refugee Convention are not being infringed. While this may be the case in a strict legal sense, many of the policies exploit the grey areas of refugee law and undermine each states' standing as a good international citizen committed to human rights. Moreover, the "closing" of state borders to refugees and asylum seekers seriously jeopardises the international refugee protection regime.

Interdiction policies are embedded in state perceptions that their obligations to refugees are territorially bound. The liberty at which such interdiction policies are conducted by states presents a significant retreat from the Refugee Convention and increasingly undermine state obligations under international law. These include interception, interdiction, safe third country rules, temporary protection and excision of migration zones—what Brennan calls "tampering with asylum" (Brennan, 2003).

Globalisation and interdiction

Soysal (1993) has argued that international human rights are based on universalistic principles which disrupt the territorial notions of nation state citizenship. Jacobson (1996) notes that globalisation has been accompanied by a de-territorialisation between nation and territorial state. Interdiction policies adopted by developed nations, however, prove otherwise. Interdiction measures display the reassertion of the primacy of the territorial sovereignty of the state, at the cost of refugee protection. The right to make a refugee claim outside the nation state is missing from the global order (Philpott 2002, 67). Globalisation has been designed to protect the freedoms of transnational corporations and not the basic human rights of people. Papastergiadis states that "the current discourse of new personal freedom and global interconnection masks complex forms of bondage and displacement" (Papastergiadis 2000, 76). Globalisation is a process of social exclusion with the rules of modern migration welcoming migrants with skills, education and capital and closing the doors on people who do not fit in with this general category, including refugees and asylum seekers (Harvey 2001, 95; Marfleet 1998, 77; Richmond 2002, 717).

Border controls play a part in the preservation of the mal-distribution of income and wealth between the developed and undeveloped countries (Bhuta 2003, 16). Talk of a cosmopolitan world order or post-national forms of membership and belonging mask the fact that citizenship rights (as evidenced by the responses of developed countries to asylum seekers) are marked by the notions of democratic citizenship (Harvey 2001, 95). Carter highlights this by stating that:

> despite the development of international law with a cosmopolitan focus on individual rights, appeals for asylum highlight the conflict between the claims of a common humanity and the political realities of the world in

which, even in an age of globalisation, the legal right to cross frontiers is still controlled by states (Carter 2001, 100).

Chimni (2000, 8) points to the development of a new global order where humanitarian interventions are selective. He argues that the objective of selective intervention is to ensure that the legitimacy of the emerging international system is not undermined. Refugee flows to the industrialised nations are stopped and the reign of transnational capital in the third world is perpetuated. The "assault" on freedom of movement and closing of borders by the more advanced industrial countries of the world has been described as a "new serfdom" (Dowty 1987) or "global apartheid" (Richmond 1994).

In the face of international condemnation by human rights groups, the creation of such categories as the "illegal" and the "legal" becomes a way of "justifying" state practices. Such discourse in turn resonates upon the average citizen so that the so called "unauthorised" asylum seeker is placed in the context of "lawlessness" while the nation state is presented as being "civilised" and "lawful", determined to "protect" its territorial "integrity" and its populace (Wazana 2004).

Conclusion

Writing in the context of Australia, but equally applicable to most developed nations, Tazreiter (2003, 17) argues that the:

> continuation of a system which extends political, social and economic rights only to members of a particular territory, is a system which can be maintained only through increasingly defensive measures.

Despite the attempts of governments to stop "unauthorised" immigration by the assertion of state primacy, many of its causes are related to the political and economic structures across the world and the relations of developed countries with those that are less developed (Castles and Miller 1998). Border controls and interdiction measures are bound to fail as they reinforce the divide and the reasons that result in refugee movements. Clearly, the movement of people within a global community requires a rethinking of the role of the nation state in regulating exit and entry and necessitates new modes of inclusion for citizens who "do not belong". A proper balance needs to be reached between border control and the obligations to refugees and asylum seekers (McMaster 2001, 9). This requires the adoption of "durable solutions" that address the root causes of mass migration (Phillips 2000; Philpott 2002).

Countries must come to grips with the fact that the characteristics and manner in which refuge is sought have changed in the post–Cold War climate and must look at the root causes of refugee movements and provide long-term solutions rather than measures designed to deter, criminalise and punish asylum seekers (McMaster 2001; Phillips 2000; Philpott 2002). The raft of amendments to the immigration acts within developed countries and the extended powers of interception and interdiction neither protect refugees, nor attack the root causes for refugee flows and ignore the fact that often asylum seekers are compelled to resort to people-smugglers and to enter developed states illegally. The tough measures implemented by developed counties unnecessarily penalise asylum seekers by denying them full enjoyment of their rights. State policies such as the Pacific Solution, safe third country practice, carrier sanctions, interdiction and interception, the TPV, and detention must be dismantled, and access to generous welfare services and family reunion rights reinstated.

References

Bhuta, N. 2003. Pass laws in the global village: Enemy aliens—Asylum Seekers, economic Migrants and Border Controls, *X Border*, 1–7, www.antimedia.net/xborder/05_globalapart.html (retrieved on 24 February 2003).

Binzegger, A. 1980. *New Zealand's policy on refugees*. Wellington: New Zealand Institute of International Affairs.

Brennan, F. 2003. *Tampering with asylum: A universal humanitarian problem*. St Lucia: University of Queensland Press.

Carter, A. 2001. *The political theory of global citizenship*. London: Routledge.

Castles, S. and M. J. Miller. 1998. *The age of migration: International population movements in the modern world*, second edn, London: Macmillan.

Chimni, B. S. 2000. Globalisation, humanitarianism and the erosion of refugee protection, *Journal of Refugee Studies*, vol. 13 (2), 243–63.

Cronin, K. 1994. Links between Human Rights Instruments and the Refugee Convention in Old Problems, New Directions. Proceedings of the Conference on Refugee Protection, University of Sydney, 18 February 1994, convened by the Australian Council of Churches and the Refugee and Migrant Services, 116–24.

Dauvergne, C. 2000. The dilemma of rights discourses for refugees, *University of New South Wales Law Journal*, vol. 23(3), 56–74.

Dowty, A. 1987. *Closed borders: The contemporary assault on freedom of movement.* New Haven: Yale University Press.
Goodwin-Gill, G. S. 1996. *The refugee in international law*, second edn, Oxford: Clarendon Press.
Haines, R. P. G. 1995. *Report on the legal condition of refugees in New Zealand*, Legal Research Foundation, Auckland, New Zealand, 1995, www.refugee.org.nz/Reference/retitle.htm, (accessed 24 September 2002).
Harvey, C. J. 2001. Refugees, rights and human security, *Refuge*, vol. 19 (4) February, 94–9.
Hathaway, J. C. 1991. Reconceiving refugee law as humanitarian rights protection, *Journal of Refugee Studies*, 1991, 2, 112–31.
Jacobson, D. 1996. *Rights across borders: Immigration and the decline of citizenship*, London: Johns Hopkins University Press.
Kneebone, S. 2002. *Refugees, natural justice and sovereignty: Fundamental or substantial justice?* Faculty of Law, Monash University, 1–14, www.eur.nl/frg/iacl/papers/kneebone.html (retrieved 14 November 2002).
Loescher, G. 1999. Protection and humanitarian action in the post Cold War era, 171–205. In A. Zolberg and P. M. Benda, ed. *Global migrants global refugees: Problems and solutions*, Berghabn Books, London.
Marfleet, P. 1998. Migration and the refugee experience, 67–90. In R. Kiely and P. Marfleet, ed. *Globalisation and the Third World.* London: Routledge.
McMaster, D. 2001. *Asylum seekers: Australia's response to refugees.* Melbourne: Melbourne University Press.
Morris, J. C. 2003. The spaces in between: American and Australian interdiction policies and their implications for the refugee protection regime, *Refuge*, vol. 21, no. 4, 51–62.
Papastergiadis, N. 2000. *The turbulence of migration.* Cambridge: Polity Press.
Phillips, M. 2000. The impact of being detained on-shore: The plight of asylum seekers in Australia, *University of NSW Law Journal*, vol. 23 (3) 2000, 288–302.
Philpott, S. 2002. Protecting the borderline and minding the bottom line: Asylum seekers and politics in contemporary Australia, *Refuge*, vol. 20 (4), August, 63–75.
Pickering, S. 2005. Crimes of the state: The persecution and protection of refugees, *Critical Criminology*, 13, 141–63.
Richmond, A. H. 2002. Globalisation: Implications for immigrants and refugees, *Ethnic and Racial Studies*, vol. 25 (5), September, 707–27.

—. 1994. *Global apartheid—Refugees, racism and the New World Order*. Oxford: Oxford University Press.

Sianni, A. 2003. Interception practices in Europe and their implications, *Refuge*, vol. 21, no. 4. 25–34.

Soysal, Y. 1993. *Limits of citizenship: Migrants and postnational membership in Europe*. Chicago: University of Chicago Press.

Stratton, J. and S. McCann. 2002. Staring into the abyss: Confronting the absence of decency in Australian refugee law and policy development, *Australian Journal of Human Rights*, vol. 8 (1), 141–56.

Tazreiter, C. 2003. Asylum seekers as pariahs in the Australian state, *Discussion Paper No. 2003/19*, United Nations University.

Wazana, R. 2004, Fear and loathing down under: Australian refugee policy and the national imagination, *Refuge*, vol. 22 (1), 83–95.

BIBLIOGRAPHY

Adelman, H. The new immigration regulations. 1–20, 2002, www.yorku.ca/crs/publications/articles.htm (accessed 2 August 2004).

Agamben, G. "Security and Terror." *Theory and Event* 5 (4) trans. Carolin Emcke (See http://muse.jhu.edu/journals/theory_and_event/v005/5.4agamben.html, 2001 accessed 10 January 2003).

—. "No to Bio-political Tattooing," *Le Monde*, www.ratical.org/ratville/CAH/totalControl.pdf, 2004 (accessed 4 August 2006)

—. *State of Exception*. Chicago: The University of Chicago Press, 2005

Aiken, S. J. *Comments on Bill C11 Related to National Security and Terrorism. Submission to the House of Commons Standing Committee on Citizenship and Immigration, 26 March 2001*. Ontario: Centre for Refugee Studies, 2001.

Albrechtsen, J. "Bungles Have Undermined Laws," *The Australian*, 25 July 2007, http://www.theaustralian.news.com.au/story/0,25197,221291305013450,00.html (accessed 10 August 2007).

Ali, T. *Rough Music: Blair, Bombs, Baghdad, London, Terror*. London: Verso, 2005.

Amnesty International and Human Rights Watch. *Statement*. Geneva: The Governing Council, International Organization for Migration, 2002.

Amnesty International Australia: *Fact sheet 14: Community based asylum seekers*. 1–4. www.amnesty.org.au/refugees/ref-fact14.html (retrieved 13 March 2003).

ANAFE. *Coquelles: Le Juge de Libertés et de la Détention Cautionne une Justice d'Exception pour les Etrangers*, 17 June 2005.

—. Les Enfants Ont Droit à un Avocat, Ils ne l'Ont Jamais, *Journal l'Humanité*, 6 January 2005.

Andrews, K. *Cooperation with Indonesia makes life harder for people smugglers*, media release, 3 May 2007, http://www.minister.immi.gov.au/media/mediareleases/2007/ka07033.htm

—. *Strengthening Australia's border, budget media release fact sheet: prospective illegal immigrants—improved arrangements in transit countries*, 8 May 2007,

http://www.minister.immi.gov.au/media/mediareleases/2007/budget0708/budget0708-prospective_illegal_immigrants.pdf.
—. *Strengthening Australia's border, budget media release fact sheet: stabilising displaced populations*, 8 May 2007, http://www.minister.immi.gov.au/media/mediareleases/2007/budget0708/budget0708-address_refugees_worldwide.pdf.
—. *Strengthening Australia's border, budget media release*, 8 May 2007, http://www.minister.immi.gov.au/media/mediareleases/2007/ka07038.htm
—. *Strengthening Australia's border, budget media release fact sheet: assistance for management and care of irregular immigrants in Indonesia*, 8 May 2007, http://www.minister.immi.gov.au/media/mediareleases/2007/budget0708/budget0708-immigration_management_facilities.pdf.
Anti-Discrimination Board. *Race for the Headlines: Racism and Media Discourse.* Sydney: Anti-Discrimination Board of NSW, 2003.
Appadurai, A. "Disjuncture and difference in the global cultural economy." In *Global Culture: Nationalism, Globalization and Modernity*, edited by M. Featherstone. London: Sage Publications, 1990.
Arendt, H. *The Origins of Totalitarianism.* London: Andre Deutsch, 1986.
Arras, J. "The Fragile Web of Responsibility: AIDS and the Duty to Treat." *Hastings Center Report* 18 (2) (1988): 10–20.
Attorney-General's Department. *Budget 2006/07: Security environment update*, 9 May 2006, http://www.ag.gov.au/www/agd/agd.nsf/Page/PublicationsBudgetsBudget_2006Information_Sheets.
AusAID. *Annual Report 2004/05*, http://www.ausaid.gov.au/anrep05/s2b.html.
—. Australian Aid to Micronesia, May 2007, http://www.ausaid.gov.au/country/country.cfm?CountryID=7578636&Region=SouthPacific&CFID=2481220&CFTOKEN=68665129.
Australian Broadcasting Coporation. *7.30 Report*, 22 May 2006, www.abc.net.au/7.30/content/2006/s1644678.htm.
—. *Newsonline.* Poll finds most Australians want Hicks home, http://www.abc.net.au/news/newsitems/200612/s1811171.htm (accessed 2 August 2007).
—. Glasgow attackers intent on suicide, http://www.abc.net.au/news/stories/2007/07/06/1971295.htm (accessed 10 August 2007).
Australian Catholic Migrant and Refugee Office. *Background paper on asylum seekers in Australia. Australian Catholic Migrant and Refugee*

Office, 25 August 2002, www.acmro.catholic.org.au/index.htm, (accessed 24 February 2003).

Australian Council for International Development. *Aid budget 2004/05 overview and analysis*, 7 July 2004.

—. *Aid budget 2006/07 overview and analysis*, 16 May 2006.

Australian Council for Overseas Aid. *Aid budget 2003/04 overview and analysis*, May 2003.

—. *Welfare issues and immigration outcomes for asylum seekers on Bridging E Visas*. Asylum Seeker Project, April 2003, www.acmro.catholic.org.au/index.htm, (accessed on 24 February 2003).

Australian Council of Heads of Schools of Social Work. *We've Boundless Plains to Share: The First Report of The People's Inquiry into Detention*, 2006, http://www.peoplesinquiry.org.au/PIDFirstReportNov_2006F[1].pdf.

Australian Government. *Australian government budget 2002/03, budget paper no. 2 part ii, expense measures immigration and multicultural and indigenous affairs*, http://www.budget.gov.au/2002-03/bp2/html/03_bp2expense_3.html#P3305_119859.

Australian High Commission Bangladesh. *Australia provides funds to combat irregular migration in Bangladesh*, 2006, http://www.bangladesh.embassy.gov.au/daca/0605_IOM_Ph2.html.

Australian Parliamentary Delegation to Palau and FSM. *Report*, 2006, http://www.aph.gov.au/house/info/pro/41P_reports/Palau%20and%20FSM.pdf.

Babacan, A. "Regulating Asylum in the Aftermath of September 11: The Case of Australia, Canada and New Zealand." In *Racisms in the New World Order: Realities of Cultures, Colours and Identity*, edited by N. Gopalkrishnan and H. Babacan, Newcastle: Cambridge Scholars Publishing, 2007.

Babacan, H. *I Still Call Australia Home: An Exploration of Issues Relating to Settlement and Racism*. Brisbane: Centre for Multicultural and Pastoral Care, 1998.

—. "Racism and Multiculturalism." In *Responding to Cronulla: Rethinking Multiculturalism*, edited by N. Gopalkrishnan and S. H. Toh, 59–76. city??? University of the Sunshine Coast and Griffith University, 2006, http://www.usc.edu.au/Research/Centres/CMCD/Responding+to+Cronulla.htm.

Bali Process. *Bali process on people smuggling, trafficking in persons and related transnational crime summary of activities*, 2006.

http://www.baliprocess.net/files/Activities/SummaryofActivites.pdf.
Barnett, M. and M. Finnemore. *Rules for the World: International Organizations and World Politics.* Ithaca: Cornell University Press, 2004.
BBC, New visas "exporting the borders", 8 August 2007. more info needed???
Beck, U. *What is Globalization?* Cambridge: Polity Press, 2000.
Benhabib, S. *The Rights of Others. Aliens, Residents and Citizens.* Cambridge: Cambridge University Press, 2004.
Bhuta, N. "Pass Laws in the Global Village: Enemy Aliens—Asylum Seekers, Economic Migrants and Border Controls." *X Border*, 1–7, www.antimedia.net/xborder/05_globalapart.html (retrieved on 24 February 2003).
Binzegger, A. *New Zealand's Policy on Refugees.* Wellington: New Zealand Institute of International Affairs, 1980.
Blackburn, J., Attorney-General's Department. Official Committee Hansard: Senate Foreign Affairs and Trade References Committee, *Australia's relationship with Papua New Guinea and Pacific Island Nations*, 25 October 2002.
Boister, N. "Regional cooperation in the suppression of transnational crimes in the South Pacific." In *International Law Issues in the South Pacific*, edited by G. Leane and B. von Tigerstrom. Aldershot and Burlington: Ashgate, 2005.
Boite, The. *The Fig Tree*, CD recording, Collingwood: The Boite, 2003.
Brake, M. and C. Hale. *Public Order and Private Lives: The Politics of Law and Order.* London: Routledge, 1992.
Brennan, F. *Tampering with Asylum. A Universal Humanitarian Problem.* St Lucia: University of Queensland Press, 2003.
Briskman, L. Continuing exclusion: Asylum seekers and refugees in Australia. Paper presented at conference on Refugees and Empire, De Montfort University, Leicester, 2007.
Briskman, L. "A tale of two racisms." In *Racisms in the New World Order: Realities of Cultures, Colours and Identity*, edited by N. Gopalkrishnan and H. Babacan, Newcastle: Cambridge Scholars Publishing, 2007.
Briskman, L. *Social Work with Indigenous Communities.* Sydney: The Federation Press, 2007.
Brouwer, A. *The New Immigration Act. More Questions Than Answers*, 1–8, The Maytree Foundation, www.maytree.com/HTMLFiles/publications_immigration_Act.html, (retrieved 13 November 2002).

Brouwer, A. and J. Kumin. "Interception and Asylum: When Migration Control and Human Rights Collide." *Refuge: Canada's Periodical on Refugees* 21 (4) (2003): 6–24.

Burke, A. "Prisoners of Paradox: Thinking for the Refugee." *Social Alternatives* 21 (4) (2002): 21–27.

Burke, T. *In Fear of Security: Australia's Invasion Anxiety*. Annandale, New South Wales: Pluto Press, 2001.

Byrne, M. *Fortifying Europe: Poland and Slovakia under the Dublin System*. The Contemporary Europe Research Centre, April 2007.

Canadian Council for Refugees. Interdiction and refugee protection: Bridging the gap, 2007, www.ccr.web.ca/interdiction.proceedings.PDF, (accessed 2 February 2007).

Canadian Council for Refugees. Submission of the Canadian Council for Refugees on the occasion of the visit to Canada of the UN Working Group on Arbitrary Detention, 8 June 2005, www.ccr.web.ca/WGAD.HTM, 2007, (accessed 2 February 2007).

Canadian Council for Refugees. Safe third country, 2007, www.ccr.web.ca/S3C.HTM, (accessed 2 February 2007).

Carrington, K. Law and order on the border in the neo-colonial antipodes. In *Borders, Mobility and the Technologies of Control*, edited by S. Pickering and L. Weber. Dordrecht, Netherlands: Springer, 2006.

Carter, A. *The Political Theory of Global Citizenship*. London: Routledge, 2001.

Castles, S. and M. J. Miller. *The Age of Migration: International Population Movements in the Modern World*, second edn, London: Macmillan, 1998.

Catholic Commission for Justice, Development and Peace. *Hordes or human beings? A discussion of some of the problems surrounding Australia's response to asylum seekers and possible solutions to those problems*. Occasional Paper no. 8, Melbourne: Catholic Commission for Justice, Development and Peace, 2003: 1–20. www.melb.catholic.aust.com/ccjdp/op08-200003.htm, (accessed 11 October 2003).

Centre for Population Mental Health Research. 2004. Media release: *Temporary protection visas compromise refugees' health: new research*, http://www.unsw.edu.au/news/pad/articles/2004/jan/TPV_Health.html (accessed 5 October 2007).

Chandler, David P. *The Tragedy of Cambodian History: Politics, War and Revolution since 1945*. New Haven: Yale University Press, 1991.

Cheran, R. "Xeno Racism and International Migration." *Refuge* 19 (6) August (2001): 1–3.
Chimni, B. S. "Globalisation, Humanitarianism and the Erosion of Refugee Protection, *Journal of Refugee Studies*, vol. 13 (2) (2000): 243–63.
Cimade. Centres et locaux de detention administrative, 2005, Paris.
Coffey, G. "Locked up Without Guilt or Sin: The Ethics of Mental Health Service Delivery in Immigration Detention." *Psychiatry, Psychology and Law* 13 (1) (2006): 67–91.
Cole, D. "Are We Safer?" New York Review of Books LIII (4) (2006): 15, 17.
Coll, Steve. *Ghost Wars: The Secret History of the CIA, Afghanistan and Bin Laden, from the Soviet Invasion to September 10, 2001*. London: Penguin, 2005.
Collins, J. Ethnic gangs, ethnic conflict and the Cronulla beach riots in Proceedings from the National Symposium information missing, 2006 (accessed 5 April 2007).
Commission on Human Security. *Human Security Now*. New York: United Nations, 2003.
Conseil National des Barreaux. *Rapport sur l'Avocat et Retention Administrative des Etrangers*. Paris, 2005.
Corlett, D. "Asylum Seekers and the New Racism." *Dissent* 8 Autumn–Winter (2002): 46–7.
Correll, B., Department of Immigration. Proof Committee Hansard: Senate Standing Committee on Legal and Constitutional Affairs, budget estimates, 21 May 2007.
Costello, T. "Seeing the Whole: Population Policy in a Global Context." In *Australia's Population Challenge: The 2002 Australian Population Summit*, edited by S. Vizard, H. J. Martin and T. Watts. Melbourne: Penguin, 2002.
Crock, M., B. Saul and A. Dastyari. *Future seekers II: Refugees and Irregular Migration in Australia*. Sydney: The Federation Press, 2006.
Cronin, K. Links between human rights instruments and the Refugee Convention, 116–24. Paper presented at Old Problems, New Directions, Conference on Refugee Protection, University of Sydney, 18 February 1994, convened by the Australian Council of Churches and the Refugee and Migrant Services.
Cunneen, C. *Conflict Politics and Crime: Aboriginal Communities and the Police*. Crows Nest, NSW: Allen and Unwin, 2001.

Dastyari, A. "Trading in Refugees." *On Line Opinion*, 28 May 2007, http://www.onlineopinion.com.au/print.asp?article=5896, (accessed 1 June 2007).

Dauvergne, C. "The Dilemma of Rights Discourses for Refugees." *University of New South Wales Law Journal* 23(3) (2000): 56–74.

Davis, M. "The Flames of New York." *New Left Review* 12 (2001): 34–50.

Dawson, E. "What the PM Owes to Hansonism." *The Age*, 8 September 2006.

De Lorenzo, M. The accountability gap in refugee protection. Keynote address at the National Network Conference of the U.S. Committee for Refugees and Immigrants, Washington, 23 May 2007.

Delanty, G. *Citizenship in a Global Age: Society, Culture, Politics*. Buckingham: Open University Press, 2000.

Dench, J. "Controlling Borders: C31 and Interdiction." *Refuge* 19 (4) February (2001): 34–40.

Department of Foreign Affairs and Trade. *Cook Islands Country Brief—July 2006*. Department of Foreign Affairs and Trade, 2006.

—. *Transnational Terrorism: The Threat to Australia*. Canberra: Commonwealth of Australia, 2004.

Department of Immigration. *Answer to question 9 taken on notice, Senate Legal and Constitutional Committee Inquiry into the Migration Legislation Amendment (Further Border Protection) Bill 2002 and Related Matters, 2002*, http://www.aph.gov.au/senate/committee/legcon_ctte/completed_inquiries/2002-04/mig_bp/qon/dimia.doc.

—. *Fact sheet 77: The movement alert list*. 21 August 2002. Canberra: Australian Government Publishing Service, 2002.

—. *Annual report 2002/03*. http://www.immi.gov.au/about/reports/annual/2002-03/report26.htm

—. *Answer to question 4 taken on notice supplementary Budget Estimates Hearing*, 25 November 2003, http://www.aph.gov.au/senate/committee/legcon_ctte/estimates/sup_0304/dimia/DIMIA%201%20-%206.pdf.

—. *Annual Report 2003/04*. Canberra: Commonwealth of Australia.

—. *Annual Report 2004/05*. Canberra: Commonwealth of Australia.

—. *Annual Report 2005/06*. Canberra: Commonwealth of Australia.

—. *Australia's APP Check-In Guide: An information booklet containing operating instructions for service providers*, November, http://www.immi.gov.au/managing-australias-borders/border-security/APP-check-in-htm

—. *Answer to question 156 taken on notice Budget Estimates Hearing*, 22 May 2006, http://www.aph.gov.au/senate/committee/legcon_ctte/estimates/bud_0607/dimia/qon_156.pdf.

—. *Answer to question 137 taken on notice Budget Estimates Hearing*, 22 May 2006, http://www.aph.gov.au/senate/committee/legcon_ctte/estimates/bud_0607/dimia/qon_137.pdf.

—. *Fact sheet 77. The Movement Alert List*, 2 April 2007, http://www.immi.gov.au/media/fact-sheets/77mal.htm.

Department of Immigration and Multicultural Affairs. *Consultations on the 2001/2002 migration and humanitarian programs*. Discussion Paper. Canberra: Australian Government Publishing Service, 2002.

Department of Immigration, Multicultural and Indigenous Affairs. *Fact sheet no. 65: The new humanitarian visa*, www.immi.gov.au/facts/65humanitrainh.tm, 2002 (accessed 29 September 2002).

DIAC. *Media release. Setting record straight about Vioxx*, http://www.dimia.gov.au/media/media-releases/2005/d05011.htm, 2005 (accessed 5 October 2007).

—. *Annual Report 2004/05*. Canberra: Commonwealth of Australia.

Diamond, J. Collapse: *How Societies Choose to Fail or Survive*. London: Allen Lane, 2005.

Dirks, G. E. *Controversy and Complexity. Canadian Immigration Policy during the 1980s*. Montreal: McGill Queens University Press, 1995.

Dodson, M. "Indigenous Australian." In *The Howard Years*, edited by R. Manne, 119–43. Melbourne: Black Inc Agenda, 2004.

Dodson, P. "An Entire Culture Is at Stake." *The Age*, 14 July 2007, http://www.theage.com.au/news/opinion/an-entire-culture-is-at-stake/2007/07/13/1183833765256.html?page=fullpage (accessed 20 July 2007).

Downer, A. *Parliamentary Debates: House of Representatives Official Hansard*, 3 December 2002.

—. *Regional counter-terrorism package*, media release FA046, 9 May 2006, http://www.foreignminister.gov.au/releases/2006/fa046_06.html

—. Inaugural lecture on national and international security, Wollongong: University of Wollongong Centre for Transnational Crime Prevention, 2006, http://www.foreignminister.gov.au/speeches/2006/060516_national_international_security.html.

—. *Australia provides support for the displaced in the Asia Pacific*, media release AA 07 013, 7 March 2007, http://www.ausaid.gov.au/media/release.cfm?BC=Media&ID=8914_6 617_5246_8028_3812.

Dowty, A. *Closed Borders: The Contemporary Assault on Freedom of Movement*. New Haven: Yale University Press, 1987.

Driessen, H. "The 'New Immigration' and the Transformation of the European–African frontier." In *Border Identities: Nation and State at International Frontiers*, edited by T. M. Wilson, H. Donnan. Cambridge: Cambridge University Press, 1998.

Du Gay, P., J. Evans and P. Redman. *Identity: A Reader*. London: Sage Publications, 2000.

Duffy, M. "Policy Where Facts Are Foreign." *Sydney Morning Herald*, 20 August 2005

Dunn, K., J. Forrest, I. Burnley and A. McDonald. "Constructing Racism in Australia." *Australian Journal of Social Issues* 39 (4) November (2004): 409–30.

Einfeld, M. Address to the ACT Launch of the People's Inquiry into Immigration Detention, Australian Catholic University, 4 May 2006.

Elliott, J. L. and A. Fleras. *Unequal Relations. An Introduction to Race and Ethnic Dynamics in Canada*. Ontario: Prentice Hall Canada Inc., 1992.

Esmaeli, H. and B. Wells. "The 'Temporary' Refugees: Australia's Legal Response to the Arrival of Iraqi and Afghan Boat People." *University of NSW Law Journal* 23 (3) (2000): 224–5.

Essed, P. *Understanding Everyday Racism: An Interdisciplinary Theory*. New York: Sage, 1991.

Evans, G. and K. Rowley. *Red Brotherhood at War: Vietnam, Cambodia and Laos since 1975*. London: Verso, 1990.

Explanatory Memorandum to the Channel Tunnel (Miscellaneous Provisions) (Amendment) Order 2004, no. 2589.

Falk, R. Human rights: "A Descending Spiral." In *Human Rights in the War on Terror*, edited by R. A. Wilson, New York: Cambridge University Press, 2005.

Fanon, F. *The Fanon Reader*. London: Pluto Press, 2006.

Farmer, B.; Department of Immigration. *Official Committee Hansard: Senate Legal and Constitutional Legislation Committee*, Budget Estimates Supplementary Hearings, 25 November 2003.

Farran, S. and J. Corrin Care. "Towards a Pragmatic Approach to the Contract or Tort Debate in the South Pacific." *Journal of South Pacific Law* 4 (8) (2000): 1–27.

Fassin, D. "Compassion and Repression: The Moral Economy of Immigration Policies in France." *Cultural Anthropology* 20 (3) (2005): 362–87.

Federation of Community Legal Centres. Submission of the Federation of Community Legal Centres (Vic) Inc. to the Parliamentary Joint Committee on Intelligence and Security, review of the listing of the Kurdistan Workers Party (PKK) as a terrorist organisation under the Criminal Code Act 2004. Carlton: Federation of Community Legal Centres, 2006.

Fiske, L. Australia's TPV policy: Inhumane, exclusionary and unnecessary unpublished paper. Perth: Curtin University Centre for Human Rights Education, 2006.

Flautre, H. Justice d'exception pour étrangers: Hélène Flautre se rendra lundi à l'audience "décoalisée" de Coquelles. Friday 10 June 2005.

Fletcher, G. "Terrorism and Security Issues in the Pacific." In *The Eye of the Cyclone: Issues in Pacific Security*, edited by I. Molloy, Sippy Downs: PIPSA and University of the Sunshine Coast, 2004.

Fraser, C., and M. Islam. "Social Identification and Political Preferences for One Nation: The Role of Symbolic Racism." Australian Journal of Psychology 52 (3) (2000): 131–7.

Fromkin, D. *A Peace to End All Peace: Creating the Modern Middle East, 1914–1922*. London: Penguin, 1989.

Galbraith, P. W. *The End of Iraq: How American Incompetence Created a War without End*. London: Pocket Books, 2007.

Gauthier, K. *Presentation to the People's Inquiry into Immigration Detention*. Sydney: Australian Council of Heads of Schools of Social Work, 2005.

Ghosh, B. *Managing Migration: The Need for a New International Regime*. Oxford: Oxford University Press, 2000.

Gibney, M. J. *The Ethics and Politics of Asylum: Liberal Democracy and the Response to Refugees*. Cambridge: Cambridge University Press, 2004.

Gibson, J. and M. Morje Howard. "Russian Anti-semitism and the Scapegoating of Jews." *British Journal of Political Science* 37 (2007): 193–223.

Giddens, A. *Runaway World: How Globalisation Is Reshaping Our Lives*. Cambridge: Polity, 2000.

Gil-Robles, A. *Report by Mr Alvaro Gil-Robles, Commissioner for Human Rights, on the Effective Respect for Human Rights in France Following His Visit from 5 to 21 September, 2005*. Strasbourg: Council of Europe, 2006.

Giroux, H. *The Terror of Neoliberalism: Authoritarianism and the Eclipse of Democracy*. Boulder: Paradigm Publishers, 2004.
Glover, D. *Orwell's Australia*. Victoria: Scribe Publications, 2003.
Goddard, C. and B. Saunders. "Journalists As Agents and Language As an Instrument of Social Control." Children Australia 26 (2) (2001): 26–30.
Goff, P. *NZ expertise to help draft PI counter-terrorism legislation*, 27 February 2003, http://www.beehive.govt.nz/ViewDocument.aspx?DocumentID=16125.
Goldstone, J. A. et al. *State Failure Taskforce Report: Phase Three Findings*. College Park, Maryland: Centre for International Development and Conflict Management, University of Maryland, 2000.
Goodin, R. *Protecting the Vulnerable*. Chicago: Chicago University Press, 1985.
Goodwin-Gill, G. "International Law and the Detention of Refugees and Asylum Seekers." *International Migration Review* Special Issue: *Refugees: Issues and Directions* 20 (2) Summer (1986): 193–219.
Goodwin-Gill, G. S. *The Refugee in International Law*. second edn, Oxford: Clarendon Press, 1996.
Gopalkrishnan, N. "Fear, Diversity and the Globalisation Paradigm." *International Journal of Diversity in Organizations, Communities and Nations* 3 (2003): 601–09.
—. "In-Fear-Tainment: The Convergence of Fear, Diversity and Governance. *International Journal of Diversity in Organizations, Communities and Nations* 5 (2) (2005): 85–90.
Gopalkrishnan, N. and H. Babacan. *Racisms in the New World Order: Realities of Culture, Colour and Identity*, Newcastle, UK: Cambridge Scholars Publishing, 2007.
Gorman, R. F. "Introduction: Refugee Aid and Development in a Global Context. In *Refugee Aid and Development: Theory and Practice*, edited by R. F. Gorman. Westport Connecticut: Greenwood Press, 1993.
Gould, W .T. S. "Population Movements and the Changing World Order: An Introduction." In *Population Migration and the Changing World Order*, edited by W. T. S. Gould and A. M. Findlay, 3–14. Chichester: John Wiley & Sons, 1994.
Gradstein, L. "Questioning Deterrence Policies in the Mandatory Detainment of Asylum Seekers", unpublished Doctor of Psychology (Forensic) thesis, Deakin University, 2006.
Grattan, M. "Labor Smells a New Tampa." *The Age*, 5 November 2003.

—. "Plumbing the Depths on Haneef." *The Age*, 27 July 2007.
Gray, J. *False Dawn: The Delusion of Global Capitalism*. London: Granta, 2002.
Guardian, The. "Sangatte Refugee Camp." 23 May 2002.
Hage, G. *Arab-Australians: Citizenship and Belonging Today*. Melbourne: Melbourne University Press, 2002.
Haines, R. P. G. *Report on the legal condition of refugees in New Zealand*, Legal Research Foundation, Auckland, New Zealand, 1995, www.refugee.org.nz/Reference/retitle.htm, (accessed 24 September 2002).
Hamilton, C., and S. Maddison, eds. *Silencing Dissent: How the Australian Government Is Controlling Public Opinion and Stifling Debate*. Crows Nest, New South Wales, Allen and Unwin, 2007
Hanks, P. Immigration history and policy: Australia and Canada. Paper from the conference held on 2 August 1989, Working papers on migrant and inter-cultural studies, Centre for Migrant and Inter-cultural Studies, Monash University, Melbourne, 1989.
Hardimon, M. "Role Obligations." *Journal of Philosophy* 91 (7) (1994): 333–63.
Harley, J., M. Allstrom and A. Phillips. 2005. Submission to the Palmer Inquiry from the Office of the Public Advocate of South Australia.
Harrison, Paul. *Inside the Third World*. London: Penguin, 1993.
Harvey, C. "Securing Refugee Protection in a Cold Climate." *Refuge* 20 (4) August (2002): 2–4.
Harvey, C. J. "Refugees. Rights and Human Security." *Refuge*, vol. 19 (4) February, (2001): 94–9.
Hathaway, J. C. "Reconceiving Refugee Law As Humanitarian Rights Protection." *Journal of Refugee Studies* 2 (1991): 112–31.
Head, M. "Military Call-out Powers Expanded: Disturbing Questions Posed." *Alternative Law Journal* 31 (2006): 83–7.
Held, D., A. McGrew, D. Goldblatt and J. Perraton. *Global Transformations: Politics, Economics and Culture*. Cambridge: Polity Press, 1999.
Herman, E. "Terrorism: Misrepresentations of Power." In T*he Politics and Imagery of Terrorism*, edited by D. Brown and R. Merrill, 47–56. Seattle: Bay Press, 1993.
Hillyard, P. *The "War on Terror": Lessons from Ireland*, http//www.ecln.org/essays/essays-1.pdf, 2005 (accessed 15 December 2005).
Hiro, D. *Iraq: The Report from the Inside*. London: Granta, 2003.
HM Chief Inspector of Prisons. *Annual Report 2004/2005*. London, 2006.

—. *Report on the Unannounced Inspections of Three Short-term Non-residential Immigration Holding Facilities—Calais Seaport, France, Coquelles Freight, France, Coquelles Tourist, France*. London, 2006.
Hobsbawm, E. *The Age of Capital*. London: Abacus, 1985.
Hocking, J. 1993. *Beyond Terrorism: The Development of the Australian Security State*. St Leonards: Allen and Unwin.
Hogg, R. "The Khaki Election." In *Beyond September 11: An Anthology of Dissent*, edited by P. Scraton, 135–42. London: Pluto Press, 2002.
Hogg, R. and D. Brown. *Rethinking Law and Order*. Sydney: Pluto Press, 1998.
Hollinsworth, D. *Race and Racism in Australia*, third edn, Melbourne: Thomson and Social Science Press, 2006.
Home Office. *Nationality, Immigration and Asylum Act 2002* (Juxtaposed Controls) (Amendment) Order 2006.
—. Statutory Instrument 2003, *The* Nationality, Immigration and Asylum Act 2002 *(Juxtaposed Controls) Order 2003*. Treaty between the Government of the United Kingdom and Northern Ireland and the Government of the French Republic concerning the implementation of frontier controls at the sea ports of both countries on the Channel and North Sea.
—. *Asylum Statistics 3rd Quarter*. Surrey: National Statistics, 2006.
—. *Operation Enforcement Manual*. 2006
—. *Asylum Statistics 1st Quarter*. Surrey: National Statistics, 2007.
Home Office press releases
—. 2003. *UK/French cooperation key to combatting terrorism and illegal immigration*, 4 February 2003.
—. 2006. *Inspection reports on short-term holding centres in Calais and Heathrow: Government response*, http://press.homeoffice.gov.uk/Speeches/005-06-calais-heathrow (accessed 31 July 2007).
—. 2007. *GB£1.2 billion to strengthen "off-shore" border*, 1 August 2007.
—. releases 2007. *Government to strengthen "off-shore" border*, 28 March 2007.
—. 2007. *Strengthening Britain's borders through international cooperation*, 18 June 2007.
Hounslow, B. *Immigration Law and Policy—Learning from the Experience of Canada, the United States and Britain. A Report to the Law Foundation of New South Wales*. Sydney: Public Interest Advocacy Centre, 1988.
House of Commons, Home Affairs Committee. *Immigration Control*. London, 2006.

House of Lords. *Select Committee on Home Affairs 5th Report, Border Controls*. 2006.

Howard, J. "Statement to the House of Representatives, August 2001." cited in Brennan, F. *Tampering with Asylum: A Universal Humanitarian Problem*. St Lucia: University of Queensland Press, 2003.

Howie, L. "The Threat of Terrorism and Social Change." *Human Rights Defender* Special Issue, 2005.

Hughes, P. *Official Committee Hansard: Senate Legal and Constitutional Legislation Committee, Additional Budget Estimates*, 13 February 2006.

—. *Official Committee Hansard: Senate Legal and Constitutional Legislation Committee, Budget Estimates*, 22 May 2006.

—. *Proof Committee Hansard: Senate Standing Committee on Legal and Constitutional Affairs, Budget Estimates*, 21 May 2007.

Hugo, G. "Australian Immigration Policy: The Significance of the Events of September 11." *International Migration Review* 36 (1) Spring (2002): 37–40.

Human Rights and Equal Opportunity Commission. *Ismae—Listen: National Consultations on Eliminating Prejudice Against Arab and Muslim Australians*. Sydney: Human Rights and Equal Opportunity Commission, 2004

—. *A last resort? National inquiry into children in immigration detention*, 2004, http://www.hreoc.gov.au/Human_Rights/children_detention_report/index.html.

Human Rights Watch. *NGO background paper on the refugee and migration interface*, 2001, http://www.hrw.org/campaigns/refugees/ngo-document (accessed 5 October 2007).

—. *By invitation only: Australian asylum policy*, 2002, http://hrw.org/reports/2002/australia/.

—. *Not for export. Why the international community should reject Australia's refugee policies*. Human Rights Briefing Paper, 1–21, 2002, www.hrw.org/press/2002/09/ausbrf0926.htm, (retrieved 14 October 2002).

Human Security Centre. *Human Security Report, 2005*. Vancouver: University of British Columbia, 2006.

Immigration Law Practitioners Association. Response by the Immigration Law Practitioners Association, 28 July 2006 Consultation document:

Private freight searching and fingerprinting at Juxtaposed Controls. 2006.

Inglis, C. "Australia's Refugee Policy in an International Context." *Australian Quarterly* Summer (1994): 15–25.

International Dual Loyalty Working Group. *Dual loyalty & human rights in health professional practice: Proposed guidelines & institutional mechanisms*, 2002, http://physiciansforhumanrights.org/library/documents/reports/report-2002-duelloyalty.pdf.

Interviews conducted by Deborah Zion for ARC Discovery Grant "Caring for asylum seekers in Australia: Bioethics and human rights". Investigators Deborah Zion, Linda Briskman and Bebe Loff, 2007–09.

International Organization for Migration. *Off-shore processing of Australia-bound irregular migrants*, 2001, http://www.old.iom.int/iomwebsite/Project/ServletSearchProject?event=detail&id=AU1Z001 (accessed 5 October 2007).

—. *Australian and Bangladeshi governments extend border management project*, 10 March 2006, http://www.iom.int/jahia/Jahia/pbnAS/cache/offonce?entryId=4706.

—. *Policies*, 2006, http://www.old.iom.int/en/who/main_policies_effrespect.shtml (accessed 5 October 2007).

—. *Amendments to the International Organization for Migration (IOM) Constitution*, Geneva: IOM, 2006.

—. *Australia*, 2007, http://www.iom.int/jahia/page511.html.

—. *Projects*, 2007, www.iom.int/australia/projects.html (accessed 5 October 2007).

International Organization for Migration Indonesia. *Irregular Migrants Assistance Program*, May 2006, http://www.iom.or.id/programmes.jsp?lang=eng&code=2&dcode=6.

Ipp, A., P. Cane, D. Sheldon and I. Macintosh. *Review of the Law of Negligence: Final Report*. Canberra: Commonwealth of Australia, 2002.

Jackson, A. "Detainees Given Banned Drug, Say Refugee Groups," *The Age*, 12 April 2005: 5.

Jacobson, D. *Rights across Borders: Immigration and the Decline of Citizenship*. London: Johns Hopkins University Press, 1996.

Jakubowski, L. M. *Immigration and the Legalisation of Racism*. Halifax: Fernwood Publishing, 1997.

Jayasuriya, K. *Howard, Tampa and the politics of reactionary modernisation*, 2006, www.australianreview/2003/03/jayasuriya.html (accessed 23 March 2007).

Jens, W. *International Immunities*. London: Stevens & Sons, 1961.

Johnson, C. *Governing Change: From Keating to Howard*. St Lucia: University of Queensland Press, 2000.

Joint Standing Committee on Foreign Affairs, Defence and Trade, Foreign Affairs Sub Committee. *Near Neighbours—Good Neighbours: An Inquiry into Australia's Relationship with Indonesia*. Canberra: Commonwealth of Australia, 2004.

Kaldor, A. "A Pragmatic Approach to Immigration." *Quadrant* xlvi (3) March 2002, http://quadrant.org.au/php/archive_details_list.php?article_id=677, (accessed 17 August 2007).

Kellner, D. *Media Spectacle*. New York: Routledge, 2003.

—. From 9/11 to Terror War: Dangers of the Bush Legacy. Colorado: Rowman and Littlefield, 2003.

Killesteyn, E., Department of Immigration. *Official Committee Hansard: Senate Legal and Constitutional Legislation Committee, Budget Estimates Supplementary Hearings*, 25 November 2003.

King, P. *West Papua & Indonesia since Suharto: Independence, Autonomy or Chaos?* Sydney: UNSW Press, 2004.

Klaits, Alex and Gulchin Gulmamdova-Klaits. *Love and War in Afghanistan*. New York: Seven Stories Press, 2005.

Kneebone, S. *Refugees, Natural Justice and Sovereignty: Fundamental or Substantial Justice?* Faculty of Law, Monash University, 1–14, 2002. www.eur.nl/frg/iacl/papers/kneebone.html (retrieved 14 November 2002).

—. "The Rights of Strangers: Refugees, Citizenship and Nationality." *Australian Journal of Human Rights* 10 (1) (2004): 33–61.

Knight, S. B. "The International Refugee Crisis: The Canadian Response." In *The International Refugee Crisis. British and Canadian Responses*, edited by V. Robinson, 17–25. London: Macmillan, 1993.

Knowles, V. *Strangers at Our Gates. Canadian Immigration and Immigration Policy 1540–1997*. Toronto: Dundurn Press, 1997.

Koo, K. L. 2005. "Terror Australis: Security, Australia and the 'War on Terror' Discourse." *Borderlands eJournal* 4, no. 1, (2005) (accessed 23 August 2007).

Kramer, R. and R. Michalowski. "War, Aggression and State Crime." *British Journal of Criminology* 45 (4) (2005): 446–69.

Kundnani, A. *The End of Tolerance: Racism in 21st Century Britain*. London: Pluto Press, 2007.

Kyriacou, L. *The Human Face of Australia's Refugee Policy*. Executive Committee of the UNHCR Programme Annual Meeting. Background papers, www.unhce.org/publ.html (accessed 19 December 2002).

Laclau, E. *New Reflections on the Revolution of Our Time*. London: Verso, 1990.

Law Council of Australia. *Law Council Criticisms of NT Emergency Plan*, 2007, hhtp://www.lawcouncil.asn.au/shared/2439777967.pdf (accessed 10 August 2007).

Lawrence, C. *Fear and Politics*. Melbourne: Scribe Short Books, 2006.

Legrain, P. *Immigrants: Your Country Needs Them*. London: Little, Brown. 2006.

Leitenberg, Milton. *Deaths in Wars and Conflicts in the 20th Century*, Occasional Paper no. 29, Peace Studies Program, Cornell University, 2006.

Lippert, R. "Canadian Refugee Determination and Advanced Liberal Government." *Canadian Journal of Law and Society* 13 (2) (1998): 177–207.

Loescher, G. "Protection and Humanitarian Action in the Post Cold War Era. In *Global Migrants, Global Refugees. Problems and Solutions*, edited by A. Zolberg and P. M. Benda, 171–205, London: Berghabn Books, 1999.

Lygo, I. *News Overboard: The Tabloid Media, Race Politics and Islam*. Sydney: Southerly Change Media, 2004.

Lynch, A. and G. Williams. *What Price Security: Taking Stock of Australia's Anti-terror Laws*. Sydney: UNSW Press, 2006.

Mac an Ghaill, M. *Contemporary Racisms and Ethnicities: Social and Cultural Transformations*. Buckingham: Open University Press, 1999.

MacCallum, M. "Girt by Sea: Australia, the Refugees and the Politics of Fear." *Quarterly Essay* (2002): 5.

Macklin, A. "New Directions for Refugee Policy: Of Curtains, Doors and Locks." *Refuge* 19 (4) February (2001): 1–4.

Maddison, A. *The World Economy: Volume 2, Historical Statistics*. Paris: OECD, 2003.

Maley, William. *Rescuing Afghanistan*. Sydney: UNSW Press, 2006.

Manne, R. "The Howard Years: A Political Interpretation." In *The Howard Years*, edited by R. Manne, 3–53. Melbourne: Black Inc Agenda, 2004.

Manne, R. and D. Corlett. "Sending Them Home. Refugees and the New Politics of Indifference." *Quarterly Essay*. Melbourne: Black Inc, 2004.

Manning, Patrick. *Migration in World History*. London: Routledge, 2005

Mares, P. "Canberra Funds Jakarta's Efforts to Stem the Tide," *The Age*, 29 August 2001.
—. Borderline: Australia's Response to Refugees and Asylum Seekers in the Wake of the Tampa, second edn, Sydney: UNSW Press, 2002.
Mares, P. and L. Newman. *Acting from the Heart: Australian Refugee Advocates for Asylum Seekers Tell Their Stories*. Sydney: Finch Publishing, 2007.
Marfleet, P. "Migration and the Refugee Experience." In *Globalisation and the Third World*, edited by R. Kiely and P. Marfleet, 67–90. London: Routledge, 1998.
Markus, A. Race, *John Howard and the Remaking of Australia*. Crows Nest: Allen and Unwin, 2001.
—. *Race politics*. Paper presented at Beyond Tolerance: National Convention on Racism, 2002, http:www.hreoc.gov.au/racialdiscrimination/beyond_tolerance/speeches/markus.html.
Marr, D. "His Master's Voice: The Corruption of Public Debate under Howard." *Quarterly Essay* 26 (2007).
Marr, D. nd M. Wilkinson. *Dark Victory*. Crows Nest, New South Wales: Allen and Unwin, 2003.
Mason, J. *Sea Change: Australia's New Approach to Asylum Seekers, US Committee for Refugees*, February 2002. www.safecom.org.au/Australia. pdf (accessed 18 November 2002).
McCulloch, J. *Blue Army: Paramilitary Policing in Australia*. Carlton: Melbourne University Press, 2001.
—. "National (In)security Politics in Australia: Fear and the Federal Election." *Alternative Law Journal* 29 (2004): 87–91.
—. "Blue Armies, Khaki Police and the Cavalry on the New American Frontier: Critical Criminology for the 21st Century." *Critical Criminology* 12 (2004): 309–26.
—. "(In)Security in the Age of Globalisation: Human Precariousness in the Move from Welfare to Warfare State." *Just Policy* 37 (2005): 19–24.
—. "State of Emergency: The Militarization of Civil Society." *Dissent* 19, Summer (2005/06): 7–9.
—. "In the Occupied Territory, Howard Targets the 'Enemy' Within," *The Age*, 6 July 2007, http://www.theage.com.au/articles/2007/07/05/1183351371041.html (accessed 7 July 2007).
—. *National insecurity politics in Australia: Fear and the federal election*, 2004,

www.statewatch.org/analyses/no-30-jude-mcculloch.pdf, (accessed 27 April 2007).
McGhee, D. *Intolerant Britain: Hate, Citizenship and Difference*. Maidenhead: Open University Press, 2005.
McKay, S. "Women, Human Security and Peace-building: A Feminist Analysis. In *Conflict and Human Security: A Search for New Approaches to Peace-building*, edited by H. Shinoda and H. Jeong. Hiroshima: Institute for Peace Science, Hiroshima University, 2004.
McKenzie, N. *High rates of mental illness among detainees*. In 7:30 Report. Australia: ABC Television, broadcast 15 May 2003.
McMaster, D. *Asylum Seekers: Australia's Response to Refugees*. Melbourne: Melbourne University Press, 2001.
Medical Justice Network. *Beyond Comprehension and Decency: An Introduction to the Work of Medical Justice*. London: Medical Justice Network, 2007.
Mellama, G. "Scapegoats." *Criminal Justice Ethics* 19 (1) (2000): 3–9.
Mendelberg, T. *The Race Card: Campaign Strategy, Implicit Messages, and the Norm of Equality*. Princeton: Princeton University Press, 2001.
Meyer, J. A. and M. G. Califano. *Good Intentions Corrupted: The Oil-for-Food Scandal and the Threat to the UN*. New York: Public Affairs Reports, 2006.
Monathai Pundrikabha. "The Royal Thai Government's Policy towards Cambodian refugees, 1978–98." *Asia Pacific School of Economics and Management Working Papers*, Canberra: Asia Pacific Press, 1999.
Morris, D. *The Human Zoo*. London: Corgi Books, 1969.
Morris, J. C. "The Spaces In Between: American and Australian Interdiction Policies and Their Implications for the Refugee Protection Regime." *Refuge* 21 (4) (2003): 51–62.
Morris, T. "Australia and Asylum: No Longer Land of the Fair Go?" *Forced Migration Review* 8 August (2000): 31.
Nattinee, Marakanond. "Coordination of Humanitarian Aid for Cambodian Refugees in Thailand: Reasons for Ineffectiveness." *Asia Pacific School of Economics and Management Working Papers*, Canberra, Asia Pacific Press, 1999.
New Zealand Ministry of Justice. *Anti-money Laundering and Countering the Financing of Terrorism APG Annual Meeting 2005 Jurisdiction Report: New Zealand*, 2005, http://www.justice.govt.nz/fatf/jurisdiction-report.html.
Ntumy, M. *South Pacific Islands Legal Systems*. Honolulu: University of Hawaii Press, 1993.
Oakley, J. "Varieties of virtue ethics" *Ratio* 9 (2) (1996): 128–52.

Oceania Customs Organisation. *The Quarterly News* 12 (2003).
Odowski, S. Immigration detention—The current position. Speech delivered at the Monash Institute for the Study of Global Movements, Monash University, Clayton, 10 October 2003, http://www.humanrights.gov.au/speeches/human_rights/immdetention.htm, (accessed 8 October 2006).
Official Committee Hansard, *Senate Legal and Constitutional Legislation Committee*.
Ofpra. *Les Demandes d'Admission sur le Territoire au Titre de l'Asile*, Rapport d'Activité, 2006.
Okely, J., Department of Immigration. *Official Committee Hansard: Senate Legal and Constitutional Legislation Committee, Consideration of Budget Estimates*, 29 May 2002.
Oxfam. *Foreign Territory: The Internationalisation of EU Asylum Policy*, 2005, http://oxfamgb.org/ukpp/resources/downloads/foreign_territory_english.pdf.
—. *A Price Too High: The Cost of Australia's Approach to Asylum Seekers*, August, Carlton and Glebe: Oxfam and A Just Australia, 2007.
—. with Refugee Council. *The Internationalisation of EU Asylum Policy: Joint Refugee Council and Oxfam Great Britain Response to the Home Affairs Committee Inquiry into Immigration Control*, 2 December 2005, Oxford.
—. Community Aid Abroad. *Adrift in the Pacific: The Implications of Australia's Pacific Refugee Solution*. http//:www.oxfam.org.au/campaigns/refugees/pacificsolution, 2002 (accessed 20 November 2007).
Pacific Immigration Directors' Conference. *Fact sheet*. July 2006, http://www.pidcsec.org/files/PIDC_Newsletters/pidcfactsheet_july2006.pdf.
Pacific Islands Forum Secretariat. *Press Statement 51/03: Expert Working Group to Coordinate the Development of a Regional Framework Including Model Legislation to Address Terrorism and Transnational Organised Crime*, 2003, http://www.sidsnet.org/pacific/forumsec/Home.htm.
Palmer, M. *Inquiry into the Circumstances of the Immigration Detention of Cornelia Rau: Report*, 2005, www.immi.gov.au/media/publications/pdf/palmer-report.pdf.
Papastergiadis, N. *The Turbulence of Migration*. Cambridge: Polity Press, 2000.

Paris, R. Human Security: Paradigm Shift or Hot Air? In *New Global Dangers: Changing Dimensions of International Security*, edited by M. E. Brown, O. R. Cote jr, S. M. Lynn-Jones and S. E. Miller. Massachusetts: MIT Press, 2004.

Parliament of the Commonwealth of Australia. *Australia and Refugees: 1901–2002: An Annotated Chronology Based on Official Sources*. Canberra: Department of Parliamentary Library, AGPS, 2003.

Paterson, D. "The Application of Common Law and Equity in Countries of the South Pacific." *Journal of Pacific Studies* 21 (1997): 1–20.

Pedersen, A., J. Beven, I. Walker and B. Griffiths. "Attitudes towards Indigenous Australians: The Role of Empathy and Guilt." *Journal of Community and Applied Social Psychology* 14 (2004): 233–49.

Penovic, T., A. Dastyari and J. Taylor. *Castan Centre Submission to the Inquiry into the Provisions of the Migration Amendment (Designated Unauthorised Arrivals) Bill 2006*. 2006, http://www.law.monash.edu.au/castancentre/publications/migration-amend-bill-06-sub1.pdf, (accessed 20 November 2007).

Perera, S. "Introduction: Acting Sovereign." In *Our patch: Enacting Sovereignty Post-2001*. edited by S. Perera, 1–22. Curtin University, Perth: Network Books, 2007.

Phillips, J. and A. Millbank. *Protecting Australia's Borders*. Canberra: Parliament of Australia Parliamentary Library, 2006.

Phillips, M. "The Impact of Being Detained On-shore: The Plight of Asylum Seekers in Australia." *University of NSW Law Journal*, 23 (3) (2000): 288–302.

Philpott, S. "Protecting the Borderline and Minding the Bottom Line: Asylum Seekers and Politics in Contemporary Australia." *Refuge* 20 (4) August (2002): 63–75.

Pickering, S. "Common Sense and Original Deviancy: News Discourses and Asylum Seekers in Australia." *Journal of Refugee Studies* 14 (2) (2001): 167–85.

—. "Crimes of the State: The Persecution and Protection of Refugees." *Critical Criminology* 13 (2005): 141–63.

—. "The Production of Sovereignty and the Rise of Transversal Policing: People-smuggling and Federal Policing." *Australian and New Zealand Journal of Criminology* 37 (2004): 362–79.

Pickering, S., D. Wright-Neville, J. McCulloch and P. Lentini. Counter terrorism policing and culturally diverse communities. Monash University and Victoria Police: Monash University, Arts.

Pollack, K. M. and D. L. Byman. "Iraqi Refugees: Carriers of Conflict." *The Atlantic Monthly*, November 2006, http://www.brookings.edu/views/articles/byman/2061101.htm (Accessed 7 February 2007).

Poynder, N. "Recent Implementation of the Refugee Convention in Australia and the Law of Accommodations to International Human Rights Treaties. Have We Gone Too Far?" *Australian Journal of Human Rights* 2 (1) (1995): 1–16.

Poynting, S. "'Bin Laden in the Suburbs': Attacks on Arab and Muslim Australians before and after 11 September." *Current Issues in Criminal Justice* 14 (1) (2002): 43–64.

Poynting, S., G. Noble, P. Tabar and J. Collins. *Bin Laden in the Suburbs: Criminalising the Arab Other.* Sydney: Sydney Institute of Criminology, 2004.

Poynting, S. and G. Noble. *The Experience and Reporting by Arab and Muslim Australians of Discrimination, Abuse and Violence since September 2001.* Report to the Human Rights and Equal Opportunity Commission, 19 April 2004, www.hreoc.gov.au/racial_discrimination/isma/research/index.html, (accessed 17 March 2007).

Pratt, A. "A Political Anatomy of Detention and Deportation in Canada." PhD thesis, Graduate Centre of Criminology, University of Toronto, 2000.

Pringle, R. "Why Lock up Dr Haneef?" *The Australian*, 26 July 2007.

Purcell, M. "Xenophobia Fuels Australia's Refugee Problem," *Anglican Media*, October 2001.

Quinn, M. "Immigrants and Refugees: Towards Anti-racist and Culturally Affirming Practices." In *Critical Social Work: An Introduction to Theories and Practices*, edited by J. Allan, B. Pease and L. Briskman. Sydney: Allen and Unwin, 2003.

Radden, J. Psychiatric Ethics. *Bioethics* 16 (5) (2002): 397–411.

Rasanayagam, A. *Afghanistan: A Modern History.* London: I. B. Taurus, 2005.

Ratcliffe, P. *'Race', Ethnicity and Difference: Imagining the Inclusive Society*, New York: Open University Press, 2004.

Raulin, N. "Associations et Syndicates Indignés," *Libération*, 14 June 2005.

Refugee Council. *Refugee Council's Response to Home Office Consultation on Juxtaposed Controls Implementation, Dover–Calais*, November 2002.

Refugee Council of Australia. *2007/08 Australian Government Budget: Spending on Programs Related to Refugees*, 2007,

http://www.refugeecouncil.org.au/docs/current/0708%20Budget%20Response.pdf.
—. *RCOA's Reflections on the 2002/2003 Federal Budget*, May 2002, http://www.refugeecouncil.org.au/docs/resources/ppapers/pp-budget2002-3.pdf.
—. *2005/06 Federal Budget Summary of Refugee Related issues*, 2006, http://www.refugeecouncil.org.au/docs/current/2005fedbudget.pdf.
Reid, L. "Risk and the Duty of care in the SARS Epidemic." *Bioethics* 19 (4) (2005): 348–61.
Reinisch, A. *International Organizations before National Courts*. Cambridge: Cambridge University Press, 2000.
Reith, P. *Transcript of the Hon Peter Reith MP Radio Interview with Derryn Hinch—3AK*, 2001, http://www.minister.defence.gov.au/ReithSpeechtpl.cfm?CurrentId=999 (accessed 16 August 2007).
Reitz, J. G. Immigration and Canadian nation building in the Transition to a Knowledge Economy. Paper prepared as a contribution to *Controlling Immigration: A Global Perspective*, second edn, ed. W. A. Cornelius, P. L. Matin and J. F. Hollifield, Stanford University Press, 1–46, www.utoronto.ca/ethnicstudies/research.htm, (retrieved 13 November 2002).
Republic of Nauru Permanent Mission to the United Nations. Press Release, *Nauru Calls for Responsibility from Australian government As Hunger Strike Worsens*, January 2004. http//:www.un.int/nauru/government.html (accessed 20 Novemeber 2007).
Richmond, A. H. *Global Apartheid—Refugees, Racism and the New World Order*. Oxford: Oxford University Press, 1994,
—. "Refugees and Racism in Canada." *Refuge* 19 (6) August (2001): 12–20.
—. "Globalisation: Implications for Immigrants and Refugees." *Ethnic and Racial Studies* 25 (5) September (2002): 707–27.
—. "Immigration and Multiculturalism in Canada and Australia: The Contradictions and Crises of the 1980s." *International Journal of Canadian Studies* 3 Spring (1991): 87–110.
—. *Global Apartheid: Refugees, Racism and the New World Order*, Oxford: Oxford University Press, 1994.
—. "International Migration and Global Change." In *Crossing Borders: Transmigration in Asia Pacific*, edited by O. J. Hui, C. K. Bun and C. S. Beng, 33–48. Sydney: Prentice Hall, 1995.

—. Immigration and Canadian nation building in the transition to a knowledge economy. Paper prepared as a contribution to *Controlling Immigration: A Global Perspective*, second edn, edited by W. A. Cornelius, P. L. Matin and J. F. Hollifield, Stanford University Press, 1–46, www.utoronto.ca/ethnicstudies/research.htm, (retrieved 13 November 2002).

—. "Globalisation: Implications for Immigrants and Refugees." *Ethnic and Racial Studies* 25 (5) September (2002): 707–27.

Richters, A. "When Ethics, Healthcare and Human Rights Conflict: Mental Healthcare for Asylum Seekers." *Cambridge Quarterly of Healthcare Ethics* 11 (3) (2002): 304–18.

Rigo, Enrica. "Implications of EU Enlargement for Border Management and Citizenship in Europe." *EUI–RSCAS Working Papers* 21 (2005).

Rizvi, F. "The Arts, Education and the Politics of Multiculturalism." In *Culture, Difference and the Arts*. edited by S. Gunew and F. Rizvi. Sydney: Allen and Unwin, 1994.

Rogalla, B. "Modern-day Torture: Government-sponsored Neglect of Asylum Seeker Children under the Australian Mandatory Immigration Detention Regime." *Journal of South Pacific Law* 7 (1) (2003) http://www.paclii.org/journals/fJSPL/vol07no1/11.shtml (accessed 17 September 2007).

Ruggie, J. G. "Taking Embedded Liberalism Global: The Corporate Connection." In *Taming Globalization: Frontiers of Governance*, edited by D. Held and Mathias Koenig-Archibugi, 93–129. Cambridge: Polity, 2003.

Saberan, H. "Coquelles, Tribunal 'Clandestin pour les Clandestins'". *Libération*, 14 June 2005.

Sachs, J. *The End of Poverty: How We Can Make It Happen in Our Lifetime*. London: Penguin. 2005.

Said, E. *Orientalism*. London: Penguin, 1995.

Sandoval, C. "Theorising White Consciousness for a Post-Empire World: Barthes, Fanon and the Rhetoric of Love." In *Displacing Whiteness: Essays in Social and Cultural Criticism*, edited by R. Frankenburg, London: Duke University Press, 1997.

Saniotis, A. "Embodying Ambivalence: Muslim Australians As Other." *Journal of Australian Studies* 82 (2004): 49–61.

Schloenhardt, A. "Australia and the Boat People: 25 years of Unauthorised Arrivals." *University of NSW Law Journal* 23 (3) (2000): 33–55.

Schmeidl, S. "(Human) Security Dilemmas: Long-term Implications of the Afghan Refugee Crisis." *Third World Quarterly* 23 (1) February (2002): 7–29.

Schuster, L. "A Sledgehammer to Crack a Nut: Deportation, Detention and Dispersal in Europe." *Social Policy & Administration* 39 (6) December (2005): 606–21.

—. *Asylum Seekers: Sangatte and the Tunnel*. Hansard Society for Parliamentary Government, Parliamentary Affairs 56 (2003): 506–22.

Secretariat of the Conference of the Parties to the United Nations Convention against Transnational Organized Crime. *Implementation of the Protocol Against the Smuggling of Migrants by Land, Sea and Air, Supplementing the United Nations Convention against Transnational Organized Crime—Analytical Report of the Secretariat*, 2 September 2005, http://www.unodc.org/pdf/ctoccop_2005/V0587652e.pdf.

Senate Foreign Affairs, Defence and Trade References Committee. *A Pacific Engaged: Australia's Relations with Papua New Guinea and the Island States of the South-west Pacific*. Canberra: Commonwealth of Australia, 2003.

Senate Legal and Constitutional Legislation Committee. *Report into the Provisions of the Migration Amendment (Designated Unauthorised Arrivals) Bill 2006*. Canberra: Commonwealth of Australia, 2006.

Seng, Theary, C. *Daughter of the Killing Fields: Asreai's story*. London: Fusion, 2005.

Shifman, P. "Trafficking and Women's Human Rights in a Globalised World." *Gender and Development* 11 (1) May (2003): 125–32.

Shukre, A. "Who Is a Refugee? The Definition of Beneficiaries Revisited." In *Crossing Borders: Transmigration in Asia Pacific*, edited by O. J. Hui, C. K. Bun and C. S. Beng, 125–39. Sydney: Prentice Hall, 1995.

Sianni, A. "Interception Practices in Europe and Their Implications, *Refuge* 21 (4) (2003): 25–34.

Simmons, A. B. "Globalisation and Backlash Racism in the 1990s: The Case of Asian Immigration to Canada." In *The Silent Debate: Asian Immigration and Racism in Canada*, edited by E. Laquian, A. Laquian and T. McGee, 29–50. Vancouver BC: Institute of Asian Research, 1997.

Singer, P. and T. Gregg. *How Ethical Is Australia? An Examination of Australia's Record As a Global Citizen*. Melbourne: The Australia Collaboration and Black Inc, 2004.

Singh, C. Personal correspondence, 2007.

Solomon, M. "Healthcare Professionals and Dual Loyalty: Technical Proficiency Is Not Enough." *Medscape General Medicine* 7 (3) (2005): 1–14.

Solomos, J. & L. Back. *Racism and Society*. London: Macmillan, 1996.

Soysal, Y. *Limits of Citizenship: Migrants and Postnational Membership in Europe*. Chicago: University of Chicago Press, 1993.
Steketee, M. "Return to Sender," *The Australian*, 1 March 2007.
Stokes, G., ed. *The Politics of Identity in Australia*. Cambridge: Cambridge University Press, 1997.
Stratton, J. *Race Daze: Australia in Identity Crisis*. Annandale: Pluto Press, 1998.
Stratton, J. and S. McCann. "Staring into the Abyss: Confronting the Absence of Decency in Australian Refugee Law and Policy Development." *Australian Journal of Human Rights* 8 (1) (2002): 141–56.
Taylor, S. "Reconciling Australia's International Protection Obligations with the War on Terrorism." *Pacifica Review* 14 (2) June (2002): 121–40.
—. "Immigration Detention Reforms: A Small Gain in Human Rights." *Agenda* 13 (1) (2006): 49–62.
Tazreiter, C. "Asylum Seekers As Pariahs in the Australian State." *Discussion Paper No. 2003/19*, United Nations University, 2003.
Thompson, M. *Images of Sangatte: Political Representations of Asylum Seeking in France and the United Kingdom*, Sussex Migration Working Paper, No. 18, 2003.
Topsfield, J. "Crackdown Planned on People Smugglers," *The Age*, 4 May 2007, http://www.theage.com.au/news/national/crackdown-on-smugglers/2007/05/03/1177788310417.html.
Touraine, A. *Can We Live Together?: Equality and Difference*, Cambridge: Polity Press, 2000.
Transcript of the Prime Minister, The Hon John Howard MP, Press Conference, Melbourne, 7 November 2001, http://www.pm.gov.au/News/interviews/2001/interview1452.htm.
Triggs, G. *International Law: Contemporary Principles and Practices*. Sydney: Lexis Nexus Butterworths, 2006.
UNFPA. *State of the World population 2006: A Passage to Hope: Women and International Migration*. 2006, http://www.unfpa.org/swp/2006/english (accessed 12 September 2006).
UNHCR. *The State of the World's Refugees 2000. Fifty Years of Humanitarian Action*. Oxford: Oxford University Press, UNHCR, 2000.
—. *Refugees by Numbers*. Geneva: Media relations and Public Information Service, 2005.
—. *2005 Global Refugee Trends*. Geneva: UNHCR, 2006.

—. *Regional Operations Plan 2007 Covering Indonesia, Brunei Darussalam, the Philippines, Singapore, and Timor-Leste*, 2006, http://www.indonesia-ottawa.org/UN/files/Regional%20Operation%20Plan%202007.pdf.
—. *Statistical Yearbook 2005: Trends in Displacement, Protection and Solutions*. Geneva: UNHCR, 2007.
—. *The Iraq Situation.* http://unhcr.org/cgi-bin/texis//vtx/iraq?page=intro (Accessed 10 July 2007).
United Nations High Commission for Refugees. *Refugee Newsletter*, UNHCR Regional Office for Australia, New Zealand, Papua New Guinea and the South Pacific, 2007.
United Nations Population Division. *World migrant stock: 2005 revision database*. 2005, http://esa.un.org/migration/p2k0data.asp (accessed 12 September 2006).
Van Acker, E. and R. Hollander. "Protecting Our Borders: Ministerial Rhetoric and Asylum Seekers." *Australian Journalism Review* 25 (2) (2003): 103–19.
Vanstone, A. *Strong Teamwork Key to Migration Management*, media release, 16 December 2005, http://www.minister.immi.gov.au/media/media-releases/2005/v05157.htm.
—. *Immigration Cooperation to Improve Regional Security*, media release, 28 June 2006, http://www.minister.immi.gov.au/media/media-releases/2006/v06156.htm.
—. *Greater Security from Enhanced Border Management System*, media release, 28 June 2006, http://www.minister.immi.gov.au/media/media-releases/2006/v06153.htm.
Vedsted-Hansen, J. *Europe's Response to the Arrival of Asylum Seekers: Refugee Protection and Immigration Control* (New issues in refugee research working paper no. 6), Geneva: UNHCR, 1999.
Watson, V. "Interpreting Asylum, Reinterpreting Refugees: An Australian Case Study." *Australian Journal of Social Issues* 33 (2) May (1998): 133–54.
Wazana, R. "Fear and Loathing Down Under: Australian Refugee Policy and the National Imagination." *Refuge* 22 (1) (2004): 83–95.
Weber, L. "The Shifting Frontiers of Migration Control." In *Borders, Mobility and Technologies of Control*. edited by S. Pickering and L. Weber, Dordrecht, Netherlands: Springer, 2006.
Weekley, K. Introduction. In *Globalisation and Citizenship in the Asia Pacific*, edited by A. Davidson and K. Weekley, 3–4. London: Macmillan, 1999.

Wellens, K. *Remedies Against International Organisations.* Cambridge: Cambridge University Press, 2002.

Westwood, S. and A. Phizacklea. *Trans-nationalism and the Politics of Belonging.* London: Routledge, 2000.

Whitaker, R. "Refugees: The Security Dimension." *Citizenship Studies* 2 (3) (1998): 413–34.

—. "Refugee Policy after September 11: Not Much New." *Refuge* 20 (4) August (2002): 29–33.

Whyte, J. "Life in the Camp: Giorgio Agamben and Australia's Mandatory Detention of Asylum Seekers", unpublished Bachelor of Social Science (Hons) thesis, RMIT University, Melbourne, 2003.

Wild, R. and P. Anderson. *Little Children Are Sacred*, 2007, http://www.partnerships.org.au/Library/littlechildrenaresacred.htm.

Wong, L. "Immigrants, the Contract State and Rights." *Just Policy* 29 April (2003): 47–56.

Woodward, K. ed. *Culture, Media and Identities: Identity and Difference.* London: Sage Publications, 1997.

Wright, N., UNHCR Regional Representative, 2005, *Statement, 9th Pacific Immigration Directors' Conference Annual Meeting*, Nadi.

Young, M. *Canada's Immigration Program*, 1–29, Parliamentary Research Branch, Law and Government Division, Parliament of Canada, 2001, www.parl.gc.ca/information/library/PRBpubs/bp190-e.htm, (retrieved 10 December 2002).

Zappi, S. "Sangatte Shutdown Signals New Anglo-French Cooperation," *Le Monde*, 1 February 2003.

Editor and Contributor Biographies

Editors

Dr. Alperhan Babacan
Alperhan Babacan is a Lecturer in Law at the School of Accounting and Law, RMIT University. Alperhan holds honours degrees in law and political science and a PhD from RMIT University. He has previously worked in the public and private sectors as researcher or solicitor and has written widely in areas of human rights law, comparative asylum and refugee policy, international law, counter-terrorism, citizenship and human security.

Professor Linda Briskman
Linda Briskman is the Dr Haruhisa Handa Chair of Human Rights Education at Curtin University of Technology. Her research interests include Indigenous policy and refugee and asylum seeker rights. Her most recent book is Social Work with Indigenous Communities (The Federation Press, 2007). She convenes the People's Inquiry into Detention for the Australian Council of Heads of Schools of Social Work.

Contributors

Professor Hurriyet Babacan
Hurriyet Babacan is the Professor of Social and Cultural Development at Victoria University. She has more than twenty years of experience as an academic, public servant, community worker, researcher and trainer in the government, community and university sectors. Publishing achievements nationally and internationally are in the areas of multiculturalism, immigration, identity, social policy, gender, racism, settlement and community development. She is the co-author of *Racisms in the New World Order: Realities of Colour, Culture and Identity* (Cambridge Scholars Publishing 2007).

Dr. Paul Battersby
Paul Battersby completed his graduate and postgraduate degrees in the School of History and Politics at James Cook University. He lectures in International Studies at RMIT University and for the last five years has led the International Studies Program. He has taught at universities and colleges in Australia and Thailand and has published articles and book chapters on topics ranging from Australia–Thailand relations to international project-based learning. His first book entitled *To the Islands: White Australia and the Malay Archipelago* was published in 2007. He is currently completing a second book on globalisation and human security.

Ms. Madeleine Byrne
Paris-based journalist and writer Madeleine Byrne specialises in asylum policy in the European Union (EU) and Australia. Her previous employment included periods at Australia's SBS TV News and ABC's Radio National. Byrne has published extensively on immigration detention in Australia and the EU. Her article on a riot at the Former Port Hedland immigration detention facility, "Black and Blue Justice" was the first to include photographic evidence of the abuse of detained asylum seekers in Australia (*The Bulletin* 2005). Byrne assisted in the establishment of the People's Inquiry into Detention.

Ms. Azadeh Dastyari
Azadeh Dastyari is an Assistant Lecturer in the Faculty of Law at Monash University and a member of the Castan Centre for Human Rights Law. She is a co-author (with Dr. Mary Crock and Dr. Ben Saul) of *Future Seekers II: Refugees and Irregular Migration in Australia* (The Federation Press, 2006). Azadeh has worked closely with various NGOs on refugee issues including in voluntary capacities with Amnesty International, the Public Interest Advocacy Centre and the Refugee Advocacy and Casework Service.

Mr. Narayan Gopalkrishnan
Narayan Gopalkrishnan is the Founding Director of the Centre for Multicultural and Community Development at the University of the Sunshine Coast. He has extensive work experience in Australia in the areas of diversity, cross-cultural development, aid and human development policy and program and service development, leadership and organisational change. He works with refugees, migrants and Indigenous people and has been involved in training, project management, teaching and researching for over twenty-five years in Australia and overseas.

Associate Professor Bebe Loff
Bebe Loff is the head of Human Rights and Bioethics in the Department of Epidemiology and Preventive Medicine at Monash University. She has taught health and human rights law and bioethics since 1994. She is currently a Victorian Health Promotion Foundation Senior Research Fellow. Her other roles include as a member of the Australian Health Ethics Committee, and the Ethical Review Committee of the World Health Organization. During 2003 she was a Human Rights Officer in the United Nations Office of the High Commissioner of Human Rights and was responsible for HIV/AIDS. She has worked with numerous community-based organisations and has been the editor of the medical journal *The Lancet*.

Associate Professor Jude McCulloch
Jude McCulloch is the Head of Criminology at Monash University. Prior to working as an academic she worked in various community legal centres for sixteen years. Dr McCulloch has researched and published on topics including police shootings, crime and the media, women and policing, family violence, women and imprisonment, policing dissent, paramilitary policing, counter-terrorism, globalisation and the "war on terror". She has published in newspapers, magazines and journals. She is also the author of a Victoria Legal Aid publication, *Sexual Assault, The Law, Your Rights*. She is currently in the process of co-editing a collection, with Professor Phil Scraton, on violence and incarceration.

Dr. Savitri Taylor
Savitri Taylor is a Senior Lecturer in the Law School at La Trobe University. She is an academic lawyer whose primary areas of research interest are international human rights and refugee law and Australian immigration law and policy. She has published numerous articles in these areas in Australian and international academic and practitioner journals. Since 1992 Savitri has been a member of the Committee of Management of the Refugee and Immigration Legal Centre and its several predecessor organisations. She also has longstanding involvements with many other non-government and community sector organisations in Australia that deal with asylum seeker, immigration and/or human rights issues.

Dr. Deborah Zion

Deborah Zion teaches ethics and health and human rights in the medical faculty at Monash University. Her current research is on the ethics of healthcare provision to asylum seekers in Australia. Her previous research has been in the area of AIDS/HIV. She is co-editor of the *Monash Bioethics Review*.